Fergus Hume

Aladdin in London

Fergus Hume

Aladdin in London

ISBN/EAN: 9783743333512

Manufactured in Europe, USA, Canada, Australia, Japa

Cover: Foto ©ninafisch / pixelio.de

Manufactured and distributed by brebook publishing software (www.brebook.com)

Fergus Hume

Aladdin in London

ALADDIN IN LONDON

A ROMANCE

BY

FERGUS HUME

LONDON
ADAM AND CHARLES BLACK
1892

*If by chance some wight ambitious
    Gained Aladdin's lamp of magic,
Fate, as now, would be capricious,
    Life would still be ever tragic.*

*Ever fade desired to-morrows,
    Curst despair supplants elation,
Wishes gained are bitter sorrows,
    Joy lies in anticipation.*

CONTENTS.

CHAPTER	PAGE
I. Cupid up to Date	1
II. Destiny	19
III. Bagdad in the West	35
IV. An Extraordinary Coincidence	51
V. The Talisman	63
VI. Janshah	79
VII. The Anger of Major Measurby	93
VIII. The Course of True Love runs Smooth	102
IX. A Treaty with the Enemy	117
X. Wedding Bells	129
XI. The Major makes a Proposal	139
XII. Pleasure and Politics	152
XIII. Conspiracy	169
XIV. Hilda gives her Opinion	180
XV. A Midnight Meeting	195
XVI. The Oriental Express	211
XVII. Villa Tvartko	226
XVIII. The Keys of St. Peter	241
XIX. A Modern Patriot	258
XX. The Calm before the Storm	275
XXI. New Rings for Old	288
XXII. The Storm breaks	305
XXIII. Sauve qui peut	319
XXIV. Boot and Saddle	331
XXV. The Power of the Ring	344
XXVI. Sanctuary	360
XXVII. Down with the Republic	371

XXVIII. Long live the Queen	. . . .	382
XXIX. The Gratitude of Princes	. .	392
XXX. Feminine Diplomacy	. . . .	407
XXXI. The Will of Brahma	. . . .	420

ALADDIN IN LONDON.

CHAPTER I.

CUPID UP TO DATE.

"In no way do I wish to force your inclinations, my dear Hilda," said Lord Kenny, taking up his favourite position on the hearthrug. "I simply point out to you that Sir Richard is rich and Mr. Dacre is poor. Your common sense should tell you which to choose."

"Common sense says the former, my heart the latter," answered Hilda sadly.

"Then take the advice of common sense!"

"And by doing so, ruin my life."

"Egad, if you choose Dacre you'll ruin mine," rejoined his lordship easily. "We are as poor as Job, my dear girl, but hardly so patient. If you do not marry money, the Havard family, as represented by me, will become hopelessly insolvent."

"We have been nothing else but insolvent, papa, since I left the schoolroom."

"Oh! long before that, my child, long before that. Do not blame me, but your grandfather! He was the Regent's friend, and that friendship cost him his fortune. He left me nothing but his extravagant tastes, without the means of gratifying them."

"But you have gratified them all the same."

"I admit it, I admit it," said her father airily; "the force of habit, my dear child, nothing more. What is bred in the bone, you know. One cannot be the son of a duke and have the tastes of a ploughman. I'm a great believer in heredity, Hilda. Oh yes! The duke was fond of the turf; so am I. He liked to buy whatever pleased him; so do I! What between this hereditary failing and your grandfather's extravagance, things have for many years been very unpleasant, in a pecuniary sense."

The Hon. Hilda Havard leaned forward and rested her elbows on her knees, a position which shocked Lord Kenny mightily.

"My dear Hilda, remember your father is present. Ah, that is better," as she lay back wearily in her chair. "Well, as I was saying," he resumed with a smile — "by the way, Hilda, what was I saying?"

"I don't know, papa. Never mind that. What is it you wish me to do?"

"I'll put it in a nutshell. Accept Sir Richard Denham."

"Has he spoken to you?"

"My dear child, they have both spoken to me," said Havard, glancing at his watch. "They paid me and you the compliment of asking me to permit them to pay their addresses to Miss Hilda Havard, — in other words, they wish to make proposals of marriage. I gave them both permission."

Hilda started angrily from her chair.

"Papa, you surely did not do such a thing."

"Why not?" replied Lord Kenny, trifling with his eye-glass. "It's strictly private and confidential, and I wished to give you your free choice. Dacre is coming to-day, Denham to-morrow. I knew you could not stand two proposals in one day, so I put them as far apart as was possible."

He was such an utterly selfish old man that he could not see but that he had acted in the most delicate manner. It never occurred to his frivolous mind that he was placing his daughter in an extremely unpleasant position. Hilda did not try to undeceive him. She knew her father too well.

"You might have told Mr. Dacre that you had other views, and so spared me the pain of refusing the man I love," she said, walking across to the window, deeply wounded by her father's want of consideration.

"No! I wish to let you choose for yourself," said the old beau complacently. "Marry whichever you please. I should prefer Denham as a son-in-law, myself."

"And I should prefer Wilfred Dacre as a husband," retorted Hilda coldly. "I do not know why you keep up this pretence of free-will. Your idea is that I should marry Sir Richard, and yet you pretend that I can choose either. It's Hobson's choice."

"Oh dear, dear, what an extremely vulgar expression," murmured his lordship in an annoyed tone. "I beg of you, Hilda, to recollect that your father is present. Your language grates on my ear. What is the matter?" he added sharply, seeing her draw back from the window.

"Mr. Dacre is at the door!" she replied in a low tone.

"Is he, indeed!" said Lord Kenny jocularly. "Happy the wooing that's not long a-doing. Send him about his business, Hilda. Remember what is at stake. Either you must accept Sir Richard's offer or the name of Kenneth Havard will figure in the Bankruptcy Court."

"I will remember," she murmured, as he advanced to embrace her. "No! do not kiss me, father."

"Hilda, this emotion is extremely ill-bred," replied Lord Kenny with great dignity. "However, your suitor is on the stair, so I have no time to argue the matter. Good-bye for the present, my child, and remember I give you a free choice of a husband."

Hilda was so disgusted with her father's hypocrisy that she could only bow her head in token of acquiescence, and Lord Kenny, satisfied that she would carry out his instructions, left the room with a benign smile. On the way down to the hall, he met Wilfred coming up the stairs, and paused to press his hand with great cordiality.

"You have my best wishes, Mr. Dacre," he said politely. "It is true I had other views for my daughter, but Hilda shall choose for herself. Yes, she shall choose for herself."

"Thank you, Lord Kenny. I know you are my friend."

Then they parted with mutual good will, Wilfred going up to the drawing-room, Lord Kenny down to his club. As he walked along the street, he smiled to himself with great satisfaction, and never gave a thought to the refined cruelty of the whole affair.

"A hand of iron in a velvet glove," he said exultingly; "that is what Hilda needs. Had I not managed things so delicately, she would have married Dacre in spite of me. As it is, I am afraid there is no chance of his becoming my son-in-law."

Meanwhile Wilfred, much elated by Lord Kenny's kind manner, had entered the drawing-room with a joyful sense of coming victory. Hilda, having recovered her usual manner, advanced to meet him with an artificial smile. Luckily, the blinds were down, and he could not see the look of pain in her eyes. All he beheld was this beautiful, queenly woman whom he worshipped, and, ignorant of Lord Kenny's tricky diplomacy, he felt confident he would leave the room her accepted lover.

On her side Hilda was suffering agonies. She loved Wilfred Dacre with the whole strength of her nature, and in any other case would have accepted him at once. Her father, however, with cruel ingenuity, had placed her, so to speak, on her honour by casting the burden of his pecuniary helplessness on her shoulders, and she resolved to sacrifice herself for his benefit at the cost of her own happiness. When she saw the happy smile on Wilfred's face, she nearly broke down, but steeling herself to the ordeal, asked him to be seated, in conventional tones, which she hardly recognized as her own.

Wilfred, however, was too anxious to know his fate to waste any time in idle conversation, and, crossing over to her side, took her hands in his own.

"Hilda!" he said, looking at her downcast face, "you can surely guess my errand here to-day."

He expected she would lift her face and let him see the love-light in her eyes, but she neither moved nor spoke. Like a statue of stone she stood before him with drooping head; and marking this apathy, a sudden dread entered his heart. Finely strung natures such as his, intuitively forecast the future; and in spite of a desperate effort to look on the bright side of things, he felt that he must be prepared for the worst.

"You cannot misunderstand me," he whispered in an agitated tone; "you must know how I love you. For months I have worshipped you in silence, but dared not speak because of my poverty. Now things are changed. I am able in all honour to ask you to become my wife."

"What do you mean?" asked Hilda, a gleam of hope in her eyes.

"I mean that I love you!" he said with feverish earnestness.

"Yes! but your position?" she faltered, looking at him anxiously.

"My position!" said Wilfred in a satisfied tone of voice. "Ah! that is quite altered and for the better. Up to yesterday I was an idle pauper with just enough to keep body and soul together. I had money when my parents died, but with the folly of youth I ran through my inheritance. That was before I saw you, else I might have been more careful. When you came into my life, I was too poor to ask you in marriage, so I went to an old friend of my father's who has much political influence. He, last week, obtained for me an appointment to a consulship in Cuba, and I have come to ask you to share it with me. It is not a great position, but it may be the prelude to better things."

Hilda's face fell as he spoke. Her momentary dream vanished, for she well knew that her father would never consent to such a penurious match. In the eyes of Lord Kenny, the post of a consul in a distant island would be nothing — worse than nothing, seeing it entailed absence from England. For herself she would have been glad to share such exile with the man she loved, but Lord Kenny had placed her duty clearly before her, and against her own inclination she was forced to obey. With a smiling face Wilfred waited to hear her exclamation of joy at his good news, but to his dismay she shrank from his embrace and flung herself sobbing into a chair. The reaction was too great, and, much as she strove to preserve her calm, all the woman in her revolted against the unnatural repression demanded by conventionality.

Much alarmed, Wilfred knelt beside her, and strove with fond endearments to restore her cheerfulness; but she pushed him away, crying the more bitterly as she thought of the pain she was about to inflict on this devout lover.

"My dear Hilda, what is the matter?" said Wilfred, pained and perplexed at this strange behaviour.

"I thought you would be pleased at such good news."

"It is good to you, but not to me," sobbed Hilda, trying to control her hysteria. "I am very sorry, Mr. Dacre — Wilfred, but — but I cannot marry you."

"Oh! surely you do not mean that," said Wilfred, doubting the evidence of his own ears. "I know you love me. You would not have listened so patiently did you not love me."

By this time Hilda had recovered herself, and, with a pale, set face, spoke the words which had been put into her mouth by her father. The effort was great, but the necessity was greater, and she uttered them with painful deliberation.

"I cannot marry you, Wilfred. It is impossible."

"But you love me, Hilda. Ah, never deny it. I can see love in your eyes."

"Yes! I do love you," she replied in a low tone, suffering him to take her hand, "but for my father's sake I dare not become your wife."

"Your father?" echoed Dacre in surprise. "Why, only now on the stairs he gave me his best wishes."

Hilda's lips curled with disdain.

"What he says and what he thinks are two very different things. He wants me to marry Sir Richard Denham."

"Impossible," said Wilfred, turning pale with emotion. "He gave me permission to pay my addresses."

"That is because he wished to leave me free

choice," replied Hilda in an ironical tone, the purport of which was quite lost on her auditor. .

"In that case you will marry me," he exclaimed joyfully. "You do not love Denham, and you do love me."

"For God's sake, do not speak any more," she cried, rising quickly. "I cannot marry you, Wilfred. Go! go! and leave me."

"To marry Denham!" said the young man fiercely. "I will not. You shall not marry that man."

"I did not say I was going to marry him."

"Not in words, perhaps, but you mean to do so. Oh," he cried, covering his face with his hands, "I cannot believe it."

Hilda noiselessly flitted across the room. She could not bear to witness the distress of her lover, and, but for the desire to keep up her womanly dignity, would have told him of her father's treachery. Letting his hands fall idly by his side, he heaved a sigh and looked gloomily at the floor. For the moment Wilfred was puzzled how to act, as he could not but see that Hilda's refusal was based on no reasonable grounds. In fact, she gave no reason whatever for her refusal, and yet she declared she loved him dearly. It was impossible to reconcile her actions with her words, and he felt greatly perplexed as to what was the best course to pursue.

While thus thinking, a low sob sounded through the room, and he lifted his eyes to see Hilda leaning against the wall in a half fainting condition. In a moment he was by her side.

"Hilda!" he said calmly, without a trace of passion in his tone, "let us talk over this matter quietly."

She bowed her head and suffered herself to be led back to her chair.

"I cannot believe you are a coquette," said Wilfred deliberately, "yet this sudden refusal almost persuades me that you are. For the last few months I have been your shadow and you did not discourage my attentions. I cannot offer you wealth, yet I can give you love and comfort. If you are the woman I believe you to be, you will become my wife; if not"—

Hilda looked up in alarm as he paused for an instant.

"If not!" she faltered.

"God knows!" replied Dacre gloomily. "You will perhaps have a ruined life laid to your charge."

"It is cowardly to talk in such a manner," she said indignantly. "If I could marry you I would, but it is impossible. You know it is impossible," she cried, with angry insistence. "My father expects me to make a good match, and I dare not disobey him."

"Your father leaves you free to choose."

Hilda twisted her hands together in hopeless despair. Duty to her father forbade her to tell the truth, so she evaded a direct answer.

"Please go, Mr. Dacre, and ask me no more questions."

"I will not go, and I will ask questions," he rejoined sternly. "No woman has a right to play with a man's heart as you have done. What do you think my life will be without you? Betrayed by a woman, can I ever believe in your sex again? If you "—

"Oh!" she cried, clenching her hands, "cease your reproaches. Is it easier for me than it is for you? You suffer, I also suffer. I love you dearly. I would give up the world for you, but I am not free to follow my inclination."

Wilfred looked at her with much perplexity.

"Oh, if you were only rich," she cried in despair. "For myself, I care not for money, but I must consider my father."

"You evidently do not consider me."

"Unjust! unjust! Do I not owe my first duty to my father?"

"Not when it concerns your life's happiness."

She wrung her hands in bitter sorrow.

"Oh! how cruel a man can be. You think only of yourself, not of me. If your life is ruined, what of mine? Do you deem for a moment that money will mend my broken heart? I would tell you all, but I dare not."

"All what?"

She made no answer.

"Do you know what I intend to do?" he said resolutely. "I intend to ask Lord Kenny the meaning of this mystery. You refuse me an explanation. He will not dare to do so."

"Wilfred!"

He had nearly reached the door, but on hearing that appealing cry, looked back with a frown. Her arms were outstretched, as to take him to her breast; and all his anger vanishing at the sight, he sprang back to her side.

"My darling! my poor darling!" he whispered, holding her tightly to his heart. "I do not blame you. I have been harsh and cruel to speak as I have done; but think what your refusal means to me. I will not accept your answer of to-day. At once I will see your father, and if he freely consents to our marriage"—

"I will marry no one but you," she whispered, interrupting him hurriedly. "He wants me to become the wife of Sir Richard Denham, but I will never consent. He shall not wreck our happiness for his selfish pleasure. I owe a duty to you — to myself, as well as to him. Go and see him, Wilfred, and tell him all. He must consent in the end. Go! Go!"

Wilfred pressed a kiss on her lips, and, not trusting himself to speak, ran quickly out of the room. Hilda hastened to the window and saw him walk rapidly down the street, then, in a state of utter exhaustion, went to her room to lie down. The ordeal had been too much for her, and, torn by conflicting doubts, she did not know how to act. Her father, her lover, — it was impossible to obey both; and the more she thought over the situation the more perplexing did it become. Despite the transparent selfishness of Lord Kenny's character, his daughter loved him dearly; and unfortunately her spirit was too weak to stand against his strong will. She was no Amazon to fight her own battles, but a tender and loving woman, with many of the weaknesses of a feminine nature. So in the present predicament she felt absolutely helpless between the two men. Yet though Hilda was not of the stuff of which heroines are made, neither did her character err on the side of feebleness. She was simply a woman of strong affections, unable to decide between father and lover. Besides, she was but twenty years of age, and had no mother to take her part.

Lord Kenny was very angry, when from behind the pink sheet of the " Globe " he saw Wilfred enter the club. He instinctively guessed that there was trouble in the wind, and, disliking scenes, would have given a great deal to have avoided the meeting. As it was, he hoped to escape observation behind his paper; but Wilfred recognized him at once, and walked straight up to his chair. The young man's demeanour was so aggressive that Lord Kenny thought he would make a scene there and then. Wilfred, however, was too wise to lose his temper, and saluted his lordship in a dangerously bland manner.

" Well, my dear Dacre ! " said the latter uneasily, " I trust you have had a satisfactory interview."

" Lord Kenny, I wish to speak to you in private ! " replied Wilfred, taking no notice of the remark, — an omission which by no means reassured the old gentleman.

" By all means ! " said his lordship with alacrity, getting on his legs. " Come to the smoking-room. There is no one there."

If there was to be a scene, it was as well to get it over at once. The old dandy did not lack courage, and had fully made up his mind that Wilfred should not come off best in the encounter. Dacre was young and hot-tempered, Lord Kenny cool and diplomatic, so he had little doubt but that the result would be in his favour. Havard, however, did not know the temper of his adversary, and found him more of a match than he expected. But what could unthinking youth do against thoughtful age, especially when the latter was selfish and unscrupulous in the extreme?

"Well, my dear fellow," began his lordship suavely, when they were seated in the smoking-room, "and what is it you wish to say?"

"I asked Miss Havard to be my wife, and she has refused me."

"I am deeply sorry, Dacre, but I cannot interfere. You had my best wishes, you know."

"Yes! I believe I had," replied Wilfred ironically, "but they did not do me much good. It is no use beating about the bush, Lord Kenny. I know too much to take your daughter's refusal seriously."

"I am at a loss to understand your meaning, sir."

"That is not impossible. However, I can easily make it clear. Miss Havard loves me and would marry me but for you."

"But for me!" said Lord Kenny with well acted surprise. "My dear sir, why bring me into the matter? My daughter's choice rests with herself."

"Oh no, it doesn't. She did not explain her meaning at any great length, but from what she said I gathered that you wish her to make a rich marriage."

"Every father wishes to do the best he can for his child," returned Lord Kenny evasively. "As a matter of fact, you must admit you are not well off."

"I have the offer of a consulship in Cuba!"

"Good Lord!" said Havard indignantly. "Do you think for a moment, Mr. Dacre, that I will permit my daughter to go to Cuba!"

"It's a very pleasant island," stammered Wilfred, finding himself at some disadvantage, for he could not but be aware that his offer sounded very far from tempting.

"A yellow-fever island," corrected Lord Kenny with great disdain. "Let us speak plainly, Mr. Dacre. I gave you permission to ask my daughter to be your wife. She has refused you; so, as a gentleman, you must retire."

"In favour of a wealthier suitor, I suppose," said Dacre, with an angry flush on his face.

"Precisely! You see I treat you with frankness."

"And would you sacrifice your daughter's happiness for a wealthy match, my lord?"

"That, sir," said the other with great hauteur, "is not a question for you to ask."

Decidedly, Wilfred was getting the worst of the argument, and in a despairing mood looked piteously at the impenetrable old gentleman.

"If you only knew how I love her," he groaned, burying his face in his hands.

"Pooh! All young men are like that," said Lord Kenny indulgently. "I was in love half a dozen times myself when I was a boy."

"I am twenty-five years of age. You can hardly call that boyish," retorted Wilfred rather nettled. "I have had my half loves, as the French call them, but this is the love of my life. If I lose Hilda my life is ruined."

"Not a bit of it, Mr. Dacre. You'll soon forget all about her in Cuba."

"I am not going to Cuba."

"Pardon me! I understood you to say you were!"

"Not now. I only accepted the appointment because I hoped your daughter would be my wife; but now — ah! it is useless to me."

"Then what do you intend to do?"

"Go to the devil!"

Lord Kenny frowned and arose from his seat with great dignity.

"I do not care about hearing such language, Mr. Dacre; so, if you permit me, I will retire."

"Is there no hope?" asked Wilfred appealingly.

"Not in the least," answered the peer frankly. "It is no use, my deceiving you, Mr. Dacre. I wish my daughter to make a rich marriage, and all my influence will be used to induce her to do so."

"She may risk your anger and marry me."

"She will not do that, nor do I think that as a gentleman you can ask her to do so. After to-day I am afraid our acquaintance must cease."

"I suppose so," said Wilfred disconsolately, "but it is very hard on me."

"So you think now, but you will soon get over it. Go to Cuba, and if you don't die of yellow fever, you will marry some one far more suited to you than Hilda would be."

"Never! I will live and die a single man. Is it only on the ground of poverty that you object to me as a son-in-law?"

"Yes, I think so. I have never heard anything against your character," replied Lord Kenny benignly. "If you were rich I would not mind the marriage at all, but as it is "—

His lordship shrugged his shoulders to express his inability to complete the sentence, and walked off. At the door, however, he glanced back, and, seeing how utterly dejected the young man looked, returned with slow dignity. He was a selfish old pagan, but for the moment he remembered that he also had been in Arcady, and laid his hand kindly on Dacre's shoulder.

"Come! come! sir, be a man. There are as good fish in the sea as ever came out of it."

Wilfred shook the hand impatiently off his shoulder.

"I shall not give up all hope yet," he muttered between his teeth.

"It will be wiser for you to do so. Unless," added Lord Kenny, looking over his shoulder, "you find the lamp of Aladdin."

He went out chuckling as though he had made an excellent joke, and Wilfred sat miserably in his chair. Then he wrote a letter to Hilda telling of the failure of his mission and beseeching her to be true to him. He sent this on to Curzon Street by a special messenger, desiring the reply, if there was any, to be brought to his chambers in the Albany.

"I won't give up all hope," he said, when this business was finished. "There's many a true word spoken in jest. I may find Aladdin's lamp after all."

CHAPTER II.

DESTINY.

At the age of twenty-five a man's character is hardly formed. It is true that to a keen observer the indications of futurity are there, but, vague and uncertain as they are, it is difficult to foresee what shape they will ultimately assume. A rake may reform to sobriety and sense, the sedate youth may in middle age fall into the snares of dissipation; but with the generality of men this change for the better or the worse takes place between twenty and twenty-five. That the child is the father of the man is undoubtedly true in the main, but there is a space between these two extremes in which the character resolves itself into chaos. The world of childhood is overwhelmed by the awakened passions of puberty, which rage unrestrained during the period of adolescence, and it is out of this incoherence that the new heavens and earth of maturity are formed. The will now growing stronger controls the passions according to the inherent nature of the being, and, sending them in the self-desired direction, thus creates, so to speak, the thinking and doing individual as he is to exist, till death once more changes his entity into we know not what.

In some cases this crisis takes place earlier, in others later, but for the generality of mankind it happens at the age above stated. Wilfred, therefore, was at the most critical point of this dangerous age, and the circumstances of love and poverty formed powerful factors in the settlement of his fate. Unfortunately, he had no one in whose experience he could find guidance. In addition to this he was gifted with the curse of a highly imaginative nature. Such a spirit sees the world in a more exaggerated light than the ordinary man. A fanciful mind endues everything with non-existing attributes, and can see miracles where the more phlegmatic temperament beholds only the common-place. The possessor of such a dangerous faculty feels the extremes of joy and pain. Gifted with an almost spiritual insight, he extracts delights and sorrows alike from trivialities, and so creates for himself an ideal world uncomprehended by the average mind. In that ideal world he is supremely happy; but contact with actuality, by jarring the delicacy of his mind, inflicts on him pains as keenly felt as are his pleasures. Such beings are out of place in the world of to-day, where everything is measured by the hard-and-fast rule of what is called common sense, and they lead a life of alternate ecstasy and torture which brings them early to the grave.

With such a nature, Wilfred was apt to overestimate all things, and with him disappointment meant despair. Thus his interview with Lord Kenny threw him into the slough of despond, and what many a man would have borne with equanimity rendered his life for the moment absolutely unbearable. Nor were his spirits soothed by the receipt of a letter from Hilda, which set the seal on his disappointment.

Evidently written at the dictation of Lord Kenny, the burden thereof was good-bye for ever. Divested of all graciousness, this meant that he would see her no more,—that everything was at an end. Wilfred saw plainly that, dominated as was her will by that of Lord Kenny, Hilda would marry Denham, and that there was absolutely no chance of stopping such a hateful marriage. He loved Hilda passionately, she returned that love, and out of their mutual affection they had constructed an ideal world, which the practical sense of Lord Kenny had shattered at one blow. The romance of their love was gone, and now but reality remained, — reality which pertained to the folly of a moneyless marriage. He saw it all now,— he could not help seeing it, so plainly was it placed before him; and, beggared of romance, of money, of love, he foresaw nothing but a future of despair.

Wilfred had two sides to his character,—the man-of-the-world side created by experience, and the imaginative side inherent in his being. This latter was now dominating his nature, and therefore, in accordance with the dictates of an excited brain, he madly went to extremes. All was over for him, nothing could restore his peace of mind,—life was hell, and the sooner he left this world the sooner would his self-torture be ended. This was but the midsummer madness of youth, though he never looked at the matter in that light. Worked up into a perfect frenzy by fancied wrongs which in his distempered mind assumed gigantic proportions, without a thought of the sin he was about to commit, he loaded his pistol. In another moment this madman would have been lying dead on the floor, when a sharp knock at the door brought him down with harsh insistence from the world of fantasy to that of fact. With an ejaculation the reverse of complimentary, he pushed the weapon under some loose papers on the table, and went to see who had disturbed him at so critical a moment.

His visitor proved to be Major Measurby, with whom he had made an engagement to go to the theatre that evening, — an engagement which had entirely escaped his memory.

"Upon my word, Dacre, you are treating me in a very shabby manner," said the major, who was an extremely irascible individual. "I have been waiting at the club for quite half an hour, and never a sight of you did I see."

"Why, what is the matter?" stammered Wilfred, whose brain was gradually cooling down.

"Matter!" echoed Measurby, taking a chair; "why, have n't we a box at the Curtain Theatre to-night?"

"Oh, the theatre," replied Wilfred mechanically. "I — I beg your pardon, Major, but I quite forgot the engagement."

"What's the matter with you, Dacre?" said the major in an astonished tone; "your face is as pale as a ghost, man. Have you had bad news?"

"No," replied Wilfred shortly, "I have not."

"Ah, then it's debts?"

"No."

"No? Then there must be a woman in the case."

"Nonsense!" retorted Wilfred sharply; "it has nothing to do with a woman."

"Well, if it's none of the three, what makes you so wild looking?"

"I have a headache."

Major Measurby laughed derisively, and placed his elbows on the table in order to make some ironical reply. In doing so he disarranged the papers and caught sight of the pistol, whereat the expression of his face changed. Dacre, seeing he was found out, dropped into his chair with a groan and covered his face with his hands. Measurby looked at him for a few moments in silence, as he did not well know what to say. An awkward pause ensued; but the major, accustomed in his adventurous life to act promptly in emergencies, was the first to recover himself. He saw that there was a spirit-stand on the sideboard, and speedily poured out a glass of brandy, with which he approached Wilfred.

"Here, my boy," he said in a persuasive tone, "just drink this up and then we will talk matters over. I may be able to help you."

Wilfred, utterly broken down by the strain of the day's events, did as he was ordered, and, having placed the empty glass on the table, looked inquiringly at the major. That old campaigner had thrown off his cloak and resumed his seat, from whence he regarded Dacre in a very critical manner. Knowing Wilfred's excitable nature, he gave him time to recover himself; and for fully two minutes they sat looking at one another in silence.

"Come now, my boy, what is the meaning of all this?" he said, at length, laying his hand on Wilfred's knee.

"Nothing that I can tell you," replied Dacre, in no wise prepared to make a confidant of the major.

"And why not? 'Open confession is good for the soul,'" said Measurby in a joking tone; then more seriously, "My dear Dacre, I have no wish to force your confidence, but, believe me, I may be of more use to you than you think. I arrived, you must admit, at a very opportune moment. This shows me," continued the major emphatically, "that you are influenced by me,— in other words, that I have been led to you by Fate."

"By Fate!" reiterated Wilfred, with a smile of disdain; "surely you don't believe in that rubbish."

"Is it rubbish?" asked Measurby calmly. "The West says 'yes,' the East says 'no.' I prefer to believe in the latter."

"Then you are a fatalist."

"I am. That comes of having lived so long in Asia. The doctrines of Islam have coloured my life. I believe that all our actions are under the control of the deity called Fate."

"Then your coming here, according to your theory, was fated."

"It was. Had I not arrived here to the second, you would now be dead."

"Only a coincidence."

"A coincidence which shows me that I have been brought into your life to help you in your troubles."

"You cannot do that,—unless you give me a fortune."

"Well, I may perhaps be able to do so," replied the major serenely. "Come; make me your father confessor."

Wilfred hesitated. This conversation was already influencing his mind, as he was in that state of indecision when men catch at straws. At such moments the ordinary currents of life are diverted by chance circumstances into other channels, and Wilfred, with a thrill of superstition, felt that this conversation would decide the course of his future life. With his imaginative mind, he was prone to superstition, and was more affected by it than he cared to admit. Measurby had arrived so pat to the moment when he was contemplating self-destruction, that it did indeed look as though Fate had guided him hither. It would perhaps be wise to confide his troubles to this messenger of Destiny. If that messenger had only been any one but Major Measurby!

The old soldier had not a good reputation. As a military man his character was irreproachable, for he had fought bravely in the frontier wars of the Empire; but, socially speaking, people were inclined to look upon the major as little better than an adventurer. He had lived most of his life in India, and, having retired of late years, was now residing in England on his pension. This was a very fair and above-board record; still his general habits were so mysterious that he was generally regarded as a dangerous person. Some one had discovered that he employed private detectives, but what use he made of them was a mystery. Still, the very name of a private detective smacks of some disreputable secret, and there were those who hinted at dark stories in connection with Measurby's career. Whether such gossip came to his ears it is impossible to say, but, if it did, he took no notice of such idle rumours, but went serenely on his way.

In person the major was tall and bulky, with a weatherbeaten face, grey hair and a grizzled moustache. He was as straight as a dart; dressed irreproachably, and had a pair of remarkably keen blue eyes which saw everything. He might have been a scamp or a good man, an adventurer or a millionaire; but whatever was his real character no one ever found it out, and the major was known as he chose to be known.

For some unaccountable reason he had taken a great fancy to Wilfred, and, having very ingratiating manners, had become quite intimate with the young man. Up to this moment, however, Wilfred had never known that Measurby was a fatalist, and the knowledge considerably startled him. Altogether he was somewhat perplexed how to act. If he refused to tell his troubles to the major, matters would remain in the same unsatisfactory condition; but if he did make him his confidant, the wily old soldier might show him a way out of his difficulties. While these thoughts were passing through his mind the major stared at him steadily with his keen blue eyes. Perhaps he hypnotized Wilfred into obedience, but at all events that distrustful man found himself telling all his troubles to the major, — with certain reservations.

"I need not mention names, Major," he said hurriedly, "nor need I relate a long history. The whole affair is very simple. I have not a penny in the world, and the woman I love is about to marry another man."

The major nodded sympathetically and lighted a strong cigar. "I guessed as much before you spoke," he said between puffs of smoke. "All clubland knows you are on your last legs as regards money, and also that Miss Havard is going to marry Denham."

"I mentioned no names," replied Wilfred stiffly, annoyed at this penetration.

"Of course not; but I am right all the same. Is that not so?" He waited for a reply, but receiving none, resumed his speech. "Silence gives consent. Well, and what do you propose to do?"

"Get out of the world."

"Nonsense! That would be the act of a coward. Besides, now that Fate has guided me to your side, I may help you."

"To marry Hilda Havard?"

"Yes!"

"My dear Measurby, if you can do that I will subscribe to your theory of Fate, in which at present I don't believe."

"I see that brandy has done you good," said the major in a tone of great satisfaction. "Now

3

you talk sensibly. You proposed to Miss Havard to-day."

"Yes, I did!" replied Wilfred defiantly, thinking it best to confess all.

"And she refused you. Oh yes! you need not deny it. That pistol would not have been there had she accepted you as her husband. Well, with all this excitement you have eaten nothing all day. Such abstinence, in connection with your disappointment, has upset you thoroughly. Hence your idea of suicide. After an hour at the theatre and a good supper you will look at the matter in a more philosophical light."

"I wish neither theatre nor supper," said Dacre sulkily.

"You don't know what is good for you," retorted the major grimly. "I am your physician, young man, and I am going to cure you. Now go and dress at once, and then we will go to the theatre; afterwards supper at my rooms, and then," added Measurby in a significant tone, "I should not be surprised if you met with an adventure."

"What do you mean?"

"I will tell you after supper. Meanwhile dress as quickly as you can."

Curiosity overpowered every other feeling, and Wilfred, half against his will, went off to put on his evening suit. The conversation had done him good, for he no longer thought of suicide, but looked forward with considerable bewilderment to the conversation after supper. It might be that the theory of Fate guidance was true after all, and the events of this night would enable him to marry Hilda in spite of her father's prohibition. At all events, he was fascinated by the major's proposition, and dressed himself with all speed.

"I have changed my mind," said Measurby, when Wilfred returned to the sitting-room. "We will go to my rooms and have supper at once. A good meal will do you more good than the theatre."

"I am quite agreeable," answered Wilfred listlessly. "Your comedy will be amusing if nothing else."

"Perhaps the comedy may turn out to be a tragedy," observed the major dryly. "Just slip this pistol into your pocket."

"And for what reason?" asked Dacre, accepting the weapon.

Measurby shrugged his shoulders and led the way out of the room. "My campaigning life has always taught me to be prepared for emergencies," he said as they descended the stair. "I wish you to try an experiment to-night, and it may lead you into queer places."

Decidedly the major was remarkably mysterious, and Wilfred had half a mind to draw back lest he should entangle himself in some trouble. When he reflected, however, that he had lost all that he valued in life, that things could not possibly be worse than they were, he no longer hesitated, but determined to follow out whatever advantage there might be, to the end.

"I cannot exactly make out what you mean," he said to his host when they were seated at the supper table, "and as a rule I would refuse to be influenced by you as I am to-night. But with me things have come to such a pass that I feel ready to indulge in whatever folly you may suggest."

"I am not going to suggest any folly," answered Measurby quietly. "I only wish by means of supper and conversation to bring you back to your normal state of mind. You are too young to think of such a mad thing as suicide. It's a cowardly course to take at the best, and a man is a fool who adopts it. To-morrow you will thank your stars that I arrived when I did and saved you from such idiotcy."

"But the adventure you promised me, Major."

"Humph! There may be an adventure and there may not. I am really promising you nothing, but am only putting you in the way of trying a little experiment which is a favourite one with myself. However, I'll tell you everything after supper. Meanwhile make a good meal, and reflect how near you have been to making a fool of yourself."

Despairing lover, actual pauper as he was, Wilfred made an excellent supper, and did full justice to Major Measurby's hospitality. He enjoyed his food and his champagne, of which wine his host kept an excellent brand. Towards the end of the meal things began to look more hopeful, and when he was established in a comfortable armchair with a good cigar between his lips, and a special liqueur at his elbow, he began to feel somewhat ashamed of his previous folly.

"Upon my word, Major, I think you were right," he said penitently. "I was a fool to think of suicide. After all, while there is life there is hope."

"There's no doubt about that," replied Measurby, puffing gravely at his cigar; "at your age it would be folly to despair. There is no bad but what there might not be a worse."

"Well, certainly, I might fall ill, which would somewhat complicate matters," said Wilfred, shrugging his shoulders; "but as it is I think things are quite bad enough. And I don't know if belief in your theory would render me any more philosophical."

"Perhaps my belief may supply the remedy."

"In what way?"

Major Measurby knocked the ashes off his cigar, and considered for a few moments.

"Of course I believe that a man's future is settled by Fate," he said at length with much deliberation; "still, there is such a thing as tempting Fate. I myself indulge in that pastime sometimes, and it has often led to curious results."

"What is your plan of operation?" asked Wilfred, urged to this question by a secret sympathy with the subject of conversation.

"I take notice of the first chance remark I hear on leaving the house, and guide my future course by its example. By doing so I cast myself on the tide of Destiny, and it carries me where it will."

"Is it not rather a rash proceeding?"

"For some cases it is. That is why I asked you to retain your pistol, — it might be useful, if you are involved in any adventure."

"And what am I to do?"

"When you leave this house," said Measurby

slowly, " keep your ears open for any chance remark. Act upon it if you can do so, — if not return here and tell me what it is. I may be able to read you a sermon on its text."

" It seems rather a ridiculous proceeding."

" To the sceptical it is. You are a sceptic, but if you try it to-night, who knows what Fate may have in store for you?"

" And is this the way you propose to assist me in my difficulties?" said Wilfred, rather nettled at the childishness of the whole affair.

" Oh no! I will come and see you to-morrow. If Fate does not help you I will: but, believe me, there is more in my fancy than you believe. Show me your hand."

Wilfred, with a disdainful smile, straightened his arm. Measurby looked carefully at the palm of his hand, and spoke in a low voice: —

" There is money in your hand. Money and a successful future. A happy marriage and a long life. Yes! Fate will be good to you."

" Oh, rubbish!" said Wilfred, snatching away his hand. " I don't believe in such nonsense. Your Fate belief is all very well, and is reasonable to a certain extent. But as for palmistry, my dear Major, I am a rational being."

Measurby arose to his feet with a laugh.

" Well, I will not try to convert you, but if my scheme of to-night succeeds you will have to admit that there is something in the theory of Fate."

" I shan't try your experiment."

" Oh yes, you will," replied the major quietly.

" If a chance sentence strikes on your ear, you will act on it out of sheer curiosity. When I see you to-morrow you will have something to tell me."

" I 'm afraid not," said Dacre, putting on his coat. " I am going straight home to bed. At all events, I have to thank you for having cured me of my folly."

" You won't think any more of it ? " queried the major, as he shook hands.

" No! I promise you that. If I lose Hilda I will try to bear it like a man. As to my poverty, I can cure that by work. I don't believe in your fatalistic theories, Major, but I believe in your kind heart."

" This is the first good word I have ever had said about it," remarked Measurby, with a grim smile, walking with his guest to the door. " Good-night, Dacre ; mind you try my experiment."

Wilfred laughed at the idea of committing such a folly, and ran downstairs. The supper and conversation had done him good, and he now felt in a much more hopeful mood. After all, Hilda had not yet accepted Denham, and, despite her father's insistence, might decline to be sold into matrimony. If she dared him thus far, she would certainly have her own way in other things. He might marry her after all, and then in the fairyland of Cuba they would pass a happy future. His man-of-the-world side was uppermost at this moment, and he looked back to his frenzy with the utmost disgust, hardly believing he could have acted so foolishly.

The idea of a possible marriage with Hilda quite exhilarated him, and he walked quickly down Half

Moon Street with a sudden hope, born of encouragement, that things might mend. Just as he turned the corner into Piccadilly he passed two men in earnest conversation by the lamp-post. Remembering the major's ridiculous idea, with a smile of scorn at his own childishness, he walked slowly past so as to overhear some chance remark.

" You will find it," said one man to the other, " at 49 Karp Street, Soho."

CHAPTER III.

BAGDAD IN THE WEST.

The two men passed onward, but Wilfred, astonished at the strange appropriateness of the remark, stood still in deep thought for a few moments. Many an observation would have presented obstacles, or been so conventional that no one could draw any meaning therefrom; but this saying afforded such an opportunity of testing the truth of the superstition that he half believed the experiment to be worth trying. In a second his brain was at work conjuring up all kinds of consequences. No longer a man of the world, he relapsed in a moment into the imaginative dreamer, and in this condition was ready to engage in the most fantastical adventures. Had he been in his normal state of mind he would assuredly have scorned the idea of committing such a folly, but what with the excitements of the day and the fantasies of the major, he felt inclined for once to indulge in an episode of the Arabian Nights. The fumes of the wine still stimulated his brain, and for the moment the man was practically helpless in the grip of a superstitious feeling. The sanest man has these moments of what may be called demoniac possession, so that Wilfred, constantly drawn as he was to the fantastical, saw nothing strange in thus obeying the instinct of a heated imagination. In the daytime it would have looked supremely ridiculous, but at this hour of midnight it assumed quite a different complexion, and as one in a dream accepts the most absurd events as only natural, so Wilfred believed this madness to be sanity.

"Let me forget that I am in London," he said, as he strolled along. "Let me think that this is Bagdad, and I, Haroun al Raschid in search of the fantastical. At Karp Street I may find the three Calenders and they will tell me their adventures."

Laughing somewhat at the folly of the whole proceeding, he walked rapidly in the direction of Soho, identifying himself for the moment with the curious Caliph. It was now nearly twelve o'clock, but the main streets were not yet deserted. Soho, however, was comparatively lonely, and when he arrived in the well-known square, he found no one to tell him the whereabouts of Karp Street. He had never heard of such a place, and indeed doubted its existence.

"I am on a fool's errand," he said, pausing irresolutely. "The wisest thing would be for me to go home and abandon such follies."

At this moment he heard the firm step of a policeman echo on the pavement, and at once determined to apply to him for information. If the man could inform him of the whereabouts of Karp Street, he would go there for the humour of the thing; if not, it would be best to return to the " Albany " at once.

"Policeman," he said, as that functionary drew

near, "do you know the whereabouts of Karp Street?"

"Yes, sir," answered the policeman unhesitatingly. "Go out on the left of the square and take the turning to the right."

"Thank you," said Wilfred, rejoicing that he had discovered this much; and, giving the policeman a shilling for his information, he took his way towards the left of Soho Square.

On turning to the right as directed, he found himself in a narrow little alley of no great length, and on glancing up at the corner plate saw by the light of the lamp that it was the place he was in search of.

"So this is Karp Street," he said, walking boldly along. "Now for No. 49, and then — well, since Fate has guided me successfully so far, I must leave the sequel to that power."

The gas-lamps showed the numbers quite plainly, and he had no difficulty in finding 49. It was a narrow house, three stories in height, standing a little distance back from the pavement. In front of the heavy door he stood hesitating, feeling quite undecided as to his next step. At last he timidly put out his hand and touched the door lightly. To his surprise it swung open, revealing a dark passage, which looked anything but tempting. The discovery was so unexpected that he recoiled in amazement.

"Is there truth in the major's theory, after all?" he muttered, wiping his brow. "Upon my soul, it looks very like it. Doors as a rule are not left open at night in London, and that this one which I discovered by a chance remark should be so is, to say the least, a strange coincidence. The adventure looks promising! Shall I advance or retire?"

Wilfred had plenty of courage for daylight dangers, but the fantasy of this affair assailed the superstitious side of his nature, and he hesitated for some minutes on the threshold of the mystery. At length he resolved to enter the passage and see whither it would lead, but, before advancing, made sure that his pistol was ready to hand. It was resting securely in his pocket, and, feeling that he was protected in the case of danger, he boldly stepped into the darkness. No sooner was he within than the door swung to again and shut with a sharp click.

"Trapped!" he said with a sudden thrill of fear. "Have I stumbled on a den of thieves? Thank Heaven, I have my pistol."

Indeed, the situation was not calculated to inspire him with confidence. He had heard of men vanishing in London and never being seen again. This was just the house in which an unwary stranger might be murdered, and he heartily regretted that he had not renounced the adventure. Luckily he had his pistol and would be able to defend himself in case of danger. It seemed to be all round him, though in the thick darkness he could not see where he was. No sound struck on his ear, and, strange to say, the whole atmosphere was impregnated with the odour of sandal wood, which suggested the romance of the East to his imaginative brain. The affair was becoming more like the Arabian Nights than ever, and, despite a certain feeling that he was environed by unknown dangers, Wilfred's breast was filled with a powerful curiosity.

Before committing himself fully to the adventure, he thought it would be just as well to secure a retreat in case of peril, and ran his hand up and down the door to find the lock so that he could open it again. To his dismay, the whole length of the door was perfectly smooth; and he realized with a shudder that it closed by a spring, the secret of which he could not discover. Clearly there was no chance of retreat in that direction; so, making the best of his position, he moved cautiously forward, pistol in hand. Every step was taken with great deliberation, as he knew not but what he might be precipitated into some abyss, and the darkness was so dense that he could not see an inch before him.

At length his foot struck against an obstacle, which by the touch he discovered to be a staircase. Up this he went slowly, the sandal-wood perfume becoming more powerful as he ascended. Suddenly the staircase ceased, and he found himself on what he supposed to be a landing. In the gloom he did not know which way to turn, and stretched out his hands to find the wall, by which he could guide his way. In place of wood he touched some silken texture, and grasping this drew what were evidently curtains to one side. Then he stepped forward, and paused thunder-struck at the strange scene before him.

Was he in London or Bagdad! Was it the East or the West? Hitherto he had never doubted; but now the place in which he found himself was so Eastern in character that he distrusted the evidence of his own senses. The curtains veiled the entrance to a kind of antechamber illuminated by a soft pink glow. Brilliant carpets covered the tessellated floor, there was a small fountain in the centre falling into a marble basin, and the walls glittered with arabesque patterns in vivid tints. The ceiling was of open fretwork, filled in with rose-coloured glass; and through this shone the light which illuminated the room. A divan ran round all sides of the apartment, stools inlaid with mother-of-pearl were scattered about, and gold-broidered cushions, carpets of Scind, mats from Ispahan, and gorgeous hangings of Indian workmanship, made up a most bizarre and striking picture.

Wilfred stared at all this magnificence with amazement; nor was his astonishment lessened when through the horse-shoe arch at the end of the room came a gigantic Nubian with a drawn sabre. Such a sight was by no means reassuring, and Wilfred drew back a step, keeping his pistol ready for use in his right hand. In place of assaulting him, however, the Nubian made a profound obeisance and drew back the silken curtains veiling the archway. Beyond, Wilfred caught a glimpse of more Oriental splendours, but, transfixed with astonishment, could make no movement.

At this moment an unseen minstrel — evidently a woman — began to sing some Arabic song, which further added to the Asian atmosphere of the place; and Wilfred, drawn as by magic in the direction of the singing, moved slowly forward. He felt as though he were in a dream, and obedient to the impulse passed between the curtains, still held aside by the slave, to the room beyond. It was an apartment similar to that which he had seen, but even more luxurious in character. Here he naturally expected to find the singer, but to his astonishment discovered the only occupant of the room to be a shrivelled old man, swathed in silken garments, who lay languidly on a pile of cushions. The moment he crossed the threshold the curtains fell behind him, the voice ceased, and Wilfred, more bewildered than ever, found himself standing before the old man, who surveyed him with a look of gratification.

"I congratulate you on your courage, sir," he said gravely in English, "but it shall not go unrewarded."

"What does it all mean?" asked Wilfred, passing his hand across his brow. "Am I dreaming?"

"On the contrary, you are very much awake," said the old man dryly. "Will you be pleased to be seated. I am sorry I cannot offer you a chair, but you must adopt Eastern fashions for once in your life."

Wilfred mechanically obeyed his host, and threw himself down on a pile of soft cushions, utterly worn out by the strain on his nerves. The interview with Hilda, the conversation with Measurby, the discovery of this fantastic apartment, all seemed figments of some monstrous dream, wild as that Coleridge dreamed of Kubla Khan. The old man saw this and clapped his hands sharply, whereat a black slave appeared.

"Pipes and coffee," said his master in a peremptory tone. "I see you are worn out," he added in a kindly manner, when the slave had retired, "but a cup of strong coffee will restore your nerve."

"For Heaven's sake, tell me what this all means," cried Wilfred in desperation. "Am I in London or in Bagdad?"

"You are in London, sir, and have by chance found a remnant of the East."

"By chance?" reiterated Dacre, smiling; "say, rather, by Fate."

"Ah!" cried his host with a keen glance, "you are a fatalist."

"From to-night I am."

"And why from to-night?"

"Because Fate directed me to this extraordinary place."

"Then Fate has done you a good turn. You must tell me how you came here, sir. At present drink a cup of coffee and let me look at you."

The Nubian had brought in pipes and coffee, the latter of which Wilfred accepted with avidity. His host refused coffee, but solaced himself with a nargileh, while he surveyed his guest long and attentively. Wilfred on his side examined the old man with no little curiosity, and began to think the adventure was not without certain romantic elements.

The proprietor of this Eastern paradise was a small, dried-up person, more like a monkey than a man, who looked extremely ill, and, crouching among his sumptuous cushions, appeared to be within a measurable distance of the grave. He wore a rich smoking-cap embroidered with gold lace, and flowing robes of silk, after the fashion of the Orientals. At first Wilfred thought he was an Eastern prince; but, on looking at him closely, he saw that despite his dark skin the contour of his features was decidedly English in character. The hand grasping the snaky curl of the nargileh resembled a bird's claw, and on one finger was a massive gold ring, containing a dark blue stone, evidently lapis lazuli. He appeared to be satisfied with his scrutiny of the young man, and withdrew his eyes, with a grunt of satisfaction.

"Permit me to introduce myself," he said at length, sinking back among his cushions with an air of lassitude. "I am Michael Lascelle, at your service."

"My name is Dacre,—Wilfred Dacre," replied the young man, who saw no reason to conceal his identity, "and I must apologize for my intrusion."

"By no means, Mr. Dacre. I expected you."

"Expected me?" echoed Wilfred, in astonishment. "How can that be, when you never saw me before?"

"Like yourself, I am a fatalist," said Lascelle, stroking his beard, "and I waited for Fate to send me a man of courage. You are that man, else you would not have dared the open door, and risked unknown dangers."

"Then the door was left open by design?"

"Yes! I wished some one to come to me for a particular purpose, and thought that was the best way to accomplish my aim. Indeed, the idea was suggested to me by a story, written by the cleverest of your present-day novelists. I am glad to see that the trap has been successful and caught you."

"Well, now I am here," said Wilfred, somewhat bewildered by this strange speech, "what do you wish me to do?"

"Nothing but converse with me. I am very ill, as you see, and my disease rarely permits me to sleep. Like Haroun al Raschid, I am fond of adventures; but as I cannot roam the streets like the Caliph, the adventure has to come to me. That door has been open for the last three weeks, but you are the first person who has had the courage to enter. Well, you will obtain your reward. Ask what you please, and it will be granted to you."

"I am afraid you would find it impossible to gratify my wishes."

"No! I think I can promise you most things."

"Supposing I asked for a fortune?"

"It is yours."

"Say fifty thousand pounds!"

"It is yours," reiterated Lascelle gravely; whereat Wilfred fell back on his cushions in a fit of laughter. The idea was in keeping with the gorgeous East, but not exactly fitted for the London of this matter-of-fact nineteenth century.

"You are pleased to jest," said the old man imperturbably, "but I assure you I speak truly. Truth is stranger than fiction."

"Not stranger than this page out of the Arabian Nights," retorted Wilfred, recovering his gravity. "Here am I, a perfect stranger, who uninvited enter your house. Instead of ordering me away, you propose to bestow a fortune on the intruder. I presume I am awake, but it is difficult to believe that such is the case."

"I could relate stranger things than this adventure of yours, and perhaps I will if I see fit to do so. Meanwhile, tell me how you were directed here by Fate."

Wilfred had no objection to relate his adventures, but he suppressed all mention of Major Measurby, as he judged it best to tell as little about himself and his surroundings as possible.

"I was conversing with a friend of mine," he said with apparent frankness, "and our conversation turned on Fate. He told me of the Eastern custom which converts chance remarks into oracles. I was so amused at the idea that I determined to obey, if I could, the first remark I heard. It chanced that I passed two men conversing earnestly, and one said to the other, 'You will find it at 49 Karp Street, Soho;' so acting upon that advice I came here, found the door open and arrived as you see."

"What was the remark?" asked Lascelle, starting up with some excitement.

"'You will find it at 49 Karp Street, Soho,'" repeated Wilfred, rather pleased that he had startled his host for once in a way.

"Strange!" muttered the old man with a frown. "I know not why such a remark should be made. I am a stranger in London. No one knows of this place. Young man," he said aloud, fixing a piercing eye on Wilfred, "you know more than you say."

'On my honour, I do not," replied Wilfred indignantly.

"What do you want from me?" asked Lascelle, irrelevantly.

"Nothing."

"Nothing!" echoed the old man in surprise. "Then why did you come to see me?"

"I didn't come to see you," retorted Dacre, feeling exasperated by this questioning. "I came here by chance, as I told you. If you doubt me I can go away."

"No, no! Sit down," cried Lascelle, waving his hand in a deprecating manner. "Do not be so hasty, Mr. Dacre. Old age is naturally suspicious. Let me think for a moment."

He thrust his hand into his beard, and began to mutter in a low tone, while Wilfred, rather perplexed by his conduct, smoked on in silence.

"Is it indeed Fate?" he murmured thoughtfully to himself. "Fate or design? No! I believe this man speaks truly; but who in London could know of this address? Never mind, I will know all to-morrow. If"—

"Well, Mr. Lascelle," interrupted Wilfred, who was beginning to grow tired of this silence, "I have told you my story, and now I would like to know yours. Are you a millionaire indulging in romance, an Indian prince exiled to England, Haroun al Raschid in the flesh, or what are you?"

"What is your opinion?" asked Lascelle with a smile, leaning forward.

"Upon my word, I have no opinion," retorted Dacre, shrugging his shoulders. "A character out of the Arabian Nights, I suppose. Judging from this Oriental paradise in the heart of London you must have the ring of Solomon, and command the tribes of the Jinn. Tell me who you are. I will accept any story, however marvellous. This is not London, but Bagdad, and I am in the land of romance. Feed my fancy with marvels, Haroun, and I will believe them all."

"I like your humour," said Lascelle smiling, " but I will not tell you my story just yet. To-morrow night I may do so."

"Oh! so you expect me to return to-morrow night?"

"Yes! if you care to."

"Of course I care to," replied Wilfred gaily. "Life is so prosaic in the nineteenth century that I welcome a romance like this with delight. I presume you are some eccentric millionaire who indulges in this Oriental freak by way of amusement. I admire your humour as you admire mine, and, were I rich, might act in the same way. It is not given to every one to realize the romances of Dumas."

" If you were rich would you do so ? "

Wilfred shrugged his shoulders.

" I don't know, M. Monte Christo! At present I have not a penny, so I know not in what follies I would indulge if rich."

" You are poor ! "

" Poor ! " echoed Wilfred with scorn. " My dear sir, I haven't got more than ten pounds in the whole world."

" Yet you are dressed well and look like a gentleman."

"Oh!· As to these clothes, they are the remains of my fine days, when I had a banking account. I am of good birth, certainly, but my money is all gone and I am in the depths of despair. 'I cannot dig, to beg I am ashamed,' so what I am to do I know not."

"Still, you have health and strength and good looks."

"All useless to me, I assure you."

"That is not a very noble sentiment."

"My dear sir," said Wilfred sarcastically, "sentiment is a luxury only to be indulged in by a millionaire like yourself. A poor gentleman is denied such consolations."

"So you are poor!" said Lascelle musingly. "What would you do if I made you rich?"

"I do not accept gifts from strangers," replied Wilfred, drawing himself up stiffly. "I know nothing of you, nor you of me, so that you should give or I accept riches is out of the question."

"Then what do you intend to do?"

"Emigrate to the colonies, I suppose," said Dacre with a sigh. "I have no care to stop in England."

"On account of your poverty?"

"Yes, and on account of a woman."

"Ah! I thought we should come to that sooner or later," remarked Lascelle, with a meaning smile. "So you are in love?"

"Full ten fathoms deep."

"And you cannot marry on account of your poverty?"

"No, I cannot. She also is poor, and is forced by circumstances — and her father — to make a rich marriage. 'T is the popular mode of to-day."

"You would give a good deal to stop that marriage, would you not?"

"I would give my soul," said Dacre impetuously. "I love her fondly, madly. But there! What is the use of talking about such things to a stranger! You are too old to sympathize with the foolish romance of a lover, and cannot help me."

"Yes, I can — and I will!"

"By giving me money? Thank you, my dear sir, but I decline to encourage such quixotism. Leave your money to your heirs."

"I have none!"

"Then to some charity, if it so pleases you. I am poor, but I am a gentleman, and proud enough to refuse wealth to which I have no right."

"I do not propose to offer you money."

"Then how can you help me?"

"I will tell you that to-morrow night, if you come here, and I still live."

"I will come here, certainly," said Wilfred, rising to his feet, "if only out of curiosity. But why 'if you still live'?"

"Because I am dying."

"I am sorry to hear that. Why do you not see a doctor?"

"I have seen all the best doctors in the world. They can do nothing. I am dying fast."

"Can I not help you?"

"Not unless you can give me a new body," replied Lascelle grimly. "No, I am beyond the power of man. I must die and leave all my wealth behind me."

"Are you rich?"

"I am as rich as a king."

"I thought so," said Wilfred, glancing round the room; "else you could not afford such a palace as this. Well, Mr. Lascelle, I am sorry for your illness, but I am afraid I can do nothing."

"You can come and see me to-morrow night."

"By all means: but it is no use your offering me money, for I will not take it."

"I promise you I won't offend in that way again. Good-night."

"Good-night. I can find my way out. Thank you for your entertainment."

"And you can find your way back to this place?"

"Easily! Good-night once more. I trust you will be better to-morrow evening."

Wilfred shook the hand extended to him by Lascelle, and walked out of the room. There was no slave in the antechamber as he passed through; so, on arriving at the head of the staircase, he lighted a match. By such a feeble light he found his way down to the door, which to his surprise was now wide open.

"The old man works it from above, I suppose," he said, as he passed out into the street. "Ah!" he continued, as the door closed again, "I thought so. Well, certainly I have had a strange adventure. Measurby is right, after all. Won't he be astonished to-morrow, when I tell him of the events of this night!"

CHAPTER IV.

AN EXTRAORDINARY COINCIDENCE.

When Wilfred awoke next morning he had considerable doubt as to the actuality of his bizarre adventure. Had he really been to Karp Street, Soho? Had he really spoken to this modern Monte Christo amid Asian splendours, or was the whole thing a vision of the night? Might not Major Measurby have drugged him with opium, and so caused him to dream such fantasies? In truth, the events had been of so extraordinary a nature that he might well doubt whether they had ever taken place. One is not as a rule transported in a moment from smoky London to the banks of the Tigris. Nubian slaves and Oriental splendours are alien to our prosaic existence, and there are no Jinns in the West to realize the magic of the Thousand and One Nights.

Between sleeping and waking Wilfred pondered over these things, and it was not until he had taken his bath that he began to really believe in the adventure of the previous night. Nor when he came to the conclusion that all had actually happened did he arrive at any solution of the mystery, beyond the fact that Lascelle was some eccentric millionaire.

"I have eaten of the insane root," said Wilfred, as he sat down to breakfast, "and it has taken my reason prisoner. Karp Street exists only in my brain; and as for this Palace of Delight, my imagination has created it out of nothing. What a pity I did not people it with women instead of a wrinkled old man! Bah! I have no control over my imagination."

But doubt his own senses as he might, facts were too strong to be thus dismissed, and he soon arrived at the conclusion that all was true. This belief gave him great satisfaction, as it inspired him with a wild hope that through the instrumentality of Lascelle he might yet make Hilda his wife. After all, he doubted whether he had been wise in refusing the generous offer of the millionaire. Here was a man who had no relatives to claim his wealth, and who freely offered to bestow it on a stranger. Eccentric certainly, but not more so than the Orientalism of the house in Soho. It is not wise to flout the gifts of grudging Fortune, for no deity is so capricious or more prone to take offence.

"If I don't take the money, some one else will," soliloquized Wilfred, as he finished his breakfast; "and as I need wealth very badly, I do not see why I should have any scruples in accepting such a quixotic offer. I asked Providence for immediate wealth in order to marry Hilda, and Providence in the most fantastical manner has granted me my wish. It would be folly to refuse, and yet I hardly like to accept. The whole thing smacks of witchcraft. I believe in 'La Peau de Chagrin,' for my adventures have been quite as odd as those of Raphael. Luckily I am not burdened with such a cursed talisman as robbed him of all enjoyment of his good fortune. My benefactor proposed no conditions, so I think it would be wise of me to take this proffered wealth and risk the consequences. To-night I will see him again and tell him of my determination. If he proposes conditions, as he might do, I will hear what they are before accepting. I don't care about selling myself to the devil, and upon my soul this business looks uncommonly like a Satanic contract. I am a youthful Faust, and he a paralytic Mephistopheles."

Meanwhile he made one resolution: that Hilda should not at once accept Sir Richard Denham's offer, and thus if anything resulted from his adventure he would at least find her free to marry him. With this idea he wrote her a letter, stating that circumstances had occurred which might possibly enable him to remove all obstacles to their union, and begging her to evade Denham's offer for at least a few days.

"By to-night," thought Wilfred, as he sent this letter off, "I shall know exactly how I stand. If I do become rich I will see Lord Kenny at once and satisfy his scruples; if not, — well, Hilda will still be able to accept Denham's offer in a few days. It is a forlorn hope truly; still, it is a hope, and drowning men like myself catch at straws."

The excitement of the previous night had left him very weary; so, in place of going out as usual, he lay down on the sofa, and gave himself up to idle thoughts. Nothing might come of his adventure; still, he cherished a certain amount of hope that he might benefit thereby, and indulged in a few day-dreams, which if not probable were at least possible. While thus engaged Major Measurby arrived, and Wilfred sprang up to give him a hearty greeting. Putting all else out of the question, Measurby had behaved in a very kind manner, and Wilfred was not the man to forget a generous action.

"I am glad to see you, Measurby. Have you had breakfast?"

"Long ago," replied the major, taking a seat. "You, I perceive, have just finished, which tells me you were up late this morning."

"Does it tell you anything else?"

"Yes! You did not come straight home, last night, after leaving my rooms."

"No, I did not, Major Measurby," said Wilfred solemnly. "I am beginning to believe in your theory of Fate."

"Ah!" replied the major, interested at once. "You had an adventure last night?"

"An adventure worthy of Gil Blas!"

"Egad! I am sorry I was not with you. Well, tell me all about it."

"You won't believe my story!"

"I'm not so sure of that. I have seen so many strange things in my time that I am less sceptical than the average man. Go on, Dacre. I am all attention."

"On leaving your rooms," said Wilfred, drawing his chair close to that of the major, "I passed two men at the corner of Half Moon Street and Piccadilly. One said to the other, 'You will find it at 49 Karp Street, Soho.'"

"Queer remark. You acted on it, of course."

"I went straight to that address, and found the door open."

"After which you came away?"

"Not at all. I went upstairs and found Bagdad in place of London. It was an Oriental paradise, Major, — magnificent decorations, Nubian slaves, and all kinds of queer things."

"Pooh!" said Measurby disdainfully, "you've been dreaming."

"No! I swear I saw it all. And the master of this place was a dried-up monkey called Lascelle."

"Called what?" shouted the major, jumping up in a rage.

"Lascelle."

"An old man with a gray beard?"

"Yes!"

"Who said he was a millionaire?"

"He did!"

"And wore a ring of lapis lazuli on his right hand?"

"Why, do you know him?"

Major Measurby sat down wrathfully in his chair and hit the table with his clenched fist. For a few moments he spluttered with rage.

"Do I know him, the villain? Of course I do. The old scoundrel comes from India. I met him at Benares ten years ago, and have been hunting after him ever since."

"Why! What has he done to you?"

"He has a ring of mine, — that one you saw on

the finger of his right hand. It's a family heirloom which was in the possession of my brother Brian. I introduced Brian to this Lascelle, and they became very friendly. When my brother died he left the ring to Lascelle, and though I have asked the old man at least a dozen times to give it up to me, he refuses to do so. If I could only find him I'd soon force him to surrender the ring."

"But if your brother left it as a legacy" — began Wilfred, when the major cut him short with a wrathful ejaculation.

"My brother had no right to leave that ring out of the family. I prize it, sir, more than anything else in the wide world, and would give my ears to get it back again."

"I don't think you will need to make that sacrifice," said Dacre, a trifle sarcastically. "Come with me to-night, and probably Lascelle will give it to you. He has no further use for it."

"What do you mean?" asked Measurby, turning pale.

"He is dying!"

"Dying?" echoed the major in a nervous tone. "I must get that ring from him before he dies."

"Well, come with me to-night and ask him to give it to you," said Dacre again, rather disdainful of the major's excitement over such a trifle.

Measurby made no answer, but, rising from his seat, began to walk about the room in a state of uncontrollable agitation. Accustomed to regard the major as a man of iron nerve, Dacre was somewhat surprised at this apparent weakness.

"You seem to attach great importance to this ring, Major," he said idly.

Something clicked in the major's throat, and he made an effort to speak. He could not do so at once, and it was fully a minute before he could answer.

"Yes — family ring — I — I — Brandy, Dacre — quick."

Wilfred thought he was about to have a fit, so ghastly grew his face, and hastily handed him a glass of brandy. The major finished it at one gulp, and the spirit brought the colour back to his ashen face.

"Excuse me, Dacre," he said, mopping his brow with his handkerchief. "I am liable to these fainting-fits when I get excited. I am all right now."

"Is it worth while troubling over such a trifle?" observed Wilfred, resuming his seat.

"No, I don't suppose it is, Dacre, I don't suppose it is. But you see that is no ordinary ring. It has a great value in my eyes on account of family associations. I have hunted after that ring for years, sir."

"Oh! that is the reason of your private detective business," said Dacre, who had overheard club gossip.

"Precisely. I have spent no end of money in hunting the old man out, — merely to get back that ring. Hitherto I have failed, and it is curious that you should be the first to tell me what I have desired to know for years. This confirms my belief in Fate more than ever."

"It is a curious coincidence, certainly."

"It is not a coincidence, sir," retorted the major

irritably; "it is Fate — nothing but Fate. Did I not tell you that my opportune arrival last night had brought my personality into your life? This proves it. Through my placing you in a certain position you have discovered what has baffled all my energies for years. Fate, sir, Fate, nothing but Fate."

"Why not see Lascelle to-night?"

"No!" answered Measurby decisively, "if he knew I wanted it he would not give it up. But you, Dacre, can obtain it for the mere asking."

"I!" said Wilfred in surprise.

"Yes. I know the man. He is eccentric in the extreme, and your bravery in daring that open door has pleased him. He would give you anything, even this ring."

"Well, he certainly offered me a fortune last night, which I refused to take; so in place of that he will surely give me a paltry trinket."

"Of course he will," replied the major eagerly, "and then you can give it to me. Probably he will tell you a lot of lies about the ring, but believe none of them, Dacre, believe none of them."

"I don't see why he should tell me falsehoods."

"You don't know the man. I do."

"Where did you meet him, Major?"

"I told you — in Benares ten years ago. He is an eccentric recluse, very wealthy indeed. It was I who introduced him to my brother, — and then I was called to Calcutta. I never saw him again, for my brother died and Lascelle disappeared. Brian left a letter for me, saying he had given the ring to the old man. At once I wrote for it to be given up, but received no answer. Again and again I addressed my letters to his Benares residence, but got no reply. Then I used detectives to trace him, and they chased him all over India, but I could never meet him face to face. Afterwards he went to Persia. I followed, but never could meet him. He crossed over into Europe, and for years I tried to find him on the Continent. Then my spies found out he had gone to England, so to England I came. I notice you have heard of my employing detectives. It was to find Lascelle, but I never could trace his hiding-place till you told me just now. How strange, — how very strange. You will help me to get back the ring, Dacre, will you not?"

"By all means," said Wilfred, astonished at the imploring tone in which the major spoke. "But as he is now dying, he would probably give it to you if you asked him."

"No! no! I tell you no!" replied Measurby, vehemently. "He would sooner throw it into the sea than give it to me. Some superstitious fancy, I believe. He knows how much I desire it, and will never let me possess it. But you — you are the one to whom he will give it. If so, promise you will bring it straight to me."

"You say the ring is yours," said Dacre, ignoring the request.

"Yes! It is a family heirloom. No use to any one except me."

"Can you describe it?"

"Easily. A thick band of gold holding a lapis lazuli stone, graven with Sanscrit characters. It came into our family through an uncle who fought at Plassy, and is supposed to be a talisman conferring happiness on the possessor. Of course I attach no importance to such superstition, but I am anxious that the ring should come once more into the possession of our family."

"If the ring is yours, I will certainly get it for you, Major."

"You swear it, Dacre?"

"I swear it."

"If you get it for me, Dacre, it will be the best day's work you ever did," said the major, feverishly. "Yes! I am not a poor man, and when it is on my finger I will give you sufficient money to enable you to marry Miss Havard. I will give you thousands of pounds."

"Really!" said Wilfred, somewhat puzzled by his eagerness. "This ring must be very valuable."

"Only to me! Only to me," replied Measurby, eagerly. "I assure you the ring is worthless to any other person. I have neither chick nor child, and I have taken a fancy to you; so get me the ring and you can take all my fortune."

"My dear Measurby, I don't want your fortune," said Wilfred in an annoyed tone. "If the ring is yours, you are the person to whom it should go. I will ask Lascelle for it to-night, and bring it to you to-morrow morning."

"Do not mention my name to Lascelle!"

"Why not?"

"Because he will guess that you intend to give me the ring, and will then refuse it. Let him think you want it for yourself, and then you can hand it over to me."

"I will do my best, Major. Come to-morrow morning, and if possible I will place the ring on your finger."

"Thank you, my dear Dacre. Thank you. One good turn deserves another; so, as I saved you from suicide, you can surely gratify a harmless fancy of mine. Besides, I will aid you by every means in my power to marry Miss Havard."

"I am afraid you can help but little," said Dacre, as the major rose to go.

"I'm not so sure about that," said the major significantly. "I have some influence with Lord Kenny, as you will find."

Wilfred laughed at this prognostication, as he hardly thought the brusque major was a man likely to be a favourite with the fastidious nobleman, However, he humoured the major in his supposition, and they parted on very good terms.

After Measurby had taken himself off, Wilfred remained in a brown study for some considerable time.

"I wonder," said he to himself aloud, "why he is so anxious to gain possession of that ring!"

The fact is, he was beginning to be suspicious of the major, as it appeared absurd that he should show emotion over such a paltry trinket as he averred the ring to be. When a man offers thousands of pounds for a bauble, that bauble must have other than an intrinsic value, and the major's story of its being a family jewel hardly seemed plausible enough. Wilfred had promised to obtain the ring for the major, but he also promised himself to find out the truth about it before handing it over to the man who desired it so eagerly.

"I have not promised to leave the major's name out of the conversation," said Wilfred, after some thought, " and as I have heard Measurby's story of the ring, I would like to hear Lascelle's. If the two stories tally, I will give the major his ring, — if not "—

He paused, and with a thoughtful look on his face returned to lie down on the sofa.

Clearly, Major Measurby was not so sure of the ring as he thought himself to be.

CHAPTER V.

THE TALISMAN.

All that day Wilfred felt restless and ill at ease. The position in which he now found himself placed was so extraordinary, that he could not but see that this was a critical moment of his life. He refused to believe that all these things were due to chance only. Rather did they look like some carefully laid plot which he was unconsciously carrying out for the benefit of some person. That person was either Measurby or Lascelle, and Wilfred could not make up his mind which of the two to suspect. Measurby's suggestion had led him to Lascelle, and Lascelle was the very person whom the major desired to discover. What if it was all schemed out beforehand, — at least so far as the major was concerned? Measurby suggested a ridiculous experiment, and in the most extraordinary manner it had resulted to his own advantage. This seemed to be rather due to design than to chance.

Altogether Wilfred had grave doubts on the subject, and began to suspect that Measurby was making use of him to recover the ring on which he set such store. The solution of the mystery lay with Lascelle, and Dacre fully made up his mind to know everything when he went to Soho that night. As to giving Measurby the ring, it depended entirely on what was told to him by Lascelle. The mention of the major's name would be enough to put the old man on his guard, and Wilfred had not bound himself to leave the name out of his conversation. In any event, things seemed likely to turn out to his advantage, for Measurby declared he would give thousands for the ring; and even if Lascelle refused to give it up there was a strong possibility that he would assist Wilfred to a fortune. Never had Dacre felt so upset; and he was glad when the long day drew to a close, bringing nearer the time of his appointment.

Several times he had felt inclined to call on Hilda, and tell her of these strange events; but he knew well enough that as Lord Kenny had forbidden him the house, he would probably be refused admission. Despondent as he was about such exclusion, he nevertheless found comfort in the thought that on reading his letter Hilda would certainly refuse to give Denham a direct answer that day. If, therefore, he gained any advantage from his second visit to Lascelle, he would still find her free to become his wife, and might be in a position to overcome Lord Kenny's scruples regarding a pauper son-in-law. This was the supreme moment of his life, and the whole of his future appeared to depend upon the conduct of two men, Lascelle and Measurby.

So impatient was he to be relieved from suspense that he could hardly eat any dinner, and his sitting down to the meal was a mere farce. To strengthen his nerves, he drank several cups of strong coffee, and about nine o'clock set off to keep his appointment with his eccentric host of the hidden Paradise.

All things happened as on the previous evening. He walked down Karp Street, found the door of No. 49 open, and, ascending the stairs, was admitted to the inner room by the Nubian slave. Lascelle was again seated among his cushions, and greeted the young man with a smile of gratification. He appeared to be much exhausted, and from time to time sipped some liquid from a cup at his elbow, as if to sustain his failing strength. Death had already set the seal of the grave on his face, and it seemed as though at any moment the end might come.

"I am glad to see you so punctual, Mr. Dacre," he said, motioning the young man to seat himself in his old place. "Will you have some coffee?"

"No, thank you," responded Wilfred, making himself comfortable among the cushions; "but I would like to smoke."

Lascelle clapped his hands; the slave appeared, and Wilfred was speedily supplied with a nargileh, which gradually soothed his nerves.

"To what conclusion have you come regarding your visit to me last night?" asked Mr. Lascelle, when the young man was ready to converse.

"It is difficult to say. When I awoke this morning I thought I had been dreaming."

"That was scarcely to be wondered at, Mr. Dacre. I am aware that this adventure of yours is hardly in keeping with London life."

"Then you will now tell me the meaning of all this," said Wilfred, with much eagerness.

"Presently, presently," rejoined the old man, producing a small note-book; "first I wish to ascertain if certain facts connected with your life are correct."

"What do you know of my life?"

"Nearly everything."

"That is impossible," replied Wilfred bluntly; "you have had no time to make any minute inquiries."

"Have I not?" said Lascelle, with a peculiar smile. "Judge for yourself, Mr. Dacre."

The young man nodded nervously, for he almost believed that the knowledge this man assumed to possess could only have been gained in some supernatural way. In another second, however, he dismissed the idea with scorn, and, shaking off the influence of the place, remembered that he was in London, not in Bagdad. Before the end of Lascelle's speech, however, he almost recurred to his first idea.

"Your name," said Lascelle, looking at his note-book, "is Wilfred Dacre, the only representative of a Herefordshire family. Your parents died when you were still a child, and you were left to the guardianship of Mr. Vane, M. P. He sent you to Eton, afterwards to Baliol College, Oxford; and when you came of age he handed over to you your property, which was comparatively small. Finding yourself your own master, in the midst of London temptations, you ran through your money. Last year you met the Honorable Hilda Havard and fell in love with her. Mr. Vane obtained for you a consulship in Cuba, and on the strength of this appointment you asked her to become your wife. She refused your proposal, and "—

" You must be the devil in person," cried Wilfred, starting to his feet with a thrill of terror. " How did you obtain all this information ? "

" Is it true, Mr. Dacre ? "

" Perfectly true. But I cannot conceive how you found out all in such a short space of time."

" I told you I was as rich as a king," said the old man, with a faint smile of triumph. " I might also add that I am as powerful as a king. There is nothing I desire to know, but what I do not learn sooner or later. But pray sit down; I have yet to come to the most important part of my information."

" About Major Measurby," said Wilfred, with a sudden intuition that the name was on the lips of Lascelle.

" Precisely. Why did you not tell me about him last night? It would have saved me endless trouble."

" I hardly thought it was necessary to bring him into our conversation."

" Now you know better, I presume."

" Yes; after my conversation with him to-day."

" Which was about this ring ? "

Lascelle stretched forward his right hand, on which glistened the ring, and Wilfred drew back with a slight start, so unexpected were the question and the gesture. The omniscience of this strange man was beginning to inspire him with dread, and he resumed his seat with a feeling of helplessness.

"Yes, it was about the ring," he admitted with reluctance. "I was to ask you to give it to me."

"Of course," said Lascelle, scornfully. "And then you were to hand it over to Major Measurby."

"Certainly. It is a family jewel."

His host laughed feebly and made a derisive gesture.

"Is it, indeed? There are some things I do not know, after all. Tell me of this conversation, Mr. Dacre, and then I will show you what a blind puppet you have been in the hands of your pretended friend."

"A puppet!" repeated Wilfred, with a frown. "I do not like that word, Mr. Lascelle."

"Nevertheless, it is the only word which can be used in connection with your conduct. I had my suspicions last night when you told me of the chance remark which guided you here. Now, those suspicions are confirmed, both by my inquiries and your own admission."

"Mr. Lascelle," cried Dacre, in a fury, "do you think I came here with a knowledge that I would see you?"

"I do not. I called you a puppet, not a scoundrel."

Wilfred fell back among his cushions, with a perplexed look on his face.

"All this is beyond me," he said at length. "Go on, Mr. Lascelle. I await your promised story."

"Nay. First tell me of this conversation."

"There is not much to tell," responded Dacre,

after a moment's thought. "This morning Major Measurby called to see me, and I gave him a full account of my visit to you. On hearing your name, he said he met you in Benares, in India, ten years ago, that there his brother had died, leaving you that ring, which is a family jewel. He told me, also, that you refused to give it up, that he had hunted you all over the world to obtain it, and at the present time he had detectives searching for your domicile in London. According to him, my chance visit had unconsciously revealed your whereabouts, and he implored me to ask for the ring, and restore it to him. I promised to do so, and intended to have asked you as requested, but that you forestalled my question by mentioning the major's name."

Lascelle listened to this long speech with a satirical look of admiration in his eyes, and at the conclusion nodded his head two or three times like a Chinese mandarin. The story seemed to amuse him greatly.

"What a wonderful man is the major!" he said ironically. "This tale does the utmost credit to his invention."

"Then it is not true?"

"It is an admirable mixture of truth and fiction," responded Lascelle, with weak emphasis. "I certainly met Major Measurby in India, but he never possessed a brother. This ring belongs solely to me, and was never at any time in the possession of your friend. How I gained this ring will be told to you by another person" —

"By another person?" interrupted Wilfred, in surprise.

"Who will call on you to-morrow morning," pursued the old man, without taking any notice of his observation. "Pray do not interrupt me, Mr. Dacre, as I require all the strength I have to tell you my story. It is true that Measurby has hunted me all over the world to obtain possession of the ring, and it is equally true that I refuse to give it to him. With a man of his character this ring would only work evil, and I do not care about leaving a legacy of woe to the world. Had the ring of Sulieman bin Daoud been given to Nero, with what supernatural cruelties — more terrible even than his actual monstrosities — would he have horrified the world!"

Worn out by his energy, Lascelle moistened his dry lips with the draught, and again resumed his speech. Fascinated as by some unknown horror, Wilfred sat in silence, listening intently to the words which fell one by one from his pale lips.

"It is true that Measurby tried to harm me, but I was, I am, protected from his malignancy. I departed from India, but not for fear of that man. I left Persia for Europe, but my enemy had no power to force me into such a journey. He followed me all over Europe. Well do I know it. For years not an action on his part has been unknown to me. I did not even attempt to conceal myself, and he could have seen me at any moment had he so desired. On my arrival in England his emissaries discovered that I was here, and for weeks he has known of my presence in Soho."

"Then why did he not come to see you, Mr. Lascelle?"

"He would only come for one thing," said the old man quietly, "and that I would not yield to him. He knew that, and, anxious to obtain possession of this ring, employed you as an unconscious emissary in the hope that through ignorance you would obtain the ring from me and give it to him. Ah! he did not guess that I had him watched. I know all, and Major Measurby is once more foiled, even while I am on the threshold of the grave."

"What do you mean?" asked Wilfred, deeply interested in the recital of this strange history.

"Have you read the Eastern tale of Aladdin?" said Lascelle with sudden energy; "of the pretended uncle who made use of Aladdin to secure the magic lamp which the genii refused to give to him personally? This is your case."

"My case?" reiterated Dacre, with a thrill of fear as he remembered Lord Kenny's scornful allusion to the lamp.

"Yes. Finding he could not obtain this ring himself, Major Measurby resolved to employ another. That was why he fixed on you. Knowing your imaginative nature, the desperate condition of your finances, he could scarcely have hit upon a better agent. He made you his friend, as you know; he haunted your steps everywhere; he made himself, so to speak, indispensable to you. Then, when the time was ripe, he made use of you to secure his ends. But we will baffle him, you and I, and the ring with all its power will be yours only."

"What powers has the ring?"

"I will tell you afterwards. Let me conclude my

story of Measurby's treachery. He asked you to his rooms last night and spoke of Fate,—of the Eastern custom of using chance remarks as oracles. He induced you to try the experiment, and at the corner of the street down which he knew you must pass he posted two men so that you should overhear this address. You did so, and in all innocence came here."

"Then those two men were employed by the major?"

"Yes. They waited there for you to pass by, and said their lesson so correctly that you could not help but hear. Measurby, having worked on the imaginative side of your nature, knew that you would act upon the remark, and that is why he called on you this morning."

"And his story of to-day?"

"All lies, as I have told you. So far he had been successful, and hoped to be so to the end. Such might have been the case had you not told me of the remark you overheard. It was too strange to be chance only; so I had inquiries made to-day, and found out all I have told you. You were his dupe, Mr. Dacre; but rest assured that you will be able to punish him bitterly for his deception."

"I fervently hope I shall."

Wilfred gnawed his nether lip angrily as he thought how egregiously he had been deceived. It is not a pleasant thing for any man to think he has been made use of by a scoundrel, and Dacre's pride was stung by the position in which he now found himself. Had Measurby been present, Wilfred would then and there have taken him to task for daring to treat him in such a manner. He bitterly resented the trickery of which he had been a victim, and involuntarily clenched his fist as he recalled how easily he had been gulled. Lascelle noticed the action, and, guessing what was passing in the young man's mind, strove to console him in a kindly manner.

"It is not worth fretting about, Mr. Dacre," he said faintly, raising himself up on his elbow. "I assure you nothing in the world is worth such a waste of energy. I have lived a long life, — a strange life, — one such is given to few men, and, believe me, I speak truly. Besides, Measurby, without knowing it, has unconsciously done you a good turn. Had he not sent you blindly to me, I would not have seen you; in which case your great good fortune would not have come about."

"What great good fortune?" asked Dacre gloomily, in no wise inclined to take a cheerful view of things.

"I am going to give you the ring," said the old man in a solemn tone of voice.

"What possible use can it be to me?"

"A great deal. If you only knew its power!"

"Measurby said that it was a talisman, the possession of which conferred happiness on the possessor."

"Did he tell you that? I am astonished that he was so unwise."

"He merely gave it as a sample of the stories you would tell about the ring."

"And warned you not to believe them, I presume?"

"Yes, he certainly did."

"Major Measurby is a clever rogue," said Lascelle, smiling; "but in this case he has overreached himself. What is your opinion of the ring, Mr. Dacre?"

"I can have no opinion in the matter, seeing I am quite in the dark. Judging from the value you attach to the ring, and the eagerness displayed by Major Measurby in trying to gain possession of it, I presume it possesses some properties which render it valuable. What those properties are I cannot in the least guess."

"I will tell you. It is a talisman."

"Pardon me. I cannot believe in such fantasies," said Wilfred, with a sceptical smile.

"It sounds impossible, I admit, but it is so. With this ring on your finger you can command the world."

"Is it the seal ring of the great Solomon?"

"I see you think I am out of my mind," observed Lascelle, marking the mocking tone of the young man; "but though on the point of death I am as sane as you are."

Wilfred, owing to the extraordinary talk of the old man, had his doubts on the subject, but, not wishing to appear offensive, held his peace.

"Tell me, Mr. Dacre," observed his host suddenly, "if I give you the ring, will you surrender it to the major?"

"Certainly not," replied Wilfred emphatically.

"Apart from the fact that he has acted with unpardonable freedom, I believe that he has spoken falsely about the ownership of the ring. Your story is more credible than his."

"I am glad you will not be so foolish as to part with it to him. But suppose he persuades you into doing so?"

"His persuasions will have but small effect on me," retorted Dacre grimly. "To-morrow I intend to see him, give him a bit of my mind, and then decline his further acquaintance."

"You won't shake the major off so easily as that. He has the pertinacity of a gadfly, and, as he has failed to obtain the ring from me, will do his best to wrest it from you."

"Let him try."

"Mind you, there is nothing he will not do to get possession of it. Fortunately the ownership of the ring, though it entails danger, also protects you from the machinations of your enemies."

"Is this ring a talisman similar to the lamp of Aladdin?"

"Something very like it. If you wear it you will have command of unlimited wealth."

"Of course. And if I rub it, a Jinn will appear," said Wilfred in a jesting tone.

"Even that is not impossible," replied Lascelle solemnly. "Oh, I assure you I speak truly. All this magnificence around you comes from the ring. Judge, then, how powerful it is to its master."

Dacre looked at him sceptically, whereat the old man sighed.

"I see you do not believe me; nor can I blame you

for such scepticism. But you will hear the whole story of the ring and its powers to-morrow."

"From whom?"

"Janshah, the slave of the ring."

"Oh, more Arabian Nights!" said Dacre, half pettishly. "Well, give me the ring, and I promise you that no one will ever take it from me."

Lascelle drew it off his finger and looked at it with a melancholy expression of countenance.

"For many years," he said sadly, "I have possessed this ring; and yet, with all its magic powers, it has not brought me happiness. Now I am dying, and before dawn will have no further need of earthly riches. Therefore, I give it to you. Use the wealth it bestows wisely, Mr. Dacre, for I am making you by this gift more powerful than any monarch on his throne. If you misuse the talisman it will bring you sorrow. I have not made such good use of it as I might have made. But it came to me when I was old. You who receive it are young and generous; so take the ring, Mr. Dacre, and with it the control of millions."

He slipped it on the third finger of Wilfred's right hand, and the young man, much puzzled at the extraordinary gift and still more extraordinary speech, could only thank Lascelle for the present. All this talk of magic bewildered him; and though he was sceptical of the powers possessed by the bauble, yet the conduct of both Lascelle and Measurby showed that the ring was no ordinary trinket.

"You are now the master of the ring," said Lascelle, in a tone of much satisfaction; "so I must introduce you to your servant."

He clapped his hands, whereat the curtains at the end of the room were drawn back, and a tall, swarthy man, dressed in an Oriental fashion, appeared. Moving swiftly towards Lascelle, he made a profound obeisance, and waited for him to speak.

"This, Janshah," said Lascelle, in a faint voice, "is the master of the ring."

Janshah turned his eyes towards Wilfred's hand, and when he saw the ring on his finger prostrated himself with the utmost humility before the young man.

"Hearkening and obedience," he said in English, with profound respect.

"Janshah has full control of all the powers belonging to the ring," resumed Lascelle, turning to Wilfred, "and so long as you wear it he will obey you. But if you lose it, you will fall again to your former poverty, and Janshah will leave you."

"I will not lose it," said Wilfred, feeling nervous at this ceremony. "It will never leave my finger."

"Many will try to obtain it from you by craft, by violence; but be on your guard, for while you are its master the world is yours."

"Nothing and no one will take it from me, I swear."

"Now, leave me," said Lascelle, falling back among his cushions, quite worn out by excitement. "We will never meet again. I am sinking into the grave in poverty, and you go out into the world a monarch of wealth. Good-by, Mr. Dacre; make good use of the ring."

"Good-bye, Mr. Lascelle," said Wilfred, pressing

the hand of the old man; "whatever virtues the ring may possess, I will try not to prove unworthy of them."

Lascelle made no reply, but waved his hand faintly in token that Wilfred was to leave him. Janshah clapped his hands, and two women came in to attend to the old man; then he preceded Wilfred with grave dignity out of the room.

"Where does the master desire to go?" he asked in the antechamber.

"Home to my rooms," replied Wilfred, wondering at the slavish demeanour of this man.

Janshah bowed, and, taking a lamp from a bracket, preceded Wilfred downstairs. To Wilfred's astonishment a carriage was waiting at the door.

"To whom does this belong?" he asked Janshah.

"To the master of the ring."

Wilfred felt the ring on his finger, and knew that it must be meant for him; so in a state of considerable bewilderment he stepped into it. As soon as he was within Janshah shut the door, and the carriage rolled away up Karp Street.

"Well," said Wilfred to himself, "I don't exactly know what all this means, but judging by this carriage I must possess Aladdin's lamp after all."

CHAPTER VI.

JANSHAH.

It must be remembered that Wilfred was as yet completely ignorant of the true value of this much desired ring. The circumstances by which he became its owner were extraordinary, but the powers attributed to its influence by Lascelle were still more so. That the wearing of such a trinket should invest its possessor with untold wealth, and give him the powers of a monarch, was manifestly absurd. In the Middle Ages such a fable might gain currency, but that a hard-headed man of the nineteenth century should subscribe to such a monstrous belief was out of the question.

There are limits to human credulity, even that of the most superstitious; and prone as Wilfred was to accept the impossible, — an acceptance begotten only by the imaginative side of his nature, — he could not believe that the ring could perform miracles. Stories of magical rings there are without doubt; such as the ring of Gyges, which rendered its owner invisible; the signet of Solomon, powerful to control the spirit world; the ring of the Nibelung, which dowered its master with the treasures of earth; and many others. All these tales, however, are pure fiction, and Wilfred never thought for a moment of placing his adventure in this category. So far as he saw, it was an ordinary piece of jewellery, by no means distinguished for beauty of workmanship.

It consisted of a broad band of dull gold, wherein was set a lapis lazuli the size of a pea; and this stone being perfectly flat was sunk in the metal to the level of the surface. On its blue face were graven certain characters, apparently Eastern; but of the purport of these, Wilfred was ignorant, though they presumably referred to the mystic powers said to be possessed by this so-called talisman. Nothing in the way of a trinket could have been plainer, yet for this Major Measurby offered a fortune. That offer, more than anything else, assured Wilfred that the ring was valuable; and though he disbelieved the wild fable of Lascelle, yet he was satisfied that something of which he was ignorant rendered the bauble of enormous importance in the eyes of such an astute man of the world as Measurby.

As to Lascelle, it was evident that he was insane on this point, and ascribed all his good fortune to the ring,—attaching thereto chimerical properties which it could not possess. Wilfred, in spite of his leaning towards romantic things, was a sane man, and he laughed aloud to think that any one could be found foolish enough to believe in such follies. Lascelle's ill health and sedentary life might certainly have affected his brain, and Dacre did not doubt that in his madness he believed his whimsical story; but that Major Measurby, cool, calculating and eminently practical, should offer thousands for what was intrinsically worth a few pounds, did indeed seem strange. It was almost impossible of belief, and yet Wilfred had personally received this astonishing offer.

It was about nine o'clock in the morning, and Dacre, not yet up, lay day-dreaming in bed, twisting the ring round and round his finger. He had looked at the matter in every possible way, yet he could account in no feasible way for the value attached to this ring by Lascelle and Measurby.

"At all events," he said aloud to himself, " I am now the owner of the ring, and will refuse to part with it either to Measurby or to any one else. If it can work me any benefit, I will soon be cognizant of its properties. It may be that I have become possessed of some talisman which in the most natural way performs prodigies. All the better for me. I shall then be a modern Aladdin and can marry Hilda. Oh, what nonsense I am talking! The ring is a ring and nothing else. I will keep it as a memento of a curious adventure."

He mused for a few moments, and then his thoughts turned in another direction.

"And yet," he resumed, after a pause, " there may be some story attached to this ring which renders it valuable. That story is known to Measurby; so, sooner or later, I will learn the truth from him. Then, again, there is Janshah, whom Lascelle called the 'slave of the ring.' He was to be here to-day, but as yet has put in no appearance. I am afraid the servants of the talisman are dilatory."

At this period of his reflections, the door of his bedroom was opened and a servant entered with a card. The name inscribed thereon was " Janshah."

" By Jove," cried Dacre, springing out of bed, " this begins to grow interesting. Tell the man to wait; I will be out shortly. It appears," he murmured sarcastically, " that the genii are up to date, — they use visiting-cards."

The servant departed, and Wilfred, having taken his tub, dressed himself as rapidly as possible. He was curious to know if the ring did indeed possess any powers, and no one could satisfy his curiosity on this point so thoroughly as the Indian. Wilfred supposed Janshah to be an Indian, though he had taken but little notice of him on the previous night, owing to the excitement of the moment.

"Some clever scamp, I expect," he murmured while completing his toilet, "who has imposed on old Lascelle, and styles himself euphoniously the ' slave of the ring.' Well, he will not impose on me, and will have to take his Arabian Nights fables to some more gullible person, — Major Measurby, for instance."

On entering his sitting-room, he found Janshah awaiting him, with true Eastern patience. Last night he had worn the flowing robes of the Orient, but now he was plainly dressed in respectable black clothes, which by no means suited his swarthy, un-English appearance. When Wilfred entered, he arose to his feet with a low bow, not a servile prostration, as formerly, but a deferential salutation such as would be given by a well-trained waiter. With his Oriental dress, he had evidently put aside his Oriental habits, and now, but for his dark skin and his piercing eyes, looked little different from an ordinary servitor of the West.

"So you are Janshah," said Wilfred, glancing at the card, for the name was somewhat difficult to remember.

"At your service, sir," responded Janshah in English, not styling Wilfred "my lord," as on the previous occasion.

"Do you know this?" observed Wilfred, stretching out the hand on which was the ring.

At this, Janshah suddenly relapsed into Oriental abasement, and bowed nearly to the ground before the signet. Then he straightened himself and became English once more. Wilfred was amused and somewhat puzzled by the duality of the man, but made no observation, otherwise than requesting Janshah to be seated. This the Indian refused to do.

"It is not meet that I should sit in the presence of my lord," he said, with another genuflexion.

"Oh, very well," responded Wilfred indifferently. "It seems that this ring has some real powers after all, seeing you treat it with such consideration."

"Do you not believe in the ring, sir?" asked Janshah, with an imperceptible smile.

"At present I do not. But tell me," added Wilfred, sitting down on the sofa; "why do you call me 'my lord' one minute and 'sir' the next?"

"I am of the East, sir, and reverence the ring. It is thus that I should always address you; but to dress and speak according to my race would attract too much attention here; therefore I prefer to act as an Englishman."

"You speak English very well."

"I speak nearly all the languages of Europe, sir.

While you remain here, I will be at hand to obey your behests; but should you go to the East, another servant of the ring will attend you in Asia."

"Oh! so you are the European slave of the ring?"

"Yes, sir."

"And will obey me in all things?"

"Yes, sir. While you retain possession of that ring, I am devoted to you body and soul."

Wilfred could not make out whether the man before him was in jest or earnest. He seemed to have a profound reverence for the ring and for himself as its master; so he began to think there was more in Lascelle's story than he thought. This idea brought the old man to his mind, and he questioned Janshah on the subject.

"How is Mr. Lascelle?"

"He is dead, sir."

"Dead?" echoed Wilfred, in surprise, though he might have expected such news. "And when did he die?"

"Last night, sir, shortly after you left. I have attended to all things, and he will be duly buried."

"Had he any relations?"

"Not one, sir, so far as I know."

"So you are now my servant?"

"While you retain that ring I am your slave."

It was all so gravely absurd that Wilfred threw back his head and burst out laughing. Nevertheless, he saw that the man was in earnest, and recovering his gravity began to question Janshah regarding the properties of the ring. Major Measurby might arrive at any moment, and he was anxious to be in full possession of all facts, so as to show his treacherous friend that he was no longer to be duped by his cunning. This was his principal idea, but in addition he was devoured by curiosity regarding the ring, in which, against his better judgment, he was beginning to believe.

"What letters are these graven on this stone? What do they mean?"

"They are Sanscrit letters," answered Janshah, again bowing before the ring, "and the interpretation in English is 'Brahma wills it.'"

"What has it to do with Brahma?"

"It is the ring of the god," said Janshah, reverently.

"Then how did it come into the possession of Mr. Lascelle?"

"That, sir, is a long story. Is it your will that I should tell it?"

"Yes, later on. But meanwhile, of what use is this ring to me?"

"It will give you whatever you desire, sir."

"Ah, will it, indeed?" said Wilfred, sceptically. "Then I desire money,—a great deal of money."

"You have it now, sir. The treasures of the ring are at your command."

"Indeed! And in whose keeping are those treasures?"

"They are still in India."

"Still in India? Then they were there originally?"

"Yes, my lord. He who wears that ring commands incalculable treasure."

"I do not understand," faltered Wilfred, staggered at the remark.

"If I tell my lord the story he will know all," replied the slave in a soft voice.

"Yes, tell me the story. But stay, who and what are you?"

"I am of the race of Irân, sir, and I am the servant of the ring."

"A Brahmin?"

"Of that religion, my lord."

"Were you born in India?"

"No, sir. My birthplace is Nishapoor, where sleeps Omar Khayyâm, beneath the roses. But though born in Persia, I am a pure-blooded Brahmin, as was my father before me. He was also a servant of the ring, and attended its then lord at Nishapoor, where I was born. When he died I was of man's estate and destined to become the servant of the ring. Those who hold the treasure made me the slave of Europe, and thither I was sent in early youth to learn all tongues. When my father died I succeeded to his post; and thus it comes round, my lord, that I am ready and willing to serve you — while you possess the ring."

Wilfred noticed the concluding sentence, and, now beginning to believe in the ring, determined more than ever that he would not give it to Major Measurby. This, then, was the reason that Measurby promised him a fortune if he restored him what he called his "family ring." No wonder he could afford to make such promises when the possession of the trinket gave the owner command of incalculable treasure. Unable to restrain his curiosity any longer, and anxious to get at the exact facts of the case, Wilfred spoke eagerly to Janshah: —

"Tell me the story," he said briefly, and then composed himself to listen. Janshah, still standing, folded his hands in Eastern fashion across his breast, and began to talk in a soft voice with a wonderful command of the Anglo-Saxon tongue. In telling the story he no longer assumed the position of an English servant, but relapsed almost imperceptibly into the Oriental slave.

"In the Peninsula of Guzerat is placed the temple of the god Soma, who disposes of the souls of men. For centuries had pious men bestowed their wealth on the temple in order to propitiate the deity; but in the year one thousand seven hundred and thirty-nine the infamous Shah Nadir — may his soul burn in Gehenna — looted the shrine, and took from thence wealth to the amount of nine crores of rupees. When the Infidel retired from Hindostan, the temple of Soma was thus left desolate, and the religion of Brahma was trampled in the dust by the sons of the camel driver. To restore that religion to its former splendour was now the aim of the priests of Brahma, and the god himself sent down to earth that ring upon which is graven his decree. From far and wide treasures were brought to the temple and placed under the guardianship of the high priest who wore the ring. With this wealth the Hindoos hoped to drive out the cursed Moslems and reëstablish the religion of

Brahma. By the will of the god, this treasure was to be absolutely at the disposal of him who wore the sacred ring, and it descended from high priest to high priest, who dealt with the treasure as they willed.

"Notwithstanding all their efforts, however, they were unable to reëstablish Hindooism, and in vain was the treasure used to such an end. The Moslem triumphed everywhere, and finally the ring was wrested from the high priest by Jahangir, the Shah of Delhi. He thus, by possessing the ring, controlled the treasure at his will forever, though the ring was in the hands of an enemy of the faith; for the decree of the god bade implicit obedience to be paid to it, and the keepers of the treasure gave up the wealth to Jahangir Shah to be used until such time as the god brought back his ring to his worshippers. The ring passed from Shah Jahangir to Shah Jaham, and then came into the possession of Arungzebe. It was then obtained by a Rajput, and rapidly passed from one person to another, until at length it fell into the power of the Emperor Mohammed Bahedur. In his time occurred the mutiny of the Sepoys, and he was banished by the English to Rangoon, where he died in exile. Seeing that his star was against him he gave the ring to Mr. Lascelle, who at that time lived at Delhi, in the employ of the East India Company. Mr. Lascelle has had the ring, till now, when he gave it to you, and thus commanded the treasure. Now you are the master of the ring, and can use the wealth it commands as you will. In all things I, the servant of the ring, will obey you, and by possessing that talisman you are greater than any king."

At the conclusion of this extraordinary story, Wilfred was perfectly bewildered, as there was no doubt that the man spoke in all good faith. Without doubt this was the secret of the ring. It gained its powers from the fanaticism of religion, and did, indeed, give to its possessor an enormous power.

"What is the amount of this treasure?" he asked at length, looking at Janshah.

"Twenty million pounds of English money."

Wilfred fell back on the sofa with a gasp of astonishment. The sum was so enormous that for a time he could not grasp the full meaning of the answer.

"And is this treasure mine?"

"Yours. While you hold the ring."

Talk about the tales of the Arabian Nights, — of Aladdin's lamp, of the hoards of Jinn, — here was an actual realization of all these wonders. He, Wilfred Dacre, sometime pauper, was now the undisputed master of twenty millions. His brain reeled at the thought of the tremendous power which this treasure conferred upon him, and he saw at a glance the meaning of Measurby's intense eagerness to possess the ring.

"How did Major Measurby learn the secret of the ring?"

"In India," replied Janshah, quietly, "from a traitor Brahmin, whose life he saved from a well-deserved death. In gratitude this Brahmin told him of the ring and its treasure, so from that day till this the English soldier has tried to get possession of the ring either by force or fraud. He could not obtain it from Mr. Lascelle" —

"Well, he certainly will not obtain it from me," said Wilfred, with a grim smile. "I will keep it and its treasure to myself. But tell me, Janshah, how is it that you can waste this treasure on unbelievers like myself and Lascelle, when it was collected for the use of Brahma himself?"

"It is the will of the god that it should be so," answered Janshah in a melancholy tone. "On the ring is written 'Brahma wills it,' and whoso possesses the talisman, him must the keepers of the treasure obey."

"But you could have seized it by force from Mr. Lascelle."

"The god wills it not. The ring must return to us as a free gift, but we dare not take it by force. The master of the ring is sacred, and no servant of Brahma would touch him. Did he so, it would be at the peril of his life."

"Do you hope to regain possession of the ring again?"

"Some day, when it is Brahma's will that it should be so. But the master of the ring must give it back freely. Mr. Lascelle would have given it back before he died had you not arrived to become its owner."

"Are you not angry, then, that I should have robbed you of the chance?"

"No," answered Janshah, with a smile. "Whatever is, is right. We can wait, and in due time the wheel will come full circle. To-day for you, to-morrow for us."

"What would you say if I gave you back the ring now?"

"That is as my lord wills it," answered Janshah, with apparent indifference. "But my lord is pleased to jest. He is young and poor; the ring makes him rich, and he will keep it for his own benefit."

"Certainly, I do not feel inclined to part with it," said Wilfred, looking at the ring with a smile of satisfaction. "No, Janshah. As the ring was given to me by Mr. Lascelle, I will certainly keep it to myself, — at least while I desire to make use of it. When I die, if I keep it so long, I would rather send it back to its rightful owner than give it to another Englishman."

"As my lord wills it," replied the servant gravely. "But what does my lord desire?"

"I cannot tell you at present. My brain cannot yet take in the magnitude of the power I now possess. Some time to-day I will tell you what I wish."

"All that my lord wishes shall be done; but let him beware of his enemy."

"Oh, you mean Major Measurby," said Wilfred, rising from the sofa. "True, he will not give up this ring without a struggle. But so long as he fights fair I do not mind."

"So that he obtains not the ring by fraud from my lord all is well," said Janshah gravely. "He cannot employ force, for my lord is protected on all sides by the servants of the ring."

"Oh! have I an invisible body-guard then?"

"Yes, my lord. You are closely watched, and while you retain the ring no one can harm you; but if the ring is obtained from you by fraud, that cannot be prevented."

"It won't be got from me that way," said Wilfred confidently. "Nothing will induce me to take it off my finger. In case of fraud I can protect myself, and if force is tried your invisible slaves can look after me; so I think that the talisman will remain in my possession for many years."

At this moment Wilfred's servant entered and announced Major Measurby.

"Now comes the first struggle for the ring," said the young man in a lively tone. "Janshah, retire into my bedroom and come out when I call you."

Janshah bowed without a word and did as he was told, leaving Wilfred alone in the room.

"Now," said Dacre to himself, "we shall see which has the most cunning, myself or Measurby."

CHAPTER VII.

THE ANGER OF MAJOR MEASURBY.

Major Measurby entered the room in a jaunty fashion, apparently quite confident that all was going as he wished. His first glance was at the ring on Wilfred's finger, his second at the young man's face. Astute in reading character, the expression thereon was by no means to the major's taste; but with considerable tact he ignored all else but the business about which he had come.

"You have the ring, I see," he said, taking a chair with well-feigned carelessness. "Had you much difficulty in obtaining it?"

"No."

The tone was so hostile that Major Measurby was forced to take notice of it, which he did with apparent astonishment.

"What is the matter, man? Anything wrong?"

"Yes, a great deal is wrong."

Intuitively Measurby guessed that Wilfred knew the secret of the ring. The game was up; but the major was not the man to give in without a struggle, and, keeping his temper well in hand, he attempted a little dexterous diplomacy.

"That is a pity; but perhaps I may be able to help you."

Wilfred made no reply, but looked scornfully at his enemy.

"It is money, I suppose," pursued Measurby, uneasily. "Your creditors have been troubling you: but don't worry yourself about that, my dear Dacre. I can help you to a fortune."

"When the ring is in your possession, I suppose," replied Wilfred, with marked emphasis.

"Oh, that is neither here nor there," said the major, shrugging his shoulders. "In any event, I will give you money. I promised you thousands of pounds when you got me the ring. Well, I see you have the ring; so hand it over, and this afternoon I will let you have sufficient to marry Miss Havard and be happy ever afterwards."

"I have no doubt that your intentions are of the best," observed Wilfred, with great deliberation, in no hurry to bring about the dénouement; "but somehow I do not feel inclined to part with the ring."

"My dear Dacre," said Measurby, trying to smile, "surely you will not keep the ring from its rightful owner?"

"By no means: but you, my astute friend, are not the rightful owner."

"What the devil do you mean, sir?" cried the major, leaping to his feet with an oath.

"Mean? That I know all, Major Measurby."

"All what?" demanded the major, blusteringly.

"All about the ring and its wonderful power."

"Lascelle has been telling you lies, I suppose."

"No. Lascelle told me but little."

"Well, whoever told you," said Measurby, making

a fight for it, " you have evidently been gulled by a pack of lies."

" Have I, indeed ! " exclaimed Wilfred, angrily. " I suppose, then, the ring is simply a jewel belonging to the Measurby family."

" Yes; I told you that yesterday," said the major, with brazen assurance.

" You did, and I was foolish enough to believe you."

" I am not accustomed to have my word doubted, Dacre."

" In this case I am afraid it must be doubted," retorted Wilfred, annoyed at the major's pretended ignorance. " It is no use fencing any further, Major. I know you are a first-class liar, but I have found you out."

" What do you mean by applying such an epithet to me ? " raged Measurby, with livid face.

" Keep your temper and your seat, Major. Blustering is no good in this case," retorted Wilfred, with the utmost calmness.

" I think your misfortunes have turned your brain, Dacre," said the major, violently. " However, I have no time to argue the matter. Give me my ring, and I will take my departure."

" You will have to take it without the ring."

" I absolutely refuse to do so," said Measurby, doggedly.

" And I absolutely refuse to give it up," replied Wilfred, with equal doggedness. " You have treated me shamefully, Major, and in place of a friend have made of me an enemy."

"Perhaps you will be kind enough to explain your meaning, sir."

"By all means. You, Major Measurby, heard about this ring, then in the possession of Mr. Lascelle, from an Indian whose life you had saved. He told you that by a strange train of circumstances — all of which are known to me — he who possessed the ring could command treasure to the extent of twenty millions."

"Lies!" muttered Measurby, savagely.

"No, it is the truth, and you know it," insisted Dacre, calmly. "When you found out this you attempted to get the ring from Lascelle. He refused to give it to you, and knowing that personally you had no chance of obtaining it, you tried to accomplish your object by using me as a tool. Oh, I know how you gulled me with your pretended belief in Fate, — how it came about that the remark upon which I was to act was made so opportunely. I know the whole of your trickery, Measurby, but I have benefited thereby. I have obtained the ring, but not for you. It was given to me by Lascelle, and I have learned the powers which it commands. Do you see it on my finger, Major? It is mine now, and mine it will remain. I, not you, am the master of the ring of Brahma."

During this speech the major's face had been changing colour like a chameleon. Red at first, it turned white, then became blue with rage, and by the time Wilfred had finished speaking, looked yellow with disappointment. He knew that his schemes had proved useless, that his treachery had recoiled on his own head, yet he fought on blindly against all hope of being successful.

"You are talking nonsense, Dacre. Who ever heard of twenty millions being at the disposal of a ring?"

"I have, and you also. And we both believe it."

"Lies! lies!" muttered Measurby, biting his fingers; "all Lascelle's lies."

"You want proof, I see," said Wilfred, clapping his hands. "Well, here is a man who can tell you all you desire to know."

Measurby swung sharply round on his heel and beheld the Indian, who in answer to his master's signal appeared at the door of the bedroom.

"Janshah!" gasped the major, falling back a pace.

"Ah, I see you know his name," said Dacre, ironically; "so, doubtless, it is useless for him to tell you his story."

"That man," cried Measurby, pointing to the dignified figure of the Indian, "is a low caste Hindoo, whom I knew well at Benares. He is a villain, a slave, a scoundrel, who seeks to gull you as he gulled Lascelle."

Janshah made no reply to this insulting speech, but, fixing his eyes on Wilfred, waited instructions with perfect calmness.

"I am quite content to be so gulled," said Wilfred coolly, "and also to keep the ring."

"It will get you into trouble."

"I will take the risk."

"And ruin your life."

"No doubt, if you can assist it to do so. Well, do your worst, Measurby. Neither force nor fraud will cause me to give up this ring. If you try fraud, I know you too well to be your dupe a second time. If force, Janshah will be able to frustrate you there. For years you tried to get the ring from Lascelle, — and failed. Try to wrest it from me, and you will be as successful as you are now."

"You boast in brave style," muttered Measurby, darting a malignant glance at his adversary; "but remember, pride goes before a fall. I will have that ring in spite of you."

"I don't think so," replied Wilfred, with supreme contempt. "However, you have my full permission to try. Begin now, if it so pleases you."

"Oh, no, I won't," said the baffled scoundrel in a hoarse voice. "I am not melodramatic enough to get up a scene of violence for your special benefit. There are surer ways than that of gaining my ends."

"No doubt. I see you declare open war."

The major clapped his hat on his head with a show of virtuous indignation and stalked in a lordly fashion to the door. Before he left the room, however, he turned to have the last word : —

"You have treated me shamefully, Dacre, and in a manner quite unworthy of a gentleman. I declare," added Measurby in a voice almost tearful, "that I believed you to be the soul of honour; but now that I know your real character, I decline to have anything more to do with you. But I warn you that I will not submit tamely to this robbery.

Protect yourself as you will, sir, I shall yet gain possession of that ring. Make use of it while you can, for I will wrest it from you sooner or later, and will hesitate at nothing to do so."

Wilfred shrugged his shoulders and turned away in disdain, upon which the major in high wrath banged the door to and departed. Heaven only knows with what feelings he went downstairs; but that he should have been beaten by a man whom he designed to use as a tool must have been a sore blow to his pride. That he had made at least one bitter enemy Wilfred knew only too well; but, protected by his knowledge of that enemy's true character and the power of the ring, he hoped to foil the major in all his subsequent schemes.

During the interview Janshah had preserved a strict silence, nor did he now venture to speak to his master, but meekly waited to be addressed. For a few minutes Wilfred said nothing, as he was thinking what was best to be done. He owned the ring and had conquered the major; so he was now in a position to make use of his good fortune.

"Janshah," he said at length, turning towards the Indian, "first and foremost I require some money. Pay five thousand pounds into my account at the Bank of Albion."

To Wilfred's surprise Janshah shook his head, and made a deprecating gesture with his hand.

"There are conditions attached to the ring," he said slowly, "and one is that the owner cannot at one time have more than one thousand pounds in the bank. If you asked for five thousand, even one hundred thousand pounds, I could pay it to you in gold, but I cannot place it to your credit, sir."

"And who made this rule?" asked Wilfred in an annoyed tone.

"The keepers of the treasure, sir. The reason is, that should the ring pass from your possession, if such large sums were paid into your account you would be able to be rich without holding the ring. The keepers of the treasure can give no moneys save to the holder of the ring. While you have it you are rich. Lose it, you become poor."

"It is an extremely inconvenient rule."

"In no wise will it curb your expenditure of money, sir," said Janshah in a soothing tone. "Order me to buy you a house, jewellery, horses, anything you please, even an estate, and I will do so; but everything must be in my name as the representative of the ring. A thousand pounds will always be lying in the bank for your personal convenience, and as soon as that one thousand is exhausted another thousand will be paid in. But all else must be in the name of Janshah."

"Then if I lose the ring everything will revert to you?"

"Everything! To hold in trust for the next possessor of the ring. It will cause you no inconvenience, sir. Order me to pay over any sum, and I will pay it: to buy anything, and I will buy it. I am, sir, your agent, and everything you order shall be done. Should you desire anything, it is yours."

"So the powers of the ring are curtailed in this way," said Wilfred in a vexed tone. "I see the genii of to-day are business spirits. But, Janshah, supposing you were to die, I should be placed in an extremely awkward position."

"Not at all, my lord. The day I died my successor would appear to do your bidding."

"Well, as I have the ring I must abide by its rules," observed Dacre in a philosophical tone. "I will let you know what I desire, very shortly. At present pay one thousand pounds into my account."

Janshah bowed.

"You can draw on it, sir, when you please," he said gravely. "Have I your permission to retire?"

"Yes! but return here this afternoon for my further commands."

Again Janshah bowed and left the room, leaving Wilfred alone to reflect over his marvellous good fortune.

"Aladdin's lamp was nothing to this," he thought exultingly. "I wonder what Lord Kenny would say if I told him all. But he must never know; I will keep the secret of my wealth to myself. Now I can marry Hilda. Shall I tell her? No! I hardly think it would be wise to do so. They say a woman cannot keep a secret, and Hilda is essentially feminine. She might tell Lord Kenny, and then it might as well be in the papers. I will keep silent, but at all events I must make up some story to satisfy any one as to the source of my wealth and the constant presence of Janshah."

CHAPTER VIII.

THE COURSE OF TRUE LOVE RUNS SMOOTH.

So far everything had gone exceedingly well, and Wilfred saw no obstacle in the way of his marriage with Hilda. It was his intention to call at Curzon Street that afternoon and tell Lord Kenny that he was now a wealthy man. This was an easy thing to do, but it was more difficult to explain whence the wealth was derived. He did not wish to relate his adventures to either Hilda or her father, as he doubted very much whether they would believe so fantastical a story. Certainly, Hilda, having full confidence in him, might do so; but Lord Kenny was too much a man of the world to give credence to such wild fables. Moreover, Wilfred desired to keep the secret of the ring to himself, as he had no wish to raise up a host of enemies, who, if they found his story to be true, would try by every means in their power to wrest the talisman from his possession.

Besides himself, Major Measurby was the only other person who knew the secret, and Wilfred felt confident that he would preserve a strict silence about the matter, for two reasons. First, he would not like to admit that he had been conquered, and second, he would prefer that the power of the ring should be known to as few people as possible. If

Wilfred was mad enough to confess the truth, he foresaw that such a marvellous story would be taken up by the daily papers, in which case the results might be serious. Every one would want to see the ring, and, knowing of the existence of such a treasure in India, the government might take steps to claim it for the crown. Therefore, with these ideas in his mind, Wilfred determined to hold his peace, and tell no one, not even Hilda, of the real source of his wealth.

Being certain in his own mind that Lord Kenny would ask him questions about the matter, Wilfred made up a little story which he thought would satisfy that suspicious gentleman. The hero of this story was an uncle, — that convenient relative, — who had gone long years ago to India, and been so busy shaking the pagoda tree that he had quite forgotten his ties in England. Then he had died and left his money to his nephew, though how this chimerical uncle came to know that he had an nephew, Wilfred did not attempt to explain. He hoped that Lord Kenny would not make too minute inquiries, but, seeing that the wealth was an actual fact, would accept the history of the Indian uncle in good faith. Wilfred composed this little history as he arrayed himself in fine raiment to call on Hilda, and did not doubt but what he would be able to account in a sufficiently plausible manner for his sudden access of wealth.

If, however, the father or daughter were sceptical, he could produce evidence of the truth of his story to any extent in the shape of money, and surely that would assure them that what he related was true. They could never suspect the real facts of the case, which were too wild for any one to dream of, save an opium-eater; so Wilfred was very certain that his little legend would pass current. Had Measurby been friendly, he would have brought him forward to substantiate the truth of the story; but the major was at present smarting under a sense of defeat. Wilfred, therefore, had to do the best he could, and, having an imaginative brain, hoped to easily baffle any too searching questions put by Lord Kenny.

As he approached Curzon Street, he was seized with a sudden qualm, lest Hilda should have placed an insuperable bar to their union by accepting Denham. It was true that he had implored her to wait before giving a decided answer, hinting at the possibility of matters turning out to their mutual benefit, but she had sent no reply to his letter; therefore he was completely ignorant as to what course she had taken, — whether she had put off Sir Richard, as desired, or, dominated by the imperious will of her father, had rashly agreed to accept the hand of a man she did not love. Wilfred felt uneasy at the thought of this possibility, and hurried to Curzon Street as speedily as possible, so as to set his doubts at rest.

Both Lord Kenny and his daughter were at home, and, thinking it best to first satisfy the father on all points, Wilfred sent up his card with a request that he might be permitted to see him on important business. Never thinking for a moment that Wilfred would attempt to reopen the matter which had been so decisively closed on the previous day, Lord Kenny consented to see him, and he was shown up to the drawing-room, where, in a short space of time, he was joined by the old gentleman. Lord Kenny's attitude towards the young man was stiff, but by no means ungracious, as he really felt sorry for the young couple; and had not Wilfred's poverty been a bar to the union, he would infinitely have preferred him, as a son-in-law, to Sir Richard Denham. The father of the baronet had made his money in trade, whereas Wilfred was gently born and bred; and, but for the desire of seeing his daughter well-off, Havard would have preferred the poor gentleman to the millionaire. As it was, however, he gave his preference to Denham, and was therefore somewhat vexed to see that Wilfred still continued to stand his ground.

Under these circumstances, he simply bowed to Wilfred, and waited to hear what reason he had to give for making this visit.

"Good day, Lord Kenny," said Wilfred, ignoring the stiffness of the old gentleman. "I have not yet given up all hope, you see."

"Are you not making a little mistake, Mr. Dacre?" replied Lord Kenny, blandly. "I understood that this matter had been finally closed."

"No doubt. But you see, my lord, something has occurred which allows me to reopen it again."

"What! Have you found Aladdin's lamp so soon?"

There was such an ironical smile on his face as he repeated his amusing witticism, that Wilfred would have dearly liked to tell him the whole truth there and then. Such a course, however, would scarcely have been wise; so, repressing the truth, which on this occasion wore the semblance of fiction, he proceeded to reel out his artfully prepared lies disguised as truth.

"No, my lord. The age of miracles is past, but I have found what is better than the wonderful lamp,— a fortune."

"I congratulate you," said Lord Kenny gravely. "Some relative, I presume."

"Yes. An uncle in India, of whom I had never heard, died some time ago, and only last night I was informed that he had left me all his money."

Lord Kenny began to grow interested. Uncles are proverbially rich, and an Indian nabob is generally wealthy beyond the dreams of men. The nobleman fidgeted in his chair. He wished to find out the amount of this fortune, but had a certain delicacy in asking such a leading question. Wilfred saw what was passing in his mind, and at once proceeded to give him all necessary information.

"Of course, Lord Kenny," he resumed politely, "after your prohibition of my suit, I would not have thought of seeking you again had I been poor. Now, however, this fortune left to me so unexpectedly has made everything smooth, and I have come to ask you for the hand of Miss Havard. She loves me, you know, and now that I am rich, there can be no objection on your part to our union."

"There are riches and riches," said Lord Kenny, cunningly. "What you may think rich I may consider poor."

"I don't think any one can consider thirty thousand a year poor."

"Thirty thousand a year!" gasped Lord Kenny, sitting bolt upright in his chair.

"Thirty thousand a year," repeated Wilfred stolidly.

The peer waited for a few minutes to recover his equanimity, which this information had taken completely away. When Lazarus suddenly calls on a friend with the astonishing intelligence that he is Dives, that friend may be excused for feeling a trifle upset.

"Thirty thousand a year!" said Lord Kenny, slowly; "that is a very nice income, Dacre."

"It is a very nice income," assented Wilfred calmly.

"And all from an uncle in India?"

"His name was John Dunlop," said Wilfred, lying in the most fluent manner. "He was my mother's brother, and went out to Hindostan in the palmy days of the H. E. I. C. Being busily engaged in collecting rupees, he had no time to write to us, and gradually dropped out of our memories. To me he is a shadow, a myth; I had vague ideas of an avuncular nabob, but deemed them tales of the genii. Now the shadow has changed into substance, the myth has turned to history. John Dunlop is dead, and all his money has been left to his dutiful nephew, Wilfred Dacre, who is profoundly grateful for the legacy, as it enables him to marry the woman he loves. Provided always," added Dacre anxiously, "that nothing has happened in the meantime to forbid the marriage."

"No, nothing has happened," observed Lord Kenny, after a pause; "but something might have happened. Sir Richard Denham proposed to her yesterday"—

"Oh!" gasped Wilfred, bounding from his seat.

"And Hilda refused him."

Wilfred sat down again and drew a long breath. Everything was going well, and, desiring to clinch the matter at once, he spoke plainly to his prospective father-in-law.

"In that case, I presume you have no objection to my seeing Miss Havard."

"By no means," replied Lord Kenny, rising with a smile. "I withdraw all opposition to the match. I suppose I ought to say that I always wished Hilda to marry you, but I will not say so. I wished her to make a good match, and you were poor. Now you are well off,— thirty thousand a year is a capital income,— and she loves you; so I will send Hilda to you, and you can marry her as soon as the settlements are all right. The settlements," added his lordship with emphasis, "must of course be to my complete satisfaction."

"You can make your own terms," said Wilfred generously, delighted that Lord Kenny had so amicably accepted his story.

The peer was touched by this open-handed way of dealing with matrimonial affairs, and shook hands heartily with Wilfred. Then he went away to find Hilda and gratify her with the intelligence. Some men would have felt virtuous over the matter, but Lord Kenny was by no means given to self-deception. Had Wilfred been poor he would still have forbidden him the house; but as he was now rich he felt pleased that Hilda could marry the man she loved. There was no virtue in letting his daughter marry a rich man, but there was a great deal of common-sense. Lord Kenny's chance of proving himself superior to the ordinary herd of fathers was entirely lost by this sudden transmogrification of a pauper into a rich man. He did not regret the change or the lost opportunity, but on the contrary was extremely pleased, as much for his own sake as that of Hilda.

As regards Wilfred when he found himself alone in the room, he began to congratulate himself on the admirable result of his necessary deviation from the truth. Lord Kenny had never for a moment doubted his word, so the fortune was everlastingly fathered on the distant Indian relative. He could obtain all necessary money from Janshah and settle it on Hilda, so that there would be no necessity for Lord Kenny to make inquiries regarding the truth of the Indian myth. Also, if necessary, he could invest a sum in the name of his father-in-law, producing that gentleman a respectable income; thus all would be well. The uncle in India, having enacted his part, could be dismissed to the shades, and then, married to Hilda, he could enjoy himself without the necessity of keeping up the mythical being of this fictitious relative.

The limitation of the ring in respect to everything being in Janshah's name was certainly irksome; still, he could always obtain as much wealth as he required, and nobody would have the right to inquire how he came by it. Lord Kenny might indeed ask how the money producing the thirty thousand a year was invested, but then a man is not compelled to explain his business affairs to his father-in-law. All that Lord Kenny wanted was a decent income for himself, and so long as he obtained that he would trouble himself but little about Wilfred's finances. Besides, he would always be able to keep up a splendid establishment, and the world is quite willing to accept a man's position, provided he is wealthy, without inquiring too closely into his private concerns. Altogether, Wilfred was very well satisfied with the explanation he had furnished to Lord Kenny, and had no doubt but what the same story would also satisfy Hilda to the fullest extent.

She came into the room with a bright flush on her face, and moved towards him with outstretched hands.

"Wilfred," she cried, as he drew her fondly to his breast, "what does it mean? Just now papa told me you were waiting in the drawing-room, and that I was to see you at once."

"All true, my dearest. You see I am waiting. Has not your father told you my good news?"

"No. He said you would tell me all, and then went away. What is it, Wilfred?"

"Simply this, Hilda,—that he withdraws all opposition to our marriage."

"Wilfred!"

"You are surprised, are you not?"

"Very much so, indeed!" she said in a perplexed

tone, as she sat down. "I never knew him to change his mind without good reason."

"Well, he has every reason in this case. He objected to me as a possible son-in-law because I was poor. Now I am rich, Hilda; I have now an income of thirty thousand a year."

"Thirty thousand pounds a year!"

"It is better than the consulship, is it not? and entails no exile to a West Indian island."

"How did you come into possession of such wealth?"

"An old uncle of mine who lived all his life in India died the other day, and I am his heir."

"Thirty thousand pounds a year!" said Hilda, putting her arm round his neck as he knelt beside her. "Oh, Wilfred, it is too good to be true."

"Nevertheless, it is true!"

"So that was why you wrote me a letter asking me to put off Sir Richard Denham."

"Yes. And you did so?"

"I refused him at once. When it came to the point, I could neither accept him nor give him any hope. My love for you was so strong, Wilfred, that I was determined if I did not marry you to marry no one."

"My dearest! And what did your father say?"

"Not very much. But what he did say was terribly cruel. You know how he speaks at times, Wilfred. Since then he has not opened his mouth to me. When he came just now I was very much astonished."

"My poor Hilda!" said Wilfred, kissing her;

"how miserable you must have been! But our troubles are all over now. Your father says we can marry as soon as the settlements are made out."

"What settlements?"

"Why, the marriage settlement on you, of course. And I do not think Lord Kenny will be averse to having an income to himself."

"But Wilfred, can you afford such a thing? Remember, papa is very, very extravagant."

"He can be as extravagant as he likes, my dear," said Dacre, with a smile; "besides the regular income there are also some loose moneys. Those we will give to your father. I don't suppose he can exist on less than two thousand a year."

"Oh, you don't know papa's capacity for spending money."

"Dear me," said Wilfred, with profound surprise, "it is to be hoped this extravagance is not hereditary. How can I support a spendthrift wife on a miserable income of thirty thousand a year?"

Hilda laughed at this sally, mild though it was. She felt so perfectly happy that she would have laughed at anything.

"It is like a fairy tale," she said in a happy tone. "I am sorry, of course, dear, for your uncle's death, but — why, Wilfred!"

"What is the matter?" he asked, alarmed at her horrified expression.

"You are not in mourning for your uncle!"

"Oh, no, I never thought of that," stammered Wilfred, beginning to think that this chimerical uncle would prove a nuisance. "I suppose I must put a band of crape on my hat. And yet I don't know. I never saw him in my life."

"Still, as you are his heir, you must show some respect for his memory."

"I will do so. At all events, I only received my good news this morning, and you would n't have me come a-wooing in crape, would you? Think what a bad omen it would be!"

"Well, when you leave here see about it at once."

"Yes, I will, dearest. But never mind my uncle; let us talk about ourselves."

In fact, Wilfred, seing that it would be necessary to carry out the deception by wearing mourning in honour of a non-existing person, determined to assume it as a compliment to the late Mr. Lascelle. To all intents and purposes, Lascelle stood in the place of the mythical uncle, as it was through him his good fortune had come.

"Yes, you are right, Hilda," he said, recurring to the subject of outward respect being shown to the dead. "I will go into mourning for the poor old man at once."

He was speaking of Lascelle, but Hilda, of course, thought his tone of regret referred to the deceased uncle.

"Do not grieve, Wilfred."

"Of course not," he replied lightly; "grateful as I am to the old man for the money, I can hardly be expected to exhibit violent grief at his death. I am like the man in 'La Peau de Chagrin,' who was to receive wealth on condition that a mandarin died in China. We will call my late uncle the deceased mandarin, by whose death I have benefited."

"What a gruesome idea!" said Hilda, with a shudder.

"Balzac's ideas generally are gruesome. But do not let us talk any more about such things. When can you marry me?"

"In six months."

"Oh, my dear Hilda, I cannot wait so long as that."

"But, Wilfred, out of respect to your uncle!"

Dacre began to heartily wish he had not invented this uncle, who seemed to come in the way every other moment; but, having done so, was forced to abide by his creation. He, however, shortened the period of mourning as much as was compatible with decency.

"Say three months, Hilda. We will be married at the end of the season."

"Oh, I don't mind the season, at all," said Hilda, hastily; "let us have a quiet wedding."

"No, my dear, we will not," said Wilfred, firmly, determined to gratify her by every means in his power. "We will have a splendid wedding, as rich as that of Aladdin to the Princess."

"Dearest Wilfred, let it be as you please. So long as I have you for my husband I am quite content."

In saying this, she took his hand, and saw thereon the ring.

"Oh, what a strange ring!" she cried, examining it.

"My uncle's ring," explained Wilfred, quickly.

"Take it off and let me look at it."

"I cannot, Hilda. It was left to me on condition that it never left my finger."

"Still — for a few minutes?"

"Impossible, my dear. Examine it on my finger."

"You need not refuse my first request, Wilfred."

"My dearest, I can refuse you nothing," said Dacre, hastily. "Ask me anything else but that."

"Well, never mind," replied Hilda, recovering her good temper. "I can see it just as well on your finger. What letters are these on it?"

"Sanscrit."

"And the meaning?"

"I — I — don't know," said Wilfred, with some hesitation. "You see, I am ignorant of Sanscrit."

"It's a very quaint ring. I quite envy you its possession."

"My dear Hilda," cried her lover with sudden dread, "do not covet this ring, I beg of you. It was left to me on condition that I never parted with it, and I am restrained by my honour from ever taking it off my finger."

"Never mind about the ring," whispered Hilda, seeing the subject was distasteful to him. "I have you; so I do not want it."

"You have us both," rejoined Wilfred, with an uneasy laugh.

The fact is, he foresaw the ring would bring him trouble as well as wealth. Hilda had taken a fancy to it, and would, some time or another, desire it for her own. If he refused she would be angry, and if he agreed there was the chance of his losing his sovereignty. He could not do that.

"Come what may," he murmured to himself, "I will not let it be taken off my finger."

CHAPTER IX.

A TREATY WITH THE ENEMY.

"Therefore," said the major, delivering the final sentence of a long speech, "I have called to see if we can come to some satisfactory arrangement."

The speech in question dealt with the events of the last few days, and these events were recapitulated by Measurby with the idea of proving to Wilfred how shamefully he had acted in keeping the ring. Dacre himself did not agree with the major's views in this matter; still, he was not unwilling to come to an understanding, and thus turn Measurby from an active enemy into a neutral party. Seeing that the major felt himself aggrieved and considered that justice could only be done by delivering up the ring, Wilfred hardly expected to gain him as a friend, nor was he very anxious to do so. Still, he recognized that fortune had dealt hardly with the man, and mentally decided to make reparation.

Unaware that his young friend had come to this decision, Measurby waited for a reply, but, receiving none, began once more to urge his claims.

"I am not the man to bear malice," he said in a dignified tone; "otherwise I could make things uncommonly hot" —

"Pardon me, Major," interrupted Wilfred, blandly, "but I think it just as well that you should refrain from using threats. They may gratify you, but they certainly do not intimidate me. When, in answer to your letter, I agreed to this interview, it was with the hope that we might come to some amicable arrangement. This, certainly, will not be the case if you lose your temper."

"I have no wish to lose my temper," growled the major, indignantly; "I have lost quite enough as it is. You have behaved very badly."

"There I don't agree with you. Self-preservation is the first law of nature, and I only looked after my own interests. Had you been in my place, Major, you would have acted in the same way."

"Sir!" exclaimed Measurby, with Johnsonian grandeur, "had I been in your place I would *not* have acted as you have done. A promise is sacred, and as you promised to give me my ring, you should keep that promise."

"I have not broken it, so far as I am aware," replied Dacre smoothly. "I certainly said I would give you your ring: but then, my dear Major, the ring is not yours, therefore I broke no promise in keeping it."

"A family jewel"—

"Oh, nonsense!" said Wilfred good-humouredly; "do not let us go over the old ground, Measurby. That family romance is rubbish. Is it not?"

"I have spent years hunting for that ring," cried the major, evading the question; "it has cost me a fortune."

"That is your own look-out, not mine. I am certainly not going to return to a state of pauperdom for your sake."

"But I promised you money."

"No doubt! but I prefer the ring. However, I am willing to admit that you have been very unfortunate, and am willing to make reparation. What amount will soothe your wounded feelings?"

"Ten millions sterling."

"What! half the treasure? Oh, nonsense; I might as well give you the ring at once. Say ten thousand pounds, Major."

"Good day, Mr. Dacre," said Measurby, seizing his hat and making for the door.

"Good day!" replied Wilfred coolly, and picked up a book.

On seeing this display of indifference Measurby returned to his seat. He recognized that Wilfred was too strong for him, and as there did not seem any prospect of his obtaining the whole loaf resolved to be content with half.

"Make it twenty thousand, Dacre," he said persuasively; "surely out of such a lot of money you can spare that paltry sum."

"Is it paltry?" said Wilfred, throwing aside his book. "Your ideas are extensive, my dear Major. However, I am not disposed to be hard. ... true that you treated me badly by making me your monkey to pull the chestnuts out of the fire; but as, in this case, the monkey has got the chestnuts to himself he can afford to be generous. I will give you twenty thousand pounds."

"Good! That will last for some time."

"It will have to last you always."

"Then I won't take it," shouted Measurby furiously. "If I asked for a million it would be only reasonable; but I 'm modest enough to be content with little."

"Then be content with twenty thousand pounds. You ought to be glad that I give you anything."

"You don't seem to be aware that I can make things unpleasant for you."

"In what way?"

"I can tell every one the true facts of the case."

"If you do I 'm afraid you will be shut up as an insane person. No one will believe such a story, particularly if I deny it."

"You cannot deny it!"

"Oh, yes, I can! This ring is a gift from my late uncle, who also left me thirty thousand a year."

"You never had an uncle!"

"Probably not; but if I swear to the existence of John Dunlop and the oath is backed up by the presence of wealth, who will disbelieve me? Tell your story, Major, and I will tell mine. Then we shall see who will be believed."

The major was furious at such plain speaking, but saw clearly that he had no chance; so, making a virtue of necessity, he surrendered without further parley.

"I will take the twenty thousand pounds," he said in a subdued voice.

"And promise to refrain from attempting to get possession of the ring?"

"Yes!" said Measurby, who had not the slightest intention of keeping his word.

"Very well! Janshah will be here directly and I will direct him to give you the money."

"In that case we are friends again," observed the major, holding out his hand.

"Oh yes, I suppose so!" returned Wilfred, coldly accepting the proffered hand. "After all, though I don't think much of your conduct, you have helped me to a fortune. Not willingly, I admit. Still, I have benefited by your treachery."

"'Self-preservation,' you know," said Measurby, recovering his good humour; "you quoted the saying yourself. Well, Dacre, we will continue our friendship — or rather acquaintanceship — as if nothing had happened. Notwithstanding that you think my conduct has been shabby, I have done you at least two good turns, — saved you from committing suicide, and enabled you to marry Miss Havard by giving you a fortune."

"Which you designed for yourself."

"Not at all. I designed the ring for myself, and would have been far more generous to you than you have been to me. However, that's all past and done with. I come to your wedding, of course."

"I'm not particularly desirous of your company," said Wilfred dryly.

"I'll come, for all that," rejoined Measurby impudently; "there is no false pride about me."

"Apparently not!"

"Hang it all, man, you might at least be civil."

Wilfred laughed. Much as he distrusted the

major, there was no getting over the fellow's good humour; so unwilling to spoil his present peace of mind by another quarrel, he assumed a graciousness which he was far from feeling.

"My dear Measurby," he said suavely, "I will do all you ask. You will be my very dear friend, to all appearances. You will come to my wedding, and visit at my house; but I fervently hope and trust that you with your twenty thousand pounds will go to Monte Carlo and keep out of my sight."

"Oh, I'll go there!" replied Measurby with a smile; "but first I must see you settled. When is the marriage to take place?"

"In about three months."

"And what do you intend to do with all your money?"

"Make use of it for my own happiness and that of others."

"Don't waste any of it on charity."

"I will certainly help poor people if I can. I don't call it a waste of money to aid the unfortunate."

"Egad, I do!" said Measurby, nodding his head. "By the way, have you told Miss Havard about the ring?"

"No! She thinks the money came from an uncle."

"I'll back you up with that uncle if you like,— say that I met him in India!"

"Say nothing of the sort," retorted Wilfred, hastily. "I prefer to tell my own lies. All I wish you to do is to keep silent about the ring, and not try to get it from me."

"I promise that! Oh, yes! Now I have twenty thousand pounds, I can amuse myself just as well as though I had a million. I'm afraid you'll find the possession of all that money a great trouble, Dacre."

"Perhaps so, but I'll try to bear up under it," said Dacre, ironically. "After all, I have no trouble in the matter. Janshah has all the worry of looking after it, and I, by possessing this ring, reap the benefit."

"Here is Janshah!" cried the major, as the Indian entered the room. "Now, Dacre, tell him what he is to do."

"I wish you to give Major Measurby the sum of twenty thousand pounds," said Wilfred, touching the ring.

"It shall be done, sir," replied Janshah, gravely.

"Not in gold," cried the major quickly. "I can't take it in specie to my bank. They would think I had committed a robbery."

"I can give you a cheque, sir," said Janshah, quietly.

"What! Does your banking account run to twenty thousand?"

"It runs to over two million, sir. I must have enough money always at my command to satisfy my lord."

"It will take a long time to use that up, Janshah," said Wilfred with a smile. "At present, give Major Measurby his cheque."

Janshah bowed gravely, and, going across to the desk, wrote out a cheque for the amount, which he handed at once to the major. Measurby looked at it doubtfully.

"You are sure they will honour this?" he said, examining the cheque closely.

"I will go with you, sir, if it so please you."

"No! no! I expect it will be all right," replied Measurby, putting on his hat. "Well, good-bye for the present, Dacre. I'll see you again, shortly."

"Whenever you please," said Dacre, smiling. "At all events you must be satisfied now."

Measurby nodded gaily and took his departure, while Wilfred, resuming his seat, conferred with Janshah regarding his own financial condition.

Some days had passed since his acceptance by Hilda, and during that period he had spoken several times with Lord Kenny as to what he wished to be settled on himself and daughter. The old lord frankly admitted that he was greatly in want of money, and suggested that Wilfred should settle on him an income of two thousand a year, which his prospective son-in-law agreed to do. At first he was doubtful whether the power of the ring would enable him to do this, but on speaking to Janshah on the subject, the Indian assured him that it could be easily accomplished. The explanation, however, had been rather a hurried one, and now Wilfred again spoke to his servant on the subject.

"I did not quite understand what you said the other day," he observed to Janshah when they were alone. "Can I settle two thousand a year on my father-in-law?"

"Yes, my lord!" answered Janshah deliberately. "All I have to do is to give you a sum which will produce the amount, and once it is made over to

Lord Kenny, of course it passes out of your possession."

"But if I lose this ring, it will be taken from him again?"

"By no means, sir. The ring gives you power to draw whatever money you desire from the treasure and pay it over to whomsoever you please; but you must not invest it for your own benefit."

"Then it seems to me that I can make every one rich but myself."

"You are the richest of all, sir, so long as you possess the ring."

"I think I could trick the ring," said Wilfred, good-humouredly, " by giving a third party a large sum of money to hold for my benefit."

"No. I could not give you money for that purpose. All moneys must be either used for your present pleasures or paid over to others, so that you cannot benefit thereby. But to invest money so as to purchase you an income would not be permitted, for by doing so, you would be independent of the ring."

"It seems to me a very ridiculous restriction."

"It is the law of the ring, my lord," said Janshah, gravely. "It gives all, it takes away all. While you wear it on your finger you are rich; if you lose it, you become poor. Such is the law of the ring."

Wilfred privately thought that there was a good deal of nonsense about these arrangements, but, talk as he might, he knew that he could not make Janshah disobey the rules of the talisman. At the same time he desired to prove to the Indian how easy it would be to evade the spirit while fulfilling the letter of the ring-law, and proceeded to do so at once.

"I desire the sum of five thousand a year to be settled on Miss Havard."

"It shall be done, my lord."

"And she shall possess that income for the rest of her life?"

"Yes, my lord!"

Wilfred burst out laughing.

"Don't you see how easily this ring can be set at defiance?" he said, with a smile. "You will not let me settle any money on myself, so as to be independent of the ring, yet you will give my wife a sufficient income to keep us both; so, even if I lose the ring, I should still have five thousand a year to live on."

"That may be so, sir," rejoined Janshah stolidly: "but such a settlement is not contrary to my instructions. If, after marriage, you settle it on your wife, there might be some doubt; but at present Miss Havard stands to you in the position of a stranger."

"But I shall marry her soon, and thereby benefit by the settlement I now desire to make."

"Probably, my lord. Still, you may not marry her in the end."

"The law of the ring is contrary to that of equity, Janshah," said Wilfred, carelessly. "Equity looks upon that as done which is intended to be done; the ring looks on nothing as certain until it is accomplished."

"That is the case, my lord."

"I'm afraid Western ingenuity can find many flaws in your ordinances of the ring. However, that is your look-out, not mine. This ring permits me to do what I please with twenty millions of money?"

"Yes, my lord."

"Then I wish two thousand a year to be settled on my father-in-law that is to be; five thousand a year on Miss Hilda Havard, my future wife; and all securities in which the capital is invested to be submitted to me for approval."

"It shall be done, sir."

"I also require a house in Grosvenor Square, with a full establishment of servants, to be ready for me when I return from my honeymoon, — horses, carriages, and everything of the kind. Pay into my bank a sum sufficient to discharge all my outstanding debts, and leave that thousand-pound account perfectly clear."

"All this I will do, without fail," said Janshah, not moving a muscle of his face at these extravagant demands. "Is that all, my lord?"

"No. I am about to see my lawyers regarding my father's property in Herefordshire, which has long since passed out of the hands of the family. I desire to buy it back again; so when my lawyers make all arrangements about the price and transfer, pay to them the sum they require."

"Yes, sir."

"I think that is all, at present," observed Wilfred, reflectively; "but tell me, Janshah: among all this treasure of Brahma, have you any jewels?"

"Yes, my lord."

"Here, in England?"

"I brought some with me, sir. Mr. Lascelle was very fond of jewels."

"Then let me see some, to-morrow. I wish a necklace for Miss Havard. Now you can go."

Janshah bowed and left the room, leaving Wilfred in a mixed state of gratification and amusement. The treasures of the Arabian Nights, brought into juxtaposition with the commonplace of English life, lost a good deal of their romance.

"If I were Aladdin, in earnest," said Wilfred to himself, "I would order a palace to be built, whereas I am content with a house in Grosvenor Square. I would ask for slave girls and basins of jewels, but find it more necessary to settle an income on my father-in-law and future wife. Decidedly, the treasures of the Jinn can be applied to very prosaic purposes. If I told this mixture of fact and fiction to any one, they would laugh, and rightly too. The East does not blend well with the West, and Arabian tales are out of place in nineteenth-century England. I am Aladdin, — a very ordinary Aladdin, it is true; nevertheless, I possess, if not his lamp, at least his ring. Aladdin in London is less romantic than his prototype in Pekin. Still, he is nearly, if not quite, as powerful."

CHAPTER X.

WEDDING BELLS.

There was great rejoicing among the aristocratic relations of Lord Kenny when it became known that his daughter was to marry Wilfred Dacre. The news of the young man's good fortune had spread rapidly, and no one questioned the truth of the uncle story. Some wiseacres did, indeed, hint that Wilfred had no wealthy relative either in India or elsewhere; but nobody paid any attention to such statements. An income of thirty thousand a year must come from somewhere, and the undeniable fact that Wilfred was in possession of it proved that he must have had an uncle. At least this was the way in which society argued the matter, and, quite satisfied that Dacre was now well off, did not trouble itself to go any deeper into the genesis of his riches. It deduced the cause from the effect, rather than the effect from the cause, and, from the fact that Wilfred was now rich, presumed such riches must have come from his uncle.

Owing to Lord Kenny's extravagant habits, he had long ago worn out the patience of his relatives in the matter of borrowing money; hence their delight at the prospect of his having a rich son-in-law on whom to sponge. They opened their purse-strings for the last time with a sigh of relief, and assisted him to give Hilda a splendid wedding; then washed their hands of him altogether. Hitherto, he had existed upon surreptitious loans which, out of respect for their name, the Havard family had to grant him; but now he could live excellently well on the two thousand a year allowed him by Dacre. On hearing of this generosity the Havards considered Wilfred a very meritorious young man, and showed their approval of his action by mustering in great force at the wedding.

Though the season was now over, the marriage was a very brilliant affair, as many people who had left town came back for the function. Besides Hilda's relatives, the many friends of Wilfred, who was an exceedingly popular young man, came to see the last of him as a bachelor, and the society papers gushed considerably over the number of aristocratic names present at St. Margaret's, Westminster.

One of the most grateful persons for this marriage was Lord Kenny's nephew, the Duke of Richborough, who had suffered considerably from his uncle's impecuniosity, and now saw a chance of keeping his income to himself. This latter he spent mostly at Monte Carlo, where he was well known in the Casino; but he came over to London for the marriage, as much on Wilfred's account as for his uncle's sake. Dacre had been up with him at Oxford, and the two young men were very intimate: therefore the duke was pleased at his favourite cousin marrying a friend of his own, independent of the fact that such friend was excellently well off.

So pleased was Richborough over the affair, that he insisted upon Hilda's being married from his town house, and, in addition, placed his country-seat in Devonshire at the disposal of the young couple for the honeymoon. Everything, therefore, smiled on Wilfred and his bride, who left town with the good wishes of all their friends.

Thanks to Janshah, and the unlimited treasures of the ring, all Wilfred's desires had been gratified to the fullest extent. A large sum had been invested for Lord Kenny, and Hilda's income of five thousand a year was settled on herself, with all due formality. Moreover, the slave of the ring purchased a magnificent mansion in Grosvenor Square, and while Wilfred was in Devonshire furnished it in a most splendid fashion. The diamonds worn by Hilda at the wedding were also very costly, and every one wondered where the bridegroom had obtained them. Janshah could have answered the question truly; but, as it was, they were supposed to be part of the legacy left to Dacre by his uncle.

In spite of Wilfred's hints, Major Measurby attended the wedding, and several times mentioned that he had met Dunlop in India; whereupon he was besieged by questioners, all of whom the major fully satisfied in the most admirable manner. It is true, that when Wilfred was afterwards called upon to confirm these stories, he displayed an astonishing ignorance of the major's statements; but then Wilfred had never known his uncle personally, and might well be pardoned for being unacquainted with his relative's history. The society papers picked up some of Measurby's stories, and repeated them, so that Wilfred found quite a literature growing around this mythical uncle, who existed but in his own imagination.

However, the wedding duly took place, and Lord Kenny performed the part of a fond parent to perfection, imposing even on his relatives who knew what a selfish old pagan he was. When the bridal pair finally took their departure from Paddington, Lord Kenny, with a sigh of relief, returned to his bachelorism, and proceeded to enjoy himself on his two thousand a year. For this purpose he proceeded to Monte Carlo, in the company of his ducal nephew, and when they were established in the Hotel de Paris, it was hard to say which was the more lively of the two; for what Lord Kenny lacked in years, he made up in spirit. He felt that he had done his duty by his child and was entitled to a little relaxation; so he trotted about with Richborough, and showed that ducal scamp that he was fully able to hold his own with the young men of the day in the matter of going the pace.

Meanwhile, quite unaware of her father's plunge into dissipation, which poverty had hitherto prevented him from taking, Hilda Dacre was enjoying herself greatly in Devonshire. There never was, according to her firm belief, so admirable a bridegroom as Wilfred, and in that country seclusion they lived only for one another. For once in their lives they tasted of perfect happiness, and both bitterly regretted that the cares of the world should ever call them back again to society.

"Not that I see why we should go back," said Wilfred, as he lounged at Hilda's feet on the seashore; "we have no call to do so."

"There are certain duties in life," replied Hilda, drawing figures on the sand with her umbrella; "we must not shirk the responsibilities of wealth."

"My dear," said her husband, lazily, "I am not a utilitarian person, and I hope you are not a woman with a mission. To my thinking, the aim of life is happiness; and as we can secure that aim by living in this manner, I do not see why we should give it up, simply because the world needs reforming."

"One can do such a lot of good with thirty thousand a year!"

"You shall do whatever you please in the way of good. I am in the giving vein to-day, Hilda; so make your demands. Shall I found a hospital, or endow an orphanage, or what not? You are Esther and I the great king. Ask what you wish, even unto half of my kingdom, and it shall be given unto you."

"Ah! such an offer requires a great deal of consideration!"

"Well, consider it now; and meanwhile I will watch Lundy Island."

They were sitting on the seashore, watching the Atlantic breakers rolling in under the soft light of the evening; in front, the sapphire sea, on which floated the huge form of Lundy Island; at the back, tall cliffs and dark woods; and far beyond, the towers of Richborough Grange sombre against the clear evening sky. All was wonderfully quiet, save for the voices of nature; for the gulls shrieked, the waves murmured on the beach, and the wind rustled through the distant trees. After the hurried town-life, this restful haven possessed a wonderful charm, and Wilfred, with his poetic imagination, felt it intensely.

"'The world is too much with us,'" he quoted absently. "Do you know, Hilda, that is a very true line; but one never believes it in town. Our artificial life there banishes all natural instincts from our breasts, and we are content to live in an unnatural manner, instead of returning to the true nature-worship of our ancestors."

"I am very fond of nature, but I would not like to live in the country altogether."

"That is because you have been brought up in town, and have acquired a love for an artificial existence. Very likely, I also, in spite of my asseveration that I love Arcadia, would tire of its placidity: but at present I am thoroughly happy. Let us not think this is Devonshire, Hilda, nor we, children of the nineteenth century. No; you are Eve, I am Adam, and this is the Garden of Eden."

"And Janshah the serpent."

"My dear Hilda, why have you taken such a dislike to that unfortunate man? He is a very harmless sort of character."

"I don't like him!" replied Hilda with a shudder; "he is so quiet and stealthy in his movements,—just like a snake. I wish you would send him away."

"I cannot! He was a servant of my uncle, and was left to my care."

"Then pension him off."

"It is impossible to do that, Hilda; but, if you like, I will send him back to town, and he can only come and see me when necessary."

"Why is it necessary for you to see him?" asked Hilda, curiously.

"Well, you see he looks after certain business, the details of which I need not enter into at present, and must make his report to me every now and then. But he will not trouble you."

The fact is, Hilda was beginning to be very curious about things; and on several occasions, Wilfred had it on the tip of his tongue to tell her the true state of affairs. Then he thought it best to be silent, as, if he revealed the secret of the ring, he could never be certain that she would keep her knowledge to herself. Lord Kenny was an inquisitive old man, and might ask her questions which Hilda would be unable to parry, and sooner or later would tell him all. If Lord Kenny learned the truth, it would soon be known all over London, and Wilfred by no means relished the idea of his private affairs becoming the gossip of clubs and drawing-rooms. He therefore judged it wiser to keep his secret, and succeeded in doing so at the cost of a considerable number of lies, which, though necessary, he very much disliked telling.

In the end, he saw plainly, he would have to tell the truth, but he delayed the necessity as long as possible. As Hilda grew older, and emancipated herself from the influence of her father, he would be able to reveal all with safety; but as it was, he preferred to remain silent, lest Lord Kenny should become suspicious, and discover that which it was not desirable for him to know.

"Besides," resumed Wilfred, anxious to come to a complete understanding regarding Janshah, "I must have some one to look after my business."

"Then why not engage an English steward?"

"He would not be so useful. Janshah is perfectly honest, and knows the details of my uncle's investments, from whence we get our income. Moreover, he speaks nearly all the European tongues, and will be very useful to us when travelling abroad. Still, if you insist upon it, I will dismiss him."

This was very artfully put, as Wilfred knew very well after his explanation Hilda would never consent to his making such a sacrifice.

"My dear Wilfred," she said, taking his hand, "I do not wish you to do that. Keep him in your employment by all means; but the less I see of him the better shall I be pleased."

"You will hardly see him at all," replied Wilfred, rejoiced at thus gaining his point; "he will only come to the house when it is necessary for me to see him on business. By the way, I received a letter from him to-day."

"About what?"

"I told him to get me a villa on the shores of the Black Sea."

"Why the Black Sea?"

"It is said to have a very charming climate, — at least the southern portion of it, — and I am anxious to spend a winter there. He has secured a villa which he says is beautifully situated, some distance above Constantinople."

"In the Bosphorus?"

"No. On the shores of the Black Sea. In the kingdom of Busk."

"Oh!" said Hilda, somewhat startled. "Is not that the place where they have been having a revolution?"

"Yes, but it is all over now. King Pierre is dead, and his daughter, the Princess Julia, is an exile in England. Busk is a republic now, so we shall be perfectly safe."

"And when do you propose to go there?"

"Oh, not for some time. Next year, if it pleases you. I am sure you will like that part of the world very much."

"So long as there is no fighting."

"There will not be any fighting. The republic, one and indivisible, is firmly established, and order prevails everywhere. This villa is perfect, according to Janshah; so we will go there next winter."

"It will be a novelty, at all events," said Hilda in a pleased tone. "Oh dear me, what a lot we have to see, Wilfred! There is our house in town, your family seat in Herefordshire, and now this villa. I am afraid thirty thousand a year will not stand all these extravagances."

"Oh, yes, it will," answered Wilfred gaily. "You have no idea how clever Janshah is in managing all these things. Now we are married, I must make up to you for your hardships."

"My hardships!"

"Well, you did not have much enjoyment in your youth, — I mean when you were with your father."

"No. That is true. Papa was so badly off."

"Then from henceforth your life shall be all sunshine."

"But in our happiness, Wilfred, we must not forget other people."

"No, we will not; but, my dear Hilda, there is plenty of time for that. Let us have two or three years of selfishness, and then you can waste money in charity to your heart's content."

"I am quite willing. How are we going to spend the next few months?"

"We will leave this place for Monte Carlo, in order to see your father. At Christmas, we will go down to Herefordshire, where you can play the part of Lady Bountiful. Afterwards we can take possession of our house in town for the season, and then" —

"And then —" said Hilda, gaily, springing to her feet.

"We will go for the winter to our villa in Busk."

"Our villa in Busk!" repeated Mrs. Dacre, laughing; "it sounds like a castle in Spain."

"More substantial, I hope," said Wilfred, offering her his arm. "We will call it, if you like, the Castle of Indolence."

CHAPTER XI

THE MAJOR MAKES A PROPOSAL.

The true joy of life lies rather in anticipation than in realization; but the truth of this statement is not apparent to the young. How can it be when they are but straining for that distant goal which their imaginations invest with all the glory and romance of the unknown? Only when the goal is attained, only when the prize is within reach, does the victor find that he has but gained Dead-Sea fruit for his reward. That which glistens like gold in the distance proves to be but tinsel on closer inspection, and the beautiful dreams of youth, unsubstantial as the fantasies of sunset, lure us onward with the promise of glories never to be realized. It is the illusions of youth which render us so happy, so ambitious, so determined to succeed; but when they are lost, the actual truth is bitter indeed.

Ask any successful man if he is happy, and without doubt he will tell you that happiness vanished with success, and that the much-desired bauble when gained proved hardly worth the struggle of years. Some few happy persons there are who can attain their ambitions and yet be happy; but the majority of mankind learn by bitter experience that the work is worth more than the reward. Solomon had all that the heart of man can desire, and wrote the Book of Ecclesiastes. Charles V., the most powerful monarch in Europe, gave up all his imperial splendours for the quiet of St. Just; and Diocletian — but why prolong the list? history is but a record of those who have been disillusioned by success. It is as enchanting as the gardens of Armida, and as lacking in true happiness.

These were sad thoughts for a young man; but they were those of Wilfred Dacre, whom all men envied for his wealth and for his beautiful wife. A year had passed since he had gained the ring and Hilda, yet he now felt more unhappy than he had ever felt before. Formerly he had wished for many things, and the constant hope that such might be gained had filled his life with joy; now he had won them all, and found but scant pleasure in their possession. It is true that he loved his wife fondly, that he was not averse to possessing wealth capable of gratifying his most extravagant whims; yet withal there seemed to be something lacking in his existence. That something, though he did not know it, was action.

Nothing stands still in the universe for a moment. It must either go backward or forward in order to fulfil the condition of its being. Owing to his wealth and satiety of desire, Wilfred was as near standing still as is possible for anything, and consequently felt very unhappy. He wanted work, he wanted action, he wanted something to lure him on through toilsome years; but as it was he simply rusted for want of use. It is a fatal mistake to think that idleness is happiness, and this Wilfred speedily discovered. The statesman engaged in creating empires, in maintaining peace, in threatening war, the artist striving to attain the unattainable of perfection, the sailor constantly in expectation of the occurrence of the unforeseen, — all these are happy because busy; but the rich man without ambition creates a hell for himself as terrible as any conceived by fanatics.

In those days of luxury, Wilfred felt very unhappy, and appreciated none of the blessings by which he was surrounded, simply because he obtained them too easily. If he formed a wish, however extravagant, he had only to summon Janshah, when what he desired was immediately granted. He was like a child with too many toys, and suffered bitterly from this plethora of delights.

On the other hand, Hilda was perfectly happy. She did not know of the immense wealth which was crushing the soul of her husband, but, dreaming him to be in the receipt of a settled income, proceeded to enjoy herself to the best of her ability. In her girlhood she had suffered much from poverty, and had always promised herself if she ever became rich to make good use of her money. Now she was in a position to fulfill her girlish dreams, and she did so. Hilda Dacre was ambitious of social success. She desired to have one of the best houses in London and entertain therein all the notabilities of the day. The first she had, for the mansion in Grosvenor Square was simply perfect; so she set to work to secure the second, and with the tact of a clever woman succeeded in her desire. During the first season in London she gave two balls and several "at homes," all of which were very successful.

Wilfred used to laugh at the number of strange people his wife collected in her salons, but he was always very much amused at the queerness of their several types. Hilda was a lion-hunter, and secured all the latest successes at her parties. Great singers, famous novelists, the latest professor of spiritualism, the newest explorer,—they were all present, and, mixed with them, fashionable ladies, tall guardsmen, and invariably a sprinkling of politicians. These latter were brought there for Wilfred's special benefit, as his wife was anxious that he should enter the House. Having no political ambition, however, he obstinately refused to think of such a thing, much to Hilda's despair, as she greatly desired to rouse him from the listless state into which he had fallen.

One constant visitor to Hilda's cosmopolitan salons was Major Measurby, who had now secured quite a position of his own. On receiving the twenty thousand pounds from Wilfred, he also had announced that he had succeeded to a small legacy, as the best way of accounting for his newly acquired wealth. So great is the power of money that this announcement did much to rehabilitate the major in the opinion of his fellow-creatures. Hitherto he had been looked upon with suspicion as little better than an adventurer; but now his wealth and his constant presence at Hilda's reunions had succeeded in gaining him an excellent social position.

Yet, withal, the major was quite as unhappy as

Wilfred. Despite his apparent friendship with Dacre he had not forgiven him the loss of the ring, and determined to gain possession of it sooner or later. Seeing that he had now plenty of money, this desire appeared to be rather selfish, as he could gain no benefit from possessing millions where he now had thousands. So it would appear; but the fact is that Measurby had in his being many characteristics of those condottieri of the Renaissance, and found modern life much too narrow for his ambitions. With twenty millions he could found a kingdom and cut a great figure in the world, while, limited as he now was to a few thousands, he could hope to do nothing save lead this aimless London life, which he detested. He regarded himself as an embryo Napoleon, and, provided he obtained the ring, hoped to emulate the conqueror of Austerlitz.

This being the case, Measurby set his wits to work in order to hit upon some method of wresting the ring from Wilfred. He despised its present possessor very much for frittering away the wealth in such idle ways as he was now doing, and conceived that he would be acting only wisely in gaining possession of the treasure, so as to use it largely for the benefit of mankind in general and himself in particular.

Nevertheless, he saw plainly that it would be a difficult task to get the ring from Wilfred, as that astute young man was proof against fraud; while in a law-ridden place like England, it was impossible to obtain it by force. The only thing to be done was to lure Wilfred out of the kingdom into some land beyond the confines of civilization, and then take advantage of the lack of law and order to accomplish the seizure. This Measurby resolved to do, and proposed to Wilfred that they should undertake an expedition to Africa. Hilda, however, forbade this, as she did not want her husband to leave her on such perilous travels; so Measurby, foiled on one point, tried another.

Knowing all the gossip of the town, Measurby had but little trouble in hitting upon a feasible scheme; and this, under the guise of a friendly act, he communicated to Wilfred at the club. He saw that the young man was devoured with ennui, and resolved to show him how to dispel the curse by leading a life of action. The major, who had all his plans cut and dried, hoped that the life of action he proposed would lead Wilfred into Eastern countries. Once there Measurby promised himself possession of the ring.

They were seated at the window of the smoking-room looking out on St. James Street, and were almost alone, as the apartment was but sparsely occupied. Buried in a large armchair, Wilfred sat smoking in an idle, dreamy fashion peculiarly exasperating to the alert major, who looked upon such inaction with disdain.

"And this fool," soliloquized the major to himself,— "this fool can command twenty millions of money,— an amount which could give him a kingdom, if he were so disposed. But he won't do anything with the ring except fritter its powers away as he is doing now. Hang it, I must get it to my-

self, come what may. I would do some good with
it, while he —"

Measurby broke off, to shrug his shoulders; an
action which attracted the notice of Dacre.

"What is the matter, Major?" he said languidly,
looking at his excellent friend; "why that shrug?"

"I was thinking of the ring," replied Measurby
pointedly.

Wilfred looked at the talisman on his finger, and
smiled complacently.

"What! Have you not given up all thoughts of
that yet?"

"Of course! Of course!" said the major, hurriedly. "I told you that twenty thousand pounds
would satisfy me. Even if you offered me the ring,
I would not take it. It does not seem to have done
you much good."

"Well, I don't know," returned Wilfred slowly,
as if he were thinking how to evade a reply; "it
has given me ease and comfort."

"Neither of which you appreciate."

"I ought to appreciate them. I have everything
to make me happy."

"My dear sir!" broke in Measurby impatiently,
"it is precisely that kind of person who never is
happy. Why don't you make use of the power that
ring gives you?"

"I am making use of it."

"Yes, like a child. You have bought a fine
house, you give grand entertainments, you lavish
jewels on your wife. My good fellow, that is not
making use of the ring."

"Well, to what better use could you put it?"

Measurby drew a long breath.

"Ah! I could do many things. For instance, I could buy myself a kingdom."

"There are none for sale," said Wilfred cynically. "The large ones decline to put up for auction, and the smaller ones are mostly turned into gambling hells."

"Your vision is narrow," retorted the major angrily; "you only see what you choose to see. If you wanted a small kingdom, you could obtain one. They say romance is dead. Pooh! the world is as romantic now as it ever was. Why now, at this moment, I could unfold to you a scheme which would transcend the wildest romance of the Middle Ages."

"Well, do so. I am only too anxious to be amused."

"There is no amusement in this, but hard work. You have had too much of the former, Dacre, and it has rendered you dissatisfied; the latter will make you a contented man once more."

"Then you do not think I am content now?"

"A glance in your mirror will answer that question," said Measurby, disdainfully. "Content? No! You are suffering from ennui, the curse of an idle existence. Oh, I speak for myself as well as for you. I, also, feel stifled in this narrow life we lead. I am not fit for your comfortable civilization, Dacre. Had I lived in the Middle Ages, I would have lived every moment of my life; now I only exist."

"Yet you say the present age is one of romance," was Dacre's commentary on this speech.

"And I say it again. Romance is all around us, hidden under the mask of the commonplace. We talked on this subject before, and I told you to go out into the streets, and seek for an adventure. You did so and found one."

"But you forget. That adventure was prepared by you."

"Partly; not altogether. But to return to our subject. Romance, I say, exists on all sides; but the special romance we need is not to be found in England. The romance of adventure, war, of life and death, must be sought for in distant lands. You are stagnating here, Dacre, and so am I. Let us go, then, to the East, and there I can promise you a life of danger — and delight."

"Is this your scheme?"

"Yes. I am going to the Black Sea, — to Busk, there to replace the Lusignan dynasty on their rightful throne."

"I am afraid you will find that task a somewhat difficult one."

"Alone and unaided I might do so, but with your money —"

The major paused and looked eloquently at Wilfred.

"My money!" repeated the young man thoughtfully. "Yes, as you say, a great deal can be done with that. Still, the task is a dangerous one."

"No doubt; but it will be something to live for! Of course, if you are afraid —"

"Afraid!" interrupted Wilfred, colouring with vexation, "no, I am not afraid, but I am prudent.

It does not do to decide a question of this sort without due reflection. Have you spoken to any one else about this idea?"

"No. It is no use speaking to any one else, Only a man of your wealth can aid me to carry out the scheme."

"Do you know the princess de Lusignan?"

"No."

"Or the marquess Paradiso?"

"No. I am acquainted with neither of them. But I know that the princess is not a woman to submit tamely to the loss of her throne. Eighteen months ago her father died, and before she could be proclaimed queen, the republican faction drove her into exile. All those eighteen months she has been scheming to return again to Busk. She has asked for the aid of England, and our present government, afraid of Russia, refuses to assist her. France, republican herself, will not aid fallen royalty. Germany dare not embroil herself with the Balkan states, lest she should offer a pretext to France for war; so on all sides this unfortunate princess has been refused help."

"In that case, as the great powers have decided to remain neutral, she will never get back her throne."

"It is questionable," replied the major, musingly; "but Julia de Lusignan is too daring a spirit to submit to such injustice. I discovered, quite by accident, that at the present time she is forming a conspiracy against the republic of Busk. Her party is a strong one: there is dissension among the leaders of the republic, and if she strikes a bold blow, who knows but what she may seize the throne before the year is out!"

"It is a forlorn hope."

"Not more so than was that of Napoleon III. when he lived in London. Yet he secured the imperial throne. I do not know this woman personally, Dacre, but on all sides she is spoken of as a daring and noble sovereign."

"Without a crown," said Wilfred, significantly. "I am acquainted with Madame de Lusignan, and she seems to be a singularly clever woman; but, it takes more than that to secure a throne."

"It does," replied the major emphatically; "it takes money, — which she has not. Dacre, we are both tired of inaction, and desire a life of adventure. Let us obtain our desire by offering to assist the princess to get back her throne."

Wilfred remained silent, stroking his chin with his hand.

"Your proposal is not unworthy of consideration," he said at length; "and I am rather in favour of doing what you say, but I will commit myself to no undertaking without due reflection. Tell me what you know of this conspiracy."

"I know nothing more than what I have told you. It was by accident I discovered so much. Meetings of the royalists are held at Madame de Lusignan's house in Portman Square. I intended to try and gain admission, but resolved to first speak to you."

"Why to me?"

"Because I don't think you are making a proper use of the ring," replied Measurby, calmly. "With such wealth, you should do more than lead an aimless existence. Besides, I see you are dull; and, for your own sake as well as my own, I desire to show you how to enjoy life."

"And you did not want to go to Madame de Lusignan empty-handed, I suppose," suggested Wilfred, sarcastically.

"No, you are quite right," returned the major, in no wise offended; "your money will be more grateful to the princess than my sword. However, if you do not like my idea, let us drop the subject."

"By no means. I am much taken with your idea, but I will not decide hastily."

"Then what are your intentions?"

"The marquess Paradiso," said Wilfred, reflectively, "is coming to an 'at home' my wife is giving this afternoon. You also are coming, Major, I presume?"

"Yes; Mrs. Dacre was kind enough to send me an invitation."

"Good! Then while society is engaged in listening to the last new singer captured by my wife, I will take an opportunity of introducing you to the marquess. I suppose he knows all about this conspiracy?"

"Everything. He is completely in the confidence of the princess."

"Then we will hold a council of three, and if I am satisfied with the facts he puts before us, I will think over the matter."

"How wonderfully cautious you have become, Dacre," said Measurby ironically. Wilfred turned towards him with a meaning smile.

"My dear Major," he said significantly, "I was talking with a cabinet minister last week, and the question of Princess Lusignan and her exile came up in the course of conversation. It was the opinion of this statesman that the first effort made by the princess for the recovery of Busk would result in a European war. With that possibility, can you wonder at my caution?"

CHAPTER XII.

PLEASURE AND POLITICS.

The Tower of Babel was responsible for the confusion of tongues, and the end of the nineteenth century is certainly accountable for the confusion of classes. In the days of old every class was distinguished by a special dress, and the lines of division were sharply defined. Then the dress distinction disappeared; and now the lines of division have been removed, with the result that society has been, so to speak, reduced to an intellectual and moral chaos. Royalty, aristocracy, gentry, and merchants all mingle with one another. The only line of demarcation is that fixed against shopkeepers : but above that, to all appearances, every one, of whatever rank, seems to be on an equal footing. This fact was never better exemplified than by the motley crowd assembled in the salons of Hilda Dacre, for there social extremes met in the most extraordinary manner.

Actors elbowed peers, clergymen chatted with actresses, journalists hunted cabinet ministers, and society ladies smiled on American millionaires. It was a case of liberty, equality and fraternity with a vengeance, and the most exacting radical would have been pleased with the spectacle. The social millennium had arrived, and the aristocratic lion was lying down with the wealthy commercial lamb. A lively scene, but depressing to the thoughtful mind, as no one seemed to have any dignity, but all were more or less familiar with one another. They were of all ranks, of all professions, and the only thing they had in common was the desire of each to get the better of his neighbour.

When Hilda set up her establishment in London it was with the firm determination to keep her " at homes " as exclusive as possible, and only to admit those of her own rank. The result was that these functions were intensely aristocratic and intensely dull ; so, in order to enliven them, a few amusing people of slightly lower rank were invited. After this the deluge. These newcomers brought their friends, who in their turn brought others; so, little by little, the strong tide of plebeianism broke down the barriers set up by Hilda and flooded her salons with doubtful respectabilities. The guests, if not very select, were at all events amusing, and as Hilda desired to make her receptions successful she was obliged, sorely against her will, to invite the professional jesters of the day. Unhappily she could not accept the inevitable with a sufficiently good grace, and complained bitterly to Lord Kenny of the extraordinary people she was compelled to receive.

" I feel like Marie Antoinette," she said disconsolately, " when the mob invaded the Tuileries. It is no use trying to keep them out. They will come and bring their friends, who are worse, if possible, than themselves. I suppose the country is on the verge of a revolution, but it seems to me that we are now anticipating its worst horrors."

"My dear child, your ideas are mediæval," said Lord Kenny, indulgently. "You would have been more at home in the Middle Ages, when sixteen quarterings were required from those who wished to enter decent society. *Nous avons changé tout cela.* Money and brains are the passports nowadays, particularly the first. I don't like it, myself; but what can one do, save bend to the inevitable? As these people won't be kept out, they must be let in : and after all they come with jests, instead of bludgeons as they did in the French revolution. There is no such thing as caste nowadays. It went out with steel armour, to be superseded by American fortunes and mushroom peerages. If you wish to be select you will have to ask half-a-dozen people whose titles do not make up for their mental deficiencies. The result will be, as you have already experienced, boredom. No, my dear Hilda; in the end you will have to admit the herd."

Taking this somewhat cynical advice, his daughter did admit the herd ; and although she strove to draw the line somewhere, it was extremely difficult to draw it at all. Still, by dint of hard work and judicious selection, she managed to keep her receptions sufficiently up to the mark, and they became immensely popular among the heterogeneous society of to-day. Lord Kenny invariably came to these entertainments, in order to support his daughter, and expressed himself highly amused with the different types of sociality which came under his notice.

"It's like Noah's Ark, you know," he was saying to an M. P. on this particular occasion; "every species of animal is represented. I suppose all the people here are fairly respectable."

"Quite as respectable, if not more so, than the aristocracy," retorted the M. P., who had risen from the ranks, and never lost an opportunity of advertising the fact. "In my opinion all the virtues of the nation are concentrated in the middle classes."

"Pooh! pooh!" rejoined his lordship, easily, "that is because no one takes any notice of their peccadilloes. If one of our people makes a slip the scandal is blazoned forth in every rag calling itself a society paper; but your middle classes can sin as they please without any one being a bit the wiser."

"All men are equal, my lord!"

"And all men are brothers, also — by Adam," said the peer, sarcastically; "but they don't seem to care much about either fraternity or equality. You are a radical, I believe?"

"Yes, a strong radical."

"Then I suppose you look upon your servants as equals."

"Certainly not," replied the radical angrily; "there is a limit."

"Of course, and the limit always seems to me to be a personal matter. Your theory is a deal better than your practice, my dear sir. To all above you you urge equality, but as regards those below, you keep silent."

"It is a matter which admits of much argument, my lord."

"No doubt, but you intend all arguments to end the same way, — according to your views. However, we will not argue at all, as neither of us would convince the other. Let us talk of other things, — Princess Julia of Busk, for instance. I see her master-of-the-household is present."

"Yes. Intriguing as usual, I suppose."

"Well, you can't expect any one to give up a throne easily, especially a woman," retorted Lord Kenny, with a chuckle. "Of course Paradiso is intriguing, and so is his mistress, but they are only winding ropes of sand, unless your government helps them."

"Certainly not. By doing so we should involve ourselves in a war with Russia."

"Ah, I forgot! Peace without honour is the motto of your party. Perhaps you are right. It is much more profitable to let the cat pull the chestnuts out of the fire."

"Princess Julia will never pull the Busk chestnut out of the Russian fire," said the M. P., spitefully. He had been introduced to Julia, and she had snubbed him severely.

"She 'll try to, at all events. A woman with the temper of Catherine the Second does not stick at trifles. She wants the throne of Busk."

"And more than that, — she wants the throne of Cyprus."

"Does she, indeed!" said Lord Kenny, nodding his head. "You can't blame her. It belonged to her family for three centuries. I suppose you won't give it to her?"

"She might as well ask for the moon."

"Women are constantly asking for that,— or its equivalent. But I see that it is the intention of the present government to remain neutral."

"Strictly neutral."

"Until Princess Julia starts a war on her own account, and then you can step in where there is any advantage to be gained. England, like Autolycus, is a picker-up of unconsidered geographical trifles. She picked up one inheritance of the Lusignans,— Cyprus; and now if she sees a chance I expect she will annex Busk."

"The Balkan states — " began the M. P., whereupon Lord Kenny cut him short with considerable impatience.

"I know what you are going to say. The balance of power and the Asian mystery. Both out of date, my good sir. Don't let us talk any more politics, they are — Ah! Wilfred," added his lordship, breaking off, "how are you? I have come to see the menagerie."

"I hope you have been amused," replied Wilfred dryly, hardly relishing the term.

"Immensely," said Lord Kenny, taking his son-in-law's arm and moving away from the M. P. "I have been talking politics with a man who knows nothing about them."

"Then don't resume the subject with me, Lord Kenny. I am equally ignorant."

"In that case you ought to go into the House."

"And advocate what?"

"The abolishment of 'at homes,'" said Lord Kenny, smiling. "They are dull functions."

"I thought you said you were amused."

"Not at the entertainment, — at the people themselves. I think Darwin must have picked up his idea of monkey descent from an entertainment of this sort. It's all chatter and tricks. By the way, there is Richborough."

"Yes. He came here to-day at Hilda's particular request."

"What! is she a conspirator also?"

"I don't understand."

"Have n't you heard? My dear Wilfred, it's quite the talk of the town. Richborough is going in for politics."

"Parliament?"

"No. The de Lusignan politics. I see the marquess Paradiso is present. You know he is intriguing for the restoration of Princess Julia."

"Yes. I know that. But what has Richborough got to do with it?"

"He is going to assist. I knew you would be surprised," added Lord Kenny, seeing the look of astonishment on Dacre's face. "I confess I was surprised myself. Richborough's training has not prepared him for a political career, particularly one which brings him into contact with Muscovite politicians. But it is true, nevertheless. He is going to offer himself and what remains of his money to this exiled queen, — exchange Monte Carlo for Busk, and his coronet for a crown!"

"He might do worse."

"Ah! ah!" said Lord Kenny, significantly. "Are you bitten also? Well, why don't you join him?"

"Perhaps I may."

"If I were younger, I might be tempted to do the same thing, Dacre. This life of ours is singularly dull and vapid. A revolution offers excitement, and excitement is the salt of life. There is Hilda beckoning to you."

"But what about yourself, Lord Kenny?"

"I will talk to Mrs. Gaveston. She is a delightful old scandal-monger, and knows something bad about every one present. Go to Hilda, my dear lad."

So Wilfred went, and Lord Kenny sat down beside his antique gossip, whom he aided to pull the character of everybody to pieces. Both of them were excellent at this work, and in a few minutes had left no one in the room with a shred of respectability.

"I wish you would stay beside me, Wilfred," said Hilda, in a whisper. "I am so tired receiving people, and I want you to take some of the work off my shoulders."

"I'll do my best," replied her husband in the same tone; "but really, Hilda, I do not know why you bore yourself with these functions."

"When one is in Rome, one must do as the Romans do," retorted Hilda, laughing. "Never mind, Wilfred; the season is nearly over, and then we can amuse ourselves in our own way."

"It certainly won't be in this style. Just listen to the conversation."

No one taking up her attention for the moment, Hilda did so, and certainly was not impressed by the scraps of talk she overheard.

"Said she would never receive her — I have it for a fact — he married a chorus girl — four thousand at Monte Carlo — of course he is determined to apply for a divorce — we went to the Palace Music Hall last night — oh, my dear, the songs — well — the duke is going to marry her if she will have him — Lusignan and Richborough — an impossible mixture —"

"What's that?" asked Hilda, quickly, overhearing the last remark.

"About Richborough?" said Wilfred, slowly. "Well, your father was just telling me that he is going to offer his services to Princess Julia."

"Is he in love with her?"

"I'm sure I don't know. It's either love or ennui. However, you can ask him for yourself; here he is."

"Hilda," said the duke, approaching at that moment, "where is the marquess Paradiso?"

"What do you want to see him about?"

"About?" said Richborough, laughing. "That is a secret."

"I'm afraid not," interposed Wilfred, quickly. "It is well known that you are going to join the Lusignan party."

Richborough shrugged his shoulders, but did not deny the statement.

"One must have excitement," he said, in a low voice. "I am bored to death with everything; so a little conspiracy will be a change."

"You'll get yourself into trouble," hinted Hilda, with the amiable candour of a near relation.

"Of course, and the excitement will be in getting myself out again," said her cousin, laughing. "But I wish to speak to you about this, Wilfred."

"Don't draw my husband into your plot."

"It is not my plot," replied the duke maliciously. "Paradiso is responsible for the whole affair. Ah, there is the marquess. Excuse me, Hilda. Wilfred, I will see you again."

When the duke went off, Hilda turned towards Wilfred in surprise.

"I hope you are not entangled in any of these mad schemes, Wilfred?" she said anxiously.

"You may be certain I will tell you everything I do. I certainly had some idea of seeing Paradiso."

"At whose suggestion?"

"Major Measurby's."

"That man is your evil genius."

"Well, then, you are my good genius," replied Wilfred, smiling. "Don't be alarmed, Hilda. Whatever may be my intention, I will commit myself to nothing without your consent and approval."

Hilda looked at him anxiously and would have spoken, but at this moment her attention was claimed by a newly arrived guest, and she was forced to turn away from her husband. When she looked again he was gone.

The fact was that Major Measurby had touched his arm and drawn him aside into a quiet corner. Some new pianist was executing a firework piece of music, notwithstanding which, with the peculiar good breeding characteristic of the fashionable world, conversation went on just as usual. A few enthusiasts had gathered round the player, but the majority of the guests were talking incessantly, hardly lowering their voices to do so; and amid the general hum of talk and music, Measurby and his young friend found an opportunity of exchanging a few words.

"Have you spoken to Paradiso?" asked the major, anxiously.

"Not yet. I have not had an opportunity, but will do so shortly. At present, he is talking to the Duke of Richborough."

"And we know what that means," said Measurby significantly. "He is bent on the same errand as ourselves."

"So I hear."

"And from whom?"

"My father-in-law. He knows everything—"

"Except how to hold his tongue," muttered the major, mightily annoyed at being forestalled in his information. "Well, Dacre, I wish you would introduce me to Paradiso at once."

"Whenever I get the chance," replied Dacre, hurriedly; "but we cannot speak of anything serious to him just now."

"Of course not. Ask him to make an appointment."

"About the conspiracy?"

"Yes; but don't hint at such a thing. If you do, he'll deny all about it."

"It seems to me hardly worth while his doing so," said Wilfred sarcastically. "Every one knows that a conspiracy is in the course of formation."

"Every one does not," answered Measurby, emphatically. "There are rumours, certainly; but nothing definite is known. Why, the Russian ambassador is keeping a close watch on the princess; so if he found out her plans, she would be checkmated in Busk. No; they are keeping the affair as quiet as possible, and there is no tangible evidence that such a thing as a conspiracy is in existence."

"But Richborough?"

"Oh, I know all about him," said the major, rapidly. "It is said that he is in love with the princess, — a mere rumour, nothing more, of which the Russian government takes no notice. Richborough has no power, no money, — nothing but his title, which goes for naught in foreign politics. His accession to the party of the princess means nothing whatever."

"Mind, I do not intend to commit myself with Paradiso."

"Then what is the use of speaking to him at all?" said Measurby in an angry tone.

"Every use! I wish to find out the truth of the matter. If it is some wild scheme, such as recommends itself to Richborough, I certainly will not pledge myself to interfere in any way. But if it is serious business and I can see some possibility of success, I will do my best to help the cause, — if my wife does not object."

"Your wife, — why, what has she got to do with it?"

"Everything. If I join in this, my wife must come with me. I have been thinking over the matter since I saw you last, and her coöperation will be very useful."

"I don't see it."

"Not now; but you will, when I explain my plans."

"Have you any plans?"

"Yes. I have a design for getting the princess to Busk without any one knowing of her presence in the country."

"But—"

"Hush, Measurby," said Wilfred, a trifle impatiently, "this is not the time to discuss these matters. You will find that I am not talking without good cause. Meanwhile let us go and speak to Paradiso."

Measurby acquiesced in silence, and followed Wilfred across the room. He did not like the imperative tone adopted by Dacre, and saw that if the young man went in for conspiracy he would do so heart and soul. If he — with the aid of his money — succeeded in placing Julia de Lusignan on the throne, it would be as difficult to obtain the ring in Busk as in England, for its owner would be as safe in the former country as in the latter. Measurby, however, had a most hopeful disposition, and so long as he induced Wilfred to go to Busk trusted that some opportunity would occur enabling him to gain possession of the ring. Once he had that, and the conspiracy could come to naught so far as he was concerned. The major was intriguing purely on his own account, and making use of Wilfred as a cat's-paw; but the young man had proved too clever for him before, and Measurby dreaded lest he should do so again. At all events the major was satisfied that, whatever obstacles stood in his way, he would do his best to obtain possession of the ring, and thus punish Dacre for having so cleverly turned the tables in the last instance.

The marquess Paradiso was a tall, bluff, soldierly-looking man with a shrewd black eye and a swarthy complexion. He belonged to one of the patrician families of Busk, and was devoted heart and soul to the house of Lusignan. Thoroughly trusted by the late king, he had justified that trust by following the princess Julia into exile when the throne of Busk was overturned. Since the happening of that event he had intrigued incessantly to subvert the republican government and restore the monarchy, but hitherto without success. It was owing to his dexterity in financial matters that Julia de Lusignan was enabled to keep up an appearance of regal state. It was royalty in exile with a curtailed establishment, unacknowledged by the government, even by society; yet all matters of etiquette were strictly attended to, and the princess was served by her household with a single-hearted devotion which proved how the misfortunes of her dynasty had endeared her to those who shared her exile.

Accustomed to intrigue, and to taking advantage of every opportunity likely to contribute to the benefit of the princess, Paradiso was always on the alert for possible chances of securing his pet ambition. Richborough was not a great acquisition; still the adherence of a great English noble was not to he despised, and both Paradiso and the princess made much of the gallant young man. Knowing the cosmopolitan society which met in the salons of Mrs. Dacre, the marquess came hither with the intention of keeping his eyes open and gaining whatever advantage offered; yet, while listening to all that went on around him, was too wise to commit himself to speech.

"How do you do, Marquess," said Wilfred, saluting Paradiso. "Will you permit me to introduce you to my friend, Major Measurby."

"I have heard of you, Major," said the marquess, shaking Measurby's hand. "You have done some good work in India."

"I have been under fire, if that is what you mean," replied Measurby, on his guard at once from this too gracious reception. "Mere frontier wars, nothing more."

"Burmah and Afghanistan," said Paradiso significantly; "something more than trifles, I think. And now you are resting on your laurels?"

"A rest which I do not require."

"Ha!" observed the Marquess, darting a piercing glance at the impassive visage of the major. "You wish to repeat your warlike deeds."

"I wish for anything that means an exciting life," said Measurby significantly.

"The fact is, both the major and myself desire to see you privately on business," interposed Wilfred abruptly.

"On business?" reiterated Paradiso with feigned surprise. "I do not understand."

" Well, we can hardly explain our meaning here, Marquess, but I think you can guess it."

Paradiso glanced anxiously round the room, being constantly in dread of spies, and then shook his head with a pretence of ignorance peculiarly irritating to a quick-tempered man like Dacre.

" I am afraid I cannot fathom your meaning."

" I refer to your meetings," said Wilfred, exasperated at this fencing.

" What meetings, monsieur ? " inquired Paradiso angrily.

" I think you know that better than we do," hinted the major significantly.

Paradiso shook his head with a bright smile, and shrugged his shoulders.

" I am really at a loss to understand these allusions, messieurs," he said quickly. " Perhaps you have reference to the receptions of my august mistress. She receives on Thursdays, and I have no doubt will be graciously pleased to admit you to an audience."

" We do not wish to come on Thursdays," said Wilfred in an annoyed tone ; " but at night."

" To-morrow night," said Measurby significantly, " at ten o'clock."

The marquess looked at him anxiously, astonished that he knew the hour of the meeting ; but, astute reader of character as he was, the stolidity of Measurby's countenance baffled him, and he still professed his inability to understand the meaning of these hints. Wilfred would have retreated in despair ; but Measurby, taking the bull by the horns, whispered rapidly in Paradiso's ear without attracting the attention of the bystanders : —

"We wish to join the royal cause. Dacre is a recruit worth gaining. Money!" With a rapid movement Paradiso moved back and looked keenly at the two men.

"You are jesting with me, gentlemen," he said in a low tone. "There is no conspiracy; the princess is content to remain quiet under the protection of England."

"In that case there is nothing more to be said."

"But," added Paradiso with emphasis, "I have a few friends coming to see me to-morrow night, about ten o'clock, — a mere friendly gathering of my compatriots; and I will be pleased if you gentlemen will do me the honour of coming."

"We will be there," said Measurby decisively.

"Merely a friendly gathering," insisted the marquess, looking round to see that no one was within hearing.

"Of course," replied Wilfred, smiling; "merely a friendly gathering."

CHAPTER XIII.

CONSPIRACY.

Notwithstanding that the marquess had made an appointment with Wilfred and the major for the next night, the former was too impatient to wait even for such a short period. He therefore insisted that Measurby should seek an interview with Paradiso the same day as that when the "at home" had taken place.

"I don't want to go to a full meeting of these conspirators," he said, when Measurby urged him to wait; "we should neither of us gain sufficient knowledge of their plans. Paradiso must tell us everything, so that we may be equal in knowledge to his compatriots; otherwise I refuse to accept his invitation for to-morrow night."

"But Paradiso will tell us nothing," objected the major pointedly.

"If he does so now he certainly won't tell us any more when those whom he humorously calls his friends are present. I have no desire to form a fifth wheel in this affair, Major. Either Paradiso will accept our aid or he will not. If he intends to do so, let him grant us an interview to-night and explain all his plans. Then we shall be in a position to accept or refuse."

"I 'm afraid we shall have gone too far to refuse, if we learn his secrets."

"I fail to see that. We are gentlemen, I trust, and can keep silent about such things. If Paradiso is not prepared to accept that amount of risk, he is less daring than I give him credit for being."

"He is cautious."

"And so am I," retorted Wilfred, coolly; "too cautious to go into this matter blindly. I must know all to-night, and when we go to the meeting to-morrow I can give my answer."

"And meantime?"

"Meantime I will think over the matter and consult my wife."

"Consult your wife!" echoed Measurby, in a vexed tone. "You are mad to think of such a thing."

"What is your objection?"

"She is a woman, and cannot keep a secret."

"She will keep secret whatever I desire," replied Wilfred, with conviction.

"In that case," said Measurby, ironically, "I wonder that you did not intrust her with the secret of the ring."

"There was no necessity for such a thing," rejoined Dacre, flushing at this home thrust. "Perhaps some day I will tell her, but at present there would be no sense in doing so. This conspiracy, however," he added in an emphatic tone, "concerns us both, and she must know all about it. Besides, I may need the assistance of my wife."

"In what way?"

"All that I will tell you in the presence of

Paradiso," said Wilfred, with marked significance. " Don't be afraid, Major. The marquess shall know all my plans when he informs me of his."

" Will you tell him of your intention to take your wife into your confidence ? "

" Assuredly. And what is more, I will gain his permission to do so."

" I don't think you will," retorted Measurby, derisively. " Paradiso has but a small opinion of women."

" In that case I wonder at his determination to place Busk under the sway of a queen."

" Pooh! that argument is a mere quibble."

" Never mind; it is a sufficient answer to your objection," replied Dacre, impatiently. " But tell me, Major, will you come with me and see the marquess to-night ? "

" Whenever you please, but I 'm afraid he will not be at home."

" Oh, yes, he will," said Dacre, triumphantly. " I sent off a note to him some time ago telling him that we intended to call to-night."

" You might have consulted me," grumbled the major, rather annoyed at the leadership assumed by his proposed victim.

" My dear Major, I did not wish to lose him. You were not present; so I sent off the note on my own responsibility, and came to your rooms at once. You can hardly accuse me of neglecting your interests."

" It 's a lucky thing you found me at home," said Measurby, evading the point. " I was going to the theatre."

"Well, are you going to the theatre now?"

"No. I will come with you. The comedy of life is more amusing than that of the stage."

"It is nine o'clock," observed Wilfred, glancing at his watch. "I told Paradiso we would call about half-past."

"In that case we had better start at once."

They went outside, and speedily found themselves in a hansom rolling in the direction of Portman Square, where Madame de Lusignan at present resided. On arriving at the house, they sent up their names, and at once were conducted into the presence of the marquess Paradiso. That astute gentleman received them with easy courtesy, and gave no hint by word or deed that he was acquainted with the object of their visit, — an object which he would have been dull indeed not to guess.

"I duly received your note, Mr. Dacre," he said suavely, in English, — a language which he spoke admirably, albeit with a slight foreign accent, — "and resolved to see you and your friend as you suggested. But why you wish to see me after what passed between us to-day I am at a loss to understand."

"I must apologize for giving you so much trouble," said Dacre, gravely; "but when I explain my reasons for this visit I have no doubt you will think them sufficiently good to warrant our intrusion."

The marquess, wary old diplomat as he was, simply bowed his head in answer to this speech, and waited to hear what his visitors had to say.

"The matter I spoke of to-day is an important one to us," observed Wilfred, consulting Measurby's face; "and, notwithstanding your invitation of tomorrow night, we wish to be acquainted with certain facts before definitely deciding to accept the same."

"Your pardon, monsieur," said Paradiso, gravely; "but I have yet to learn what is the matter to which you refer."

"I can explain that," broke in Measurby at this moment; "though I think you can guess what that explanation will be. It is no use fencing any longer, Marquess. Dacre and myself desire to offer our services to the princess for the purpose of replacing her on the throne of Busk. You need not look so astonished, Marquess. We are in earnest, else we would not have come here."

"Alas!" said the marquess in a melancholy tone, "such an offer is worse than useless. The princess has long since given up all hope of regaining the kingdom of her ancestors."

"Yet, if report speaks truly," observed Wilfred, bluntly, "meetings take place at this house for that very purpose."

"And if such were the case, do you think I would admit the fact to strangers like yourselves?" said Paradiso, rising to his feet. "The emissaries of the so-called republic of Busk are in London; the English government, to its eternal shame, has acknowledged the political existence of the traitors who drove Princess Julia from her country. With these dangers around, I should be mad, indeed, to admit anything to you, lest you might make use of it in the interest of our enemies."

"Your objection," said Wilfred, in calm tones,

"is certainly just; but in this instance your suspicions are ill-founded. Instead of betraying you or your royal mistress to your enemies, we desire to assist her in regaining her throne."

"And how can you do that?" said Paradiso, with a sceptical smile.

"I can give you unlimited wealth."

"Unlimited wealth?"

"Aye. To the extent of millions."

Paradiso looked at him keenly and made a deprecatory gesture with his shoulders.

"My dear M. Dacre, I trust you did not call on me at this hour in order to make jokes."

"I am perfectly in earnest," said Wilfred firmly.

"And I can vouch for the truth of the statement," added Measurby, with great deliberation.

Paradiso walked across to the fireplace and stared vaguely into the mirror for some moments, while he pondered over his reply. This sudden visit took him somewhat by surprise, and he felt greatly perplexed how to answer these two strangers who had so unexpectedly offered their services. Surrounded as he was on all sides by treachery, he was afraid to speak too boldly, and yet did not desire to let them go without making sure of the honesty of their intentions. The royalists of Busk were not by any means a strong party, and it would never do to lose the accession of a man who could bring money to the amount of millions to forward the cause. He meditated over the matter for some time, and then turned to survey his guests with an inquiring look on his face.

"If you speak truly — " he began with marked hesitation.

Wilfred interrupted him impatiently.

"Of course we speak truly. Do you think, Marquess, that either I or my friend look like traitors? We desire to do this thing through a love of adventure; and rest assured that both my money and the major's services will be of great value to the cause."

"I will trust you," said Paradiso, extending a hand to each. "Yes, I will trust you without bonds or oaths of any kind. You are gentlemen, I know, and would not betray an unhappy princess whose fortunes are now at their lowest ebb."

Old servant as he was of the house of Lusignan, the thought of such a thing caused his voice to shake with emotion; but, speedily recovering himself, he went on, speaking in firmer tones.

"You are right in your surmise regarding meetings at this house. Most of the members of our party are in London, and we meet here to concert measures for replacing the princess once more on the throne. The republic is now anything but popular. Its leaders, consulting their own selfish interests, are oppressing the people, and the army is thoroughly demoralized. With a few brave spirits ready to act with us at the right time, we hope to raise the royal standard, and, while the country is yet in confusion, seize on the capital for Queen Julia."

"It is a splendid idea," said Wilfred, his eyes flashing at the prospect. "And when do you expect to do this?"

"We cannot say, for just now we have no money. Money! money!" repeated the marquess in despair, "we need a great deal. Several of the republican leaders, particularly Upravado, can be bribed, and would then assist us to restore the queen; but without money we can do nothing."

"I will supply the money, Marquess."

"How much can you give?" asked Paradiso, eagerly.

"As much as you require, — a million, if need be."

"Impossible!" said the marquess, recoiling. "A private English gentleman cannot have so much money at his disposal; or if so, it cannot be realized at once. We want ready money."

"You shall have ready money."

The marquess turned towards Measurby with an inquiring look.

"It is true," said that individual, with a confident nod of his head. "My friend, Mr. Dacre, is able to get the money you want."

The marquess, hardly believing the evidence of his own ears, still looked doubtful.

"Come, Marquess," said Wilfred, growing tired of all this suspicion, "are you going to accept my offer, or shall I withdraw?"

"No, no," stammered Paradiso, seizing his hand. "I do accept, and that thankfully, on behalf of my royal mistress."

"One thing I must ask," said Wilfred, returning the pressure, — "that my offer be kept secret from all save the princess."

"But I must tell the leaders of our party. It is necessary. Unless they know that the money is certain, not one of them will dare to strike a blow."

"A mercenary lot," grunted the major, who had no morality himself.

"Inform the council," said Wilfred, after a pause, "that money to the amount of one million will be guaranteed to the royal cause; but do not mention my name."

"No. I will keep silent on that point."

"And you will tell the princess of my offer?"

"Yes, to-morrow I will do so; and I have no doubt that she will grant you an audience. Do you propose to remain neutral?"

"By no means," cried Wilfred, quickly. "I and the major both wish to participate in your schemes. We will go with you to Busk."

"Then you will have to be disguised," said Paradiso, significantly.

"Not at all," said the major quickly. "Did I not hear you say, Dacre, that you had a villa on the Black Sea?"

"Yes. I am going there at the end of the season."

"The very thing," cried Measurby, striking the table with his clenched fist. "We can go there in the ordinary course of things, and it can be made the headquarters of the movement."

"Capital!" said Paradiso, who had been listening to all this with sparkling eyes. "Nothing could be better. Once you are settled there, all suspicion will be at an end, and then the princess, later on, can take up her abode at the villa. With your money, Mr. Dacre, we can sow dissension among the republican troops far and wide. All those we gain over to the cause can meet at your villa, and when all is ready we can strike."

"You don't think the present government of Busk will suspect me?" asked Wilfred anxiously.

"By no means. Why should they? To all appearance, the country is comparatively at peace. You are a wealthy foreigner who has bought a villa there for pleasure. They will suspect nothing, and the princess can go disguised, — say as the maid of your wife. Oh, it will be all right, believe me, monsieur. What with your money, your villa, and the present dissension among the republicans, we will gain our cause without almost a blow."

"And then?"

"And then we will proclaim Queen Julia. Once she is on her throne, she will not forget you, Mr. Dacre, or you either, Major."

The marquess was quite excited at the glorious prospect which he foresaw, and paced to and fro tugging vigorously at his iron-grey moustache. His guests, also, shared in his excitement; for there was no doubt that in order to bring things to a successful issue, there would be plenty of danger and difficulty. Wilfred felt his heart beat tumultuously at the idea of such stirring times, and foresaw that for once, at least, his possession of the ring would enable him to accomplish a great deed. Hitherto, he had but dealt with the small things of private life; but now, through being concerned in this conspiracy, he was juggling with crowns, — controlling the fate of kingdoms and the destinies of queens.

If the conspiracy succeeded, it meant a glorious restoration; but if it failed, there was a chance of his losing his head. Thoughts like these thrill a man's heart and wake him out of lethargy; so Wilfred, roused from discontented broodings, welcomed the dangerous prospect with infinite delight.

"You must come to-morrow, Mr. Dacre," said the marquess, as they arose to go, "and see the princess. This will put new life into her. Tell no one of your visit here to-night, and keep silent, for we are watched on all sides."

"We will be careful," replied Measurby, sturdily; "and as to these spies of the republicans, Dacre will find out all about them."

"Impossible!" said the marquess in perplexity. "You can have no idea of their dexterity."

"I think I can match them in that," replied Wilfred, with a grim smile. "As you can see from my offer, Marquess, I can command money; and he who does that commands the world."

CHAPTER XIV.

HILDA GIVES HER OPINION.

It had been Wilfred's intention to tell his wife everything that same evening; but as the interview with Paradiso had taken longer than he expected, he did not arrive home till late at night. Hilda, tired with the fatigue of holding a reception, had retired to bed somewhat earlier than usual, and, unwilling to disturb her, Wilfred delayed his revelations until the morning. When he awoke, however, he found that it was already late, and his wife had an appointment with her dressmaker; so they had only time to exchange a few words before parting. Wilfred was vexed at these untoward circumstances; but, knowing that Hilda would be certainly present at luncheon, he rested, content that he would then be able to tell her all at the meal. Meanwhile, he went to his study and shut himself up, in order to think over the events of the previous night.

He could not but see that his connection with this affair promised to be somewhat serious. In the opinion of a prominent politician, the first attempt made by Julia de Lusignan for the recovery of her crown would be the signal for a European war. If this was the case, the affair would not be so purely local as he hoped it would be. In itself it was so, as the government of the country concerned no one but the people of Busk themselves. The princess Julia had right on her side, as she had been wrongfully driven from her ancestral throne; and it was but just that she should try by every possible means to regain her rightful position. On the other hand, the republican party, deeming that the kingdom was misgoverned by the house of Lusignan, had destroyed the monarchy from purely patriotic motives, and would do their best to prevent a restoration. The question, therefore, lay solely between the royalists and republicans of a small Eastern state, and, as before stated, concerned no other government but the parties interested. In itself, it was nothing; but the results arising from this storm in a teacup were to be dreaded, — a spark may kindle a conflagration, a riot increase to a war.

For years, these petty Balkan states have given Europe endless trouble, and over them hangs a constant war-cloud, menacing the peace of the continent. Roumania and Bulgaria, Servia and Busk, they have all in their turn been the cause of terrible disturbances. Now the first three states were comparatively tranquil; but the eyes of all diplomats were eagerly fixed upon the last, which was in a state of fermentation, ready at any moment to break out into civil war. The new republic, only established eighteen months, was yet in its infancy, and, surrounded on all sides by hostile neighbours, seemed at times to be on the verge of destruction. Indeed, it was a miracle how it had held its own so long; and, but for the dexterous diplomacy of the president, it would doubtless have collapsed in the first year of its existence.

The royalists were endeavoring to restore the monarchy, the republicans were fighting bravely to maintain the existing form of government, and between these parties interposed Russia, looking after her own interests. Ostensibly aiding the republic, she was doing her best to destroy its influence, and trusted, when the crash came, to seize on the distracted kingdom. The royalists would be sure to appeal to arms in the long run, and in the event of a civil war nothing was more probable than that the opposing forces would end in destroying one another. Then Russia would step in, and the existence of Busk as an independent kingdom would end. Meanwhile, the great powers stood aloof, and waited some decisive movement by one of these three parties before interfering in the matter.

Looking at the matter in this light, Wilfred saw plainly that his action in supplying the royalists with funds to carry on the campaign would probably end in setting Europe in a blaze. As soon as the monarchists raised the standard of revolt against the existing government, those in power, too feeble to rely on their unaided strength, would enlist the sympathy of Russia. That power, to gain her own ends, would lend her best endeavours to stamp out the danger to the republic. Seeing that the royalists were helped by English gold, sooner or later that government would be entangled in the dispute, and come into collision with Russia. The shores of the Black Sea would again become the theatre of a great European war, and the disasters of the Crimea would be repeated.

Again, in the event of such a war taking place, the sympathies of Germany, united to England by dynastic ties, would undoubtedly lead her to throw in her influence with that country; whereupon France, out of hatred for her hereditary enemy, the Teuton, would form a league with Russia. Austria, in the centre of all these quarrelsome powers, would find it difficult to remain neutral, and while it was hard to say which party she would embrace, she would undoubtedly fight to maintain her prestige and the integrity of her empire.

Consequently, Europe would be in a blaze from one end to the other; and this gigantic catastrophe depended upon the decision of a foolish young man in possession of a ring which placed twenty millions of money at his command.

In his conversation with Paradiso, Wilfred had been carried away by the vivid pictures of a glorious restoration drawn by that astute statesman; but now, uninfluenced by the oratorical power which the marquess undoubtedly possessed, he saw the matter in a more reasonable light, and dreaded lest an ill-considered step on his part should be the means of deluging the continent with blood. For the moment, owing to this mastership of the ring, he had the privilege of a monarch in proclaiming war, but shrank from taking such a responsibility on his shoulders.

In this dilemma he was more determined than ever to consult Hilda, and trust to her judgment in the matter. As a rule, women give excellent advice, and Hilda was a remarkably clear-headed young person, who did not deliver her opinion without due reflection. Wilfred was quite ignorant of the major's premeditated treachery with regard to the ring, and merely thought that his desire to help the princess de Lusignan was caused by his craving for adventure. But even looking at it in this aspect, he saw plainly that Measurby was an impetuous swashbuckler who did not count the cost of the enterprise in which he desired to be engaged. War was the major's trade, and he thought nothing of it; but Wilfred, more noble-minded in his ideas, dreaded lest he should be the cause of a universal catastrophe.

"I will tell Hilda everything," he said to himself, as the gong sounded for luncheon, "and she will advise me what to do. As yet I have committed myself in no way, and if she disapproves of the matter I can draw back. If, on the other hand, she thinks it would be just to replace Julia de Lusignan on her throne, then I will supply the money and do my best to accomplish the restoration without bloodshed."

All this self-communing worried him greatly, and when he appeared at the luncheon-table Hilda was quite startled to see how haggard was his face.

"My dear Wilfred," she said in alarm, kissing him, "how ill you look!"

"The effect of late hours, I suppose," replied Daere, wondering how he was to broach the all-important subject. "I have not sufficient stamina to sit up all night."

"At what time did you come in last night? I forgot to ask you this morning."

"About midnight."

"My dear husband, you should not keep such late hours," said Hilda gently. "Remember, you are anything but strong. Where did you go last night?"

"To see the marquess Paradiso."

"Really!" observed his wife, with a glance of surprise. "That is strange. I met Richborough as I was returning this morning, and he stopped the carriage to talk about the marquess, or rather about the princess."

"Why, what has he to say about the princess?"

"A great deal," replied Hilda demurely. "He is in love with Madame de Lusignan."

"Oh, nonsense!"

"It is true," said his wife decisively. "I saw it at once. You know women are quick in these matters. Why, when I taxed him with it he could not deny that I was right."

"And does he hope to marry this exiled queen?"

"Really, I do not know; but he is going to help her to get the throne again, and afterwards, — well, who can say what may happen!"

"Don't you think such a course is rather foolish?" asked Dacre, anxious to indirectly obtain Hilda's opinion of the matter.

His wife pondered for a few moments.

"Yes, and no," she said at length; "so far as regards his love, it is the desire of the moth for the star. Julia de Lusignan is a royal personage and one of the proudest women in Europe; so it is not likely she would ever lower herself to marry a mere noble, even though he be as well born as Richborough. But as to his desire to replace her on the throne of Busk, I must say that I think it is a chivalrous way in which to act. We women love romance, you know, notwithstanding that men look on us as terribly practical in many ways. In taking up the cause of the princess, I think that Richborough is doing a wise thing."

"Why a wise thing?"

"Hitherto he has frittered his life away: and if he only finds some object worthy of his ambition, it will develop his latent talents. Most people look on my cousin as simply a frivolous man; but I know him better. Circumstances have made him what he is, and circumstances will shape his future life. As a London idler, a Monte Carlo gambler, he is nothing; but now that he has undertaken the task of replacing Princess Julia on the throne, you will be astonished how his character will reveal itself. Perhaps I am unduly prejudiced in his favour, but you will see that I am right."

"And yet in the end he will gain nothing by it."

"You mean that the princess will refuse to marry him? Well, I am not so sure about that. Gratitude carries a woman a long way, and if he gives her a throne, she may well reward him with her hand."

"I doubt it, seeing she is so proud. So Richborough is conspiring!"

"What a nasty name for a romance!" said Hilda, laughing.

"It is the true one, notwithstanding," replied Wilfred, quietly. "Well, Hilda, I must say I admire your cousin for what he is doing. What do you say to our helping him in his wooing?"

"I do not see how we can do so."

"Oh, yes, we can, and in the simplest way. As you know, we are going to Busk this year to occupy our villa."

"Are you sure it is safe to do so?" asked Hilda, anxiously. "The country is in a very disturbed state."

"Well, to tell the truth, I am tired of this humdrum London life, and a little danger will be a pleasant change."

"Are you weary of me, Wilfred?" she asked reproachfully.

"My dear, you know I am never weary of you; but confess, are not our surroundings a trifle wearisome?"

"Yes," assented Hilda, frankly. "I must say I am very tired of balls and theatres, and drawing-rooms and 'at homes.' There is such a family likeness between them all that they are apt to become monotonous."

"Then let us go to Busk, and make our villa the headquarters of the conspiracy."

"My dear Wilfred, that is playing with fire. We might lose our heads."

"And you have no desire to act the part of Marie Antoinette?"

"I cannot say that I feel so heroic. But you seem quite interested in this princess, Wilfred. Is it on her account that you saw the marquess last night?"

"Partly,— and partly on my own. I am weary of this life of frivolity, Hilda, and wish for a wider sphere of action. Therefore, I proposed to the marquess that our villa should be the headquarters of the royalist party."

"And does he accept?"

"On his own part he does, but the princess Julia has yet to be consulted. Well, Hilda, and what do you say?"

"Why ask my opinion, if you have already made up your mind?" she said in a slightly annoyed tone.

"I have not made up my mind. It is not yet too late for me to withdraw my offer, if I feel so disposed. The decision rests with you."

"It is a terrible risk to undertake, Wilfred."

"Yes," he answered calmly. "I do not disguise that fact. Once we stand committed to the cause of the princess Julia, we must carry it through at whatever cost. Myself, Richborough and Major Measurby are all willing to help her to regain the throne; but unless you freely consent to my engaging in the affair, I will have nothing to do with it. It is a serious matter, and may lead to nothing less than a European war."

Hilda thought for a few moments, and tapped her foot on the ground.

"I hardly know what to say," she said at length. "I see plainly that our possession of that villa renders us valuable to the cause. No one will suspect us of being conspirators, and we can form all our plans without hindrance. Frankly, Wilfred, I am weary of this tame London life; so if your mind is set on this matter, I do not see why I should refuse my consent."

"Then we will go to Busk and take Richborough with us."

"Yes; but I would like to see my cousin before finally deciding the matter. I asked him to luncheon, but he was engaged. However, I expect him immediately afterwards, — about two o'clock."

"At that rate," said Wilfred, glancing at his watch, "he ought to be here shortly. It is nearly two o'clock now."

Hilda went to the window, from whence she could command a view of the street, and Wilfred remained in his seat, thinking how he could best inform his wife of the money he proposed to give to the cause. Her very next remark paved the way to a conversation on the subject.

"Wilfred," she said, turning towards him, "from what my cousin said last night, the great thing wanted by Madame de Lusignan and her followers is money."

"I know that, and I am going to give them money."

"But can you afford to do so?" said Hilda dubiously.

"Oh, yes. You must not think that thirty thousand a year represents our entire wealth. My uncle, as you know, was a millionaire; and as Janshah knows all about the moneys, I spoke to him on the subject, so as to be certain how I stood, in the event of deciding to go into this matter. He assured me that I could safely venture on a million."

"A million sterling!" cried Hilda in astonishment.

"Yes; more or less."

Hilda looked at him steadily.

"I did not know you had so much money," she said at last. "Wilfred, you do not tell me everything."

"My dear, you know all there is to tell."

"I thought you had only the thirty thousand a year."

"Yes, but if you remember, I told you there were some odd moneys."

"Oh, yes. An amount, as I thought, of some thousands. But a million of money! It is enormous!"

"Well, Hilda," he replied, with feigned weariness, "all I can do is to satisfy you thoroughly on the matter. Examine Janshah, and he will tell you the fullest extent of my uncle's fortune."

"Oh, I can take your word for it," said Hilda, a trifle coldly. "As you know, I cannot bear Indians, and do not care about speaking to him. But I must say I would like to be more in your confidence."

"Hilda! My dear Hilda!" cried Wilfred, much distressed. "You are completely in my confidence."

"I am not so sure about that," she replied doubtfully. "However, we can talk of this another time, for I see my cousin is coming."

"Hilda," whispered Wilfred, crossing over to her

at once, "whatever there is to tell you — you shall know at Busk."

"Then there is something?" she said quickly.

"A mere triviality," replied her husband, shrugging his shoulders. "I would tell it to you now, only —"

"His Grace, the Duke of Richborough," announced the servant at this moment; and immediately afterwards the duke made his appearance. Wilfred was grateful for the interruption, as it spared him the necessity for an embarrassing explanation. As he shook hands with Richborough, however, he mentally determined to tell Hilda all, when they were at Busk.

"I came in here instead of going into the drawing-room," said Richborough, linking his arm in that of his cousin. "Wilfred, give me some luncheon."

"Why, have you not had luncheon?" asked Hilda in dismay.

"No. I have been talking to Paradiso, and the time passed so quickly that I quite forgot about eating. Paradiso asked me to stay to luncheon, but I thought I would come on here."

"Let me ring for some more dishes," said Wilfred, hospitably.

"No, thanks, this will do. I am so hungry, I could eat anything."

Whereupon the duke sat down gaily at the table and began to eat, talking all the time like a schoolboy.

"I want to see you, Wilfred. I suppose Hilda told you of my being a conspirator."

"Yes. She said you had made up your mind to be a queen-maker."

"Now don't you be sarcastic," said Richborough, good-humouredly. "I am going to occupy myself with politics, because I am tired of everything else."

"Is that the only reason?" asked Hilda, mischievously.

"Well, yes, for the present," replied the duke, reddening. "Keep my secret, Hilda, or I'll never forgive you."

"What secret is this?" said Wilfred, pretending ignorance.

"Oh, nothing, nothing. I will tell it to you on another occasion," said Richborough, indifferently. "At present I want to know why you and Measurby went to see Paradiso last night."

"How do you know we were there? Did Paradiso —"

"No, he didn't. He's too artful to say anything about such a visit, but I saw you leave the house."

"And what were you doing about the house at such an hour?"

"I am a conspirator, you know," said Richborough, serenely. "Consequently my movements are erratic."

"At that rate, if you judge by erratic movements, both myself and Measurby must also be conspirators."

"Now you are jesting."

"No. I am a convert."

The duke laid down his knife and fork to take a good look at his friend.

"You don't mean to say you are going to join Paradiso's conspiracy?"

"And why not?"

"Because — Oh well — it involves danger; and for your wife's sake —"

"His wife is also going to be a conspirator," said Hilda, taking Wilfred's hand.

"Nonsense, Hilda, nonsense!"

"It's not nonsense at all," retorted Hilda, piqued at his scepticism. "We were just talking about the matter when you came in."

"And do you really mean to say that both of you are going to mix yourselves up in a dangerous conspiracy?"

"Yes, we really mean it."

"Then I, for one, will never countenance such folly," said the duke, roughly. "This is not child's play. It may end on the scaffold, or in being shot by the enemy."

"Yet you are in the conspiracy yourself," said Wilfred, lightly.

"I have nothing to lose; but you — Think of your wife!"

"My dear Gerald," said Hilda, resting her hands on her cousin's shoulders, "this is the extent of my conspiracy. We have, as you know, a villa on the shores of the Black Sea near the capital of Busk, and we are going there this summer. Wilfred, who, like yourself, is tired of the inanities of London life, proposes to make it the headquarters for this movement in favour of the princess. As I am there I will merely be a spectator; so I do not see why you should feel angry about it. I do not propose to be Charlotte Corday or Louise Michel. You men can conduct the matter, and I will simply look on."

"The villa!" muttered the duke, without attending to the latter part of this speech. "A good idea! Have you mentioned it to Paradiso, Wilfred?"

"Not yet. At least, I have not done more than hint at the thing."

"Then do so to-night. You will be summoned to a meeting about ten o'clock."

"I suppose that is the result of my visit to Paradiso," said Wilfred, carelessly. "Well, I will be there, and you —"

"Oh, I will not fail to be present, you may be sure."

"What about the princess?" asked Hilda, looking at her cousin.

"Oh," he said in a lively tone, "she will preside over the meeting herself. She is a woman of masculine control, — a Semiramis, — Catherine of Russia. With her at the head nothing can fail. Long live Queen Julia, and down with the republic."

"I would not be surprised," said Hilda, reflectively, "if shortly I had a king for my cousin."

CHAPTER XV.

A MIDNIGHT MEETING.

THE history of the Lusignan dynasty is as romantic as that of the Stuarts, but hardly so widely known. From the time of Guy de Lusignan, whose good looks gained for him the hand of Baldwin's daughter and the throne of Jerusalem, the race has been renowned for its personal charm. Brave men and fair women were those Lusignans who ruled the island of Cyprus; yet some curse hung over the race, and they lost their new heritage as they had lost the old. Driven from Jerusalem, Guy de Lusignan became king of Cyprus, where his dynasty reigned for three centuries, until Catherine Coronaro abdicated in favour of the grasping Venetian republic. But she was the wife of an illegitimate son of the house; and the true heir to the honours of this famous family is the house of Savoy, who inherit through Charlotte, the daughter of Jean II.

Thus far it is a matter of history; but one fact has hitherto escaped the historian, namely, that Janus, the father of Jean II., had another son, who founded the kingdom of Busk. This son, Amaury by name, was supposed to be illegitimate; but on his deathbed Janus acknowledged the boy as his legitimate offspring and heir. Notwithstanding this, his brother

Jean II. succeeded to the throne and drove Amaury from the kingdom. After many adventures of the most romantic nature, Amaury, gaining a small band of followers by virtue of his royal descent, succeeded in establishing himself in the little territory of Busk, where he remained unmolested for some time. With the fall of Constantinople, however, came trouble; for the Turks, having captured the city on the Bosphorus, at once proceeded to reduce the surrounding country to a state of bondage.

The young kingdom, yet in its infancy, was threatened by the sultan; but Amaury managed to secure at least the nominal freedom of his country by apparent submission to the precepts of Mahomet. It was a judicious act, for the sultan, eager to conquer fairer provinces, was content with this barren confession of faith, and withdrew his armies from Busk on condition that Amaury professed Islam, assumed the lower title of pacha, and acknowledged the sovereignty of the sultan. Gifted with no ordinary degree of diplomatic talent, the young adventurer accepted these conditions in default of utter extermination, and, being thus protected by a powerful monarch, employed his time of safety in consolidating his kingdom.

Outwardly a Mahometan, he was in reality a Christian, as were all his descendants, though they conformed to the precepts of the Arabian prophet in order to preserve the favour of the sultan. As virtual Moslems, as pachas, as subject to the Ottoman dynasty, they continued till the middle of the eighteenth century, when, owing to the decay of the

Turkish power, the then king, Hugues V., found himself able to proclaim his real belief, and assume the title to which he was entitled both by descent and position.

He professed the faith of the Latin church, re-converted the principal mosque of Varzo, the capital of Busk, into the cathedral it had previously been, and was crowned therein as king by a papal legate. This behaviour enraged the sultan greatly, but, being engaged in preserving his tottering throne, he was obliged to acknowledge the freedom of the little kingdom, promising himself revenge on some future occasion.

That occasion never came, as Turkey, hemmed in on all sides by enemies, kept with difficulty the foe from the gates of Stamboul; so Busk, under its lawful sovereign, flourished and grew great. From father to son the sceptre descended in due course, and they ruled their country with a rod of iron. Owing to the diplomatic skill of these sovereigns, Busk held her own amid the troubles which plunged the Balkan states into war; and, notwithstanding the menaces of Russia, of the newly created kingdoms of Servia and Roumania, and the unconcealed hatred of the Sublime Porte, Busk remained a free and independent state.

Unfortunately, however, the country proved ungrateful to those who had preserved its liberty through so many ages, and Pierre II. was besieged in his capital by his rebellious subjects. With unusual skill he managed to ward off the catastrophe, but the end came when he died. Then the reforming party, — as they called themselves, — headed by Methodios, a Greek Phanariot, drove Princess Julia, the only living representative of the Lusignans, into exile, and proclaimed Busk a republic. Methodios was the first president, and managed to maintain his basely won position with great difficulty ; while the rightful ruler of the country waited her opportunity to regain the throne of her ancestors.

Then, indeed, did Busk find what a mistake she had made in dethroning those who had hitherto ruled her so successfully ; for Methodios was quite incapable of managing affairs at the present dangerous juncture. He would have sold his country to the Russians, had it not been that those who served him kept a keen watch over his every movement. As it was, he knew not how long he could remain president, and, to secure his own safety, would have sacrificed everything. In Varzo the citizens began to talk openly about the possible restoration of the Lusignan ; and, informed of this fact by means of her spies, Princess Julia saw that the time had come for her to act. The provinces were devoted to her house ; discontent reigned in the streets of Varzo ; so all promised well for the restoration of the monarchy.

Julia was a woman of masculine understanding. Young and beautiful, she possessed everything save a heart ; and she used all the charms of which she was mistress — and they were many — to gain her ambition. Queen Elizabeth, without the coquetry of that great sovereign ; Catherine of Russia, with no sensual leanings ; Mary of Scotland, divested of romantic tendencies, — this woman of twenty-five years of age deemed that there was one destiny in the world for her, to be a queen and reign as a queen. Never the slave of her passions, always astute and alert, gifted with unerring foresight and consummate tact, she was a woman to be admired — and dreaded. Paradiso, who knew her better than any one else, said that she would sacrifice all to her ambition; and he was right in this reading of her character. She was born to reign, and the weaknesses of her sex were not for her. Physically she was a woman, in all else a man.

Adoring such a woman, it can be easily seen what an unhappy future Richborough was laying up for himself. Gallant and ardent, he believed that he could awaken in this iceberg responsive warmth to his passion; but he was mad, to dream of such a thing. She saw in him a useful tool, and bound him to her interests by letting him think that she was not deaf to his sighing; when all the time her head governed her heart, and she would have killed him, with pleasure, had the condition of his death gained her the throne of Busk.

Paradiso saw how mistaken was the young man, and, despite his devotion to the princess, could not help hinting to Richborough that he was making a mistake in thus hoping for the impossible. The duke never heeded him. He thought Julia de Lusignan the most perfect of her sex, and hoped when he gave her a throne she would reward him with a heart. He did not know the woman with whom he had to deal.

Blinded by passion, those who loved Madame de Lusignan for her beautiful face did not estimate her character truly; but her political opponents both knew and dreaded it.

"It will be a bad time for peace, when Julia de Lusignan gets her throne again," said a veteran statesman to Paradiso; "for she is too ambitious to rest content with Busk, and will never be satisfied till she has reconstructed the Byzantine empire, and seated herself on the throne of the Eastern Cæsars."

Paradiso laughed at this, but did not deny the truth of the remark, knowing in his own heart how true it was. He was devoted to the Lusignan dynasty; he admired his mistress for her brilliant qualities; but he also knew that she was a pitiless woman, who would spare neither friend nor foe, so that she could gain her ends. Love! — the very idea was ridiculous. She would marry for political purposes, for the sake of perpetuating the Lusignan dynasty, but not for love; and therefore was Paradiso sorry for Richborough, to whom he had taken a great fancy.

Needless to say, Princess Julia was delighted at the chance of securing a wealthy follower like Wilfred. Hitherto, a want of money had been the great stumbling-block in all her schemes; but, now that she had a chance of obtaining a million sterling, she deemed — and justly — that the worst part of her troubles were over. Force could doubtless do a good deal in the way of regaining her throne; but cunning could do more, and she quite agreed with

Philip of Macedon regarding the power of gold. That handful of adventurers which now governed Busk were by no means incorruptible, and a little judicious bribery would go a long way towards turning them from republicans into royalists. Once this transformation was achieved, she would be proclaimed queen; then, — well, those who knew the merciless nature of Princess Julia could guess that she would bitterly revenge herself on the traitors who sold their services for money.

Such, then, was the woman who presided over the meeting at the house in Portman Square. She sat in the drawing-room, surrounded by her friends, and listened to the various opinions expressed regarding the projected attempt. Even in exile, she kept up her regal state, and not until she gave the signal did those around venture to seat themselves in her presence. The only woman present, she bore herself with queenly dignity, and looked as though she were presiding over a council of states, instead of being a dethroned sovereign, discussing desperate schemes with a dozen or so political adventurers. For the most part, she kept silent; but every now and then she threw in a word which showed that she fully understood the various views put forward by her devoted adherents. Catherine de Medici had not more statecraft than Julia de Lusignan. Each person, as he wished to address the assemblage, arose to his feet; and just now the marquess Paradiso was standing by the chair of his mistress, informing his colleagues of the offer made by Wilfred Dacre. Neither that gentleman nor Major Measurby had as yet arrived, and it was the object of Paradiso to prepare those present for their visit.

"This Monsieur Dacre," said Paradiso in French, "is, I am informed, extremely rich, and his offer to join our band is purely voluntary. I need not enlarge on the wisdom of accepting his help, as hitherto we have suffered greatly from the want of money. Once we are in Busk, in Varzo, we can doubtless do a great deal towards undermining the devotion of the army to the interests of the infamous republic, but there are many who can only be bribed. Yes, messieurs, these stainless patriots, who destroyed the monarchy for the sake of their republican principles, are willing to be corrupted with gold. Force and cunning can do much, gold can do everything; therefore, it will be wise for us to accept the offer of M. Dacre and enrol him among our members."

"M. Dacre," observed the princess in a clear, firm voice, "is married, I understand."

"Yes, your Majesty," replied Paradiso, who scrupulously gave his mistress her rightful title; "he is married to the Honourable Hilda Havard, daughter of Lord Kenneth Havard."

"Mrs. Dacre is my cousin," said Richborough at this moment. "May I ask your Majesty why you allude to the marriage of Dacre?"

"A wife has, in many instances, a great influence over her husband," responded the princess slowly. "M. Dacre may be now willing to join us, but should his wife disapprove, he may draw back at the eleventh hour."

"He will not draw back," exclaimed Paradiso with fiery earnestness. "I will stake my life on his fidelity."

"And I," added the duke smiling, "can guarantee that my cousin will not induce her husband to draw back."

"She favours the scheme, then?" asked the princess quickly.

"More than that, she intends to take an active part in your Majesty's happy restoration."

"In what way?"

"M. Dacre will explain that to your Majesty, himself," said Paradiso, at this moment; "for he is now waiting your gracious permission to enter."

"Is he alone, Marquess?"

"No. Your Majesty also condescended to receive Major Measurby."

"Let them be admitted, Marquess."

Paradiso turned and left the room, while a murmur went through the ranks of the conspirators, who were much excited by the good news. For a long time their scheming had seemed almost hopeless; but now, this unexpected offer promised them a fair amount of success.

"M. le duc," said Madame de Lusignan, beckoning to Richborough, "is it true that this M. Dacre can do what he says?"

"Yes, your Majesty. I know he is rich, and as he has promised to aid the cause, you may be sure he will not fail you."

"Good. We will accept his help, and if we regain our throne, M. Dacre will not find us ungrateful."

"And myself, madame," murmured Richborough in a low tone, bending towards her.

Julia de Lusignan darted a meaning glance at the young man, which hinted that his reward would be the highest of all. She well knew that the only way to keep the duke true to her cause was to encourage his romantic passion, and, therefore, affected an interest in him which she did not feel. Any woman would have been touched by Richborough's devotion, but this exiled princess had a heart of flint. She was a queen, not a woman.

Wilfred and Measurby, both somewhat agitated, were duly introduced to Madame de Lusignan, who graciously permitted them to kiss her hand. This ceremony was strictly enjoined on the pair by Paradiso, who insisted that his mistress should be treated as a royal personage, though her rank was not recognized by the great powers.

"I am glad to see you, gentlemen," said the princess in English, a language which she spoke admirably. "Now I receive you in London, but I hope with God's help to see you shortly in my palace of Varzo."

"All that I can do to aid your Majesty is at your service," said Wilfred, bowing. "My friend Major Measurby offers his sword; I lay treasures at your feet."

"I accept both, monsieur. Here you see all that remain faithful to us; but we have also friends in Varzo. This infamous rebel Methodios already sees signs that his power is at an end. With your help, M. Dacre, and with the help of those present, I hope to regain my throne; and then — Ah!" added Julia, drawing a long breath, "I will bitterly punish those who drove me from Busk."

"Death to the traitors!" cried all present enthusiastically.

"Yes, death!" said the princess, with flashing eyes; "death on the gallows! We must be diplomatic, messieurs, we must work in secret and bribe with gold; but the end once gained, and you will see that the Queen of Busk knows how to punish her foes, how to reward her adherents."

When the princess had ended her speech she sank back in her chair with a laugh of triumph and signed to Paradiso that business might be proceeded with. The marquess turned towards Wilfred.

"Will you be so kind, M. Dacre," he said suavely, "as to tell these gentlemen of the offer you propose to make?"

"Can I speak in English?"

"Certainly. Most of our friends here understand your tongue. Proceed, monsieur."

Wilfred bowed and began to speak: —

"My friend Major Measurby," he began in a firm voice, "informed me that a party was being formed in London to restore the rightful sovereign of Busk to her throne. Such a cause is sacred, and I determined to join your ranks. Thanks to the marquess Paradiso, I have learned wherein lies your strength and your weakness. You are few in number, gentlemen, but your devotion to your queen makes you strong. As to your weakness, it is want of money. It will be my task to aid you in that respect, and I here offer her Majesty the sum of one million pounds to be expended in restoring her to the throne of Busk."

One million pounds! The assemblage was struck with astonishment at the mention of such an enormous sum, and even the imperious princess seemed to scarcely comprehend the magnitude of the offer.

"One million!" she said in a low voice; "you can give us that sum, monsieur?"

"Yes. It is at your service whenever you require it."

"But you will beggar yourself for our sake, M. Dacre!"

"No, your Majesty. I shall still have sufficient for my wants even after expending that sum."

A murmur of satisfaction ran through the apartment, and the princess, rising from her seat, clasped Wilfred's hand.

"Monsieur," she said with an emotion which she really felt, "I accept your magnificent offer and thank you for your generosity. Now, I am a dethroned sovereign and cannot recognize your services as they deserve; but if with your aid, monsieur, I rule once more in Busk, then ask what you will and it shall be granted.

"I wish for nothing, madame, but permission to help in your restoration."

"I look upon that as an accomplished fact," cried Richborough with enthusiasm. "Well, your Majesty, now we have the money, what means will you adopt to get to Busk?"

"The marquess will explain," replied Julia, resuming her seat.

"M. Dacre," began Paradiso, rising to his feet, "has placed us all under deep obligations in offering to advance this money; but he has nobly decided to do even more. About four miles from Varzo is the Villa Tvartko."

"It is known. It is known."

"The royal residence," murmured Julia bitterly, "now occupied by M. le president."

"That villa, messieurs, is the property of M. Dacre, who goes there with madame his wife to spend the winter; and he has generously placed his house at the disposal of her Majesty."

"But I cannot show my face in Busk until my party is strong enough," said Julia in dismay.

"Your Majesty will go thither in disguise."

"In what disguise?"

"As the maid of Mrs. Dacre. That is, if your Majesty will so far condescend."

"Condescend!" repeated the Princess with energy; "I will condescend to anything, provided it leads to the throne."

"Your Majesty," pursued Paradiso, delighted at having so readily gained her consent, "will disguise yourself by staining your face and changing your costume. As the maid of an English lady no one will suspect you, and besides, at the Villa Tvartko you will still be surrounded by your faithful subjects."

"Meaning yourselves."

"Yes, madame," said Wilfred quickly. "I propose to make the Villa Tvartko the headquarters of our scheme. All these gentlemen present will stay there as my friends, and thus your Majesty's party will be in the very heart of the kingdom quite unsuspected."

" And afterwards ? "

" Then," said Paradiso, taking up the tale, " we will use the gold of M. Dacre to bribe the leading officials of the republic. Methodios, Upravado, Culin, Geiza, they can all be bribed; and once secured, we can proclaim your Majesty's presence in Busk with safety."

" But the army, Marquess ? "

" The army, madame, is devoted to Upravado, and if we gain him to our cause we shall gain the army. When these leaders are secured, M. Dacre will give a grand ball, to which all will be invited. At the time appointed Queen Julia will be proclaimed, and your Majesty, wearing the royal crown of Busk, will appear before the assemblage. Their loyalty and ours will do the rest."

" It is a desperate scheme," said the princess thoughtfully.

" It is a coup d'état," said Richborough joyously; " and if it can be carried without bloodshed, so much the better; but if it comes to blows, why, I think your Majesty can depend upon being well defended."

" With you by my side I am not afraid," murmured the princess in a low voice. " But, gentlemen," she added aloud, " one part of your scheme is rather difficult. I have not the royal crown."

" It is in the possession of Cardinal Gregory," cried Paradiso, " and I will get it from him. The rebels have forced him to acquiesce in the republic, but heart and soul he is devoted to your Majesty. They desired the crown jewels, but he refused to give them up; and they are still in the treasure-vault of San Hilarion."

"All objections then are removed, Marquess. Gentlemen, what do you say to this scheme?"

One after another her adherents arose and approved of the plot; upon which the princess, with a smile of delight, arose from her chair and said two words which settled everything: —

"I accept."

A cheer burst from those present, and exhausted by emotion the princess withdrew to her apartments, leaving the marquess to complete his task.

"Now, M. Dacre," said Paradiso gaily, "about this money."

"Do you want it all at once?"

"Why, no! If you give us sufficient to carry on we will wait till we get to Busk before asking for the remainder. After all, it is the bribing of Methodios and his crew that takes the money."

"Come to my house to-morrow, then," said Wilfred quickly, "and I will give you a few thousands. The rest you will receive at Busk when it is necessary."

"So far, so good," said Major Measurby at this moment, "but when do we start for Busk?"

"We must go as soon as possible," cried Paradiso decisively. "Methodios already dreads an insurrection, and if one occurs the queen's party must be there to take advantage of it. When can you start, M. Dacre?"

"Next week!"

"Next week?" said Richborough in his ear. "Will Hilda consent to that?"

"Yes," replied Wilfred in the same tone. "She is anxious to get away from London as soon as possible."

"Do we go by land or water?" asked Measurby.

"By land, of course," said Paradiso quickly. "We shall arrive in Busk sooner by rail than by a long voyage up the Dardanelles."

"And how do we go?"

"By the Oriental Express. And now, gentlemen, as you have consented to all these plans, we must part for the present. There is much for me to do. Good night, messieurs; we meet again on Monday night, when I hope to tell you that all is prepared. Long live Queen Julia!"

"Long live the queen!" echoed the assemblage, and dispersed.

"Egad!" said Measurby to Wilfred as they walked home together. "I don't think Brahma thought his treasure would be used for this purpose."

"It is a noble purpose."

"Eh! Yes, I suppose it is," replied the major, shrugging his shoulders; "but I confess I am rather republican myself."

"Don't confess that in Busk," said Wilfred grimly, "or you may get into trouble. At present it is a lawless place."

"As you say," answered the major significantly, "it is a lawless place, and who knows what may happen!"

CHAPTER XVI.

THE ORIENTAL EXPRESS.

The result of the meeting was duly reported to Hilda, and she was delighted to find things had progressed thus far in so satisfactory a manner. She was a woman with a natural aptitude for intrigue, and hailed with joy the prospect of endless complications likely to arise from the restoration of the princess de Lusignan. At once she called on that royal lady, and was most graciously received. Together they arranged the details of the plot, and it was duly settled that Princess Julia should go to Busk as the maid of Mrs. Dacre. Once in her capital of Varzo, she determined that she would either mount the throne or the scaffold, for she was perfectly weary of being exiled from her native land, and her proud spirit could ill brook the petty slights to which, as a dethroned sovereign, she was constantly subjected.

Meanwhile Paradiso sent spies to Varzo in order to report on the condition of the country, which proved to be in a greatly disturbed state. Methodios was becoming very unpopular with his party, the leaders of the populace were intriguing among themselves for the supreme power, and the archbishop of Busk was secretly fomenting all this discontent, in the hope that it would lead to the return of his exiled mistress. This report was eminently satisfactory to Paradiso, who saw plainly that if he were on the spot he would be able to forward the cause of the Lusignans by dint of dexterous diplomacy and lavish use of gold.

With regard to this latter Wilfred had seen Janshah, and obtained from him some thousands of pounds, which he at once handed over to the marquess for immediate use. Paradiso did not want to be overwhelmed with money, and was quite content that nothing more should be paid until it was necessary to bribe the rebel leaders at the Villa Tvartko. Wilfred, on his part, permitted Janshah to retain the money he required, knowing that it would be produced at the proper time on the authority of the ring.

Things being thus satisfactorily settled, arrangements were made by the royalists to leave for Busk at as early a date as possible. The season was nearly over; so Hilda gave a farewell ball to her friends, and announced her determination to leave London for Busk. The society papers contained an announcement that Mr. and the Hon. Mrs. Dacre would entertain a few friends at the Villa Tvartko, near Varzo, on the Black Sea; but the spies of the republic took no notice of the paragraph, little knowing that it meant the overthrow of their government. Thanks to the astuteness of Paradiso their enemies were completely ignorant of the princess's intended journey to Varzo. It was announced in several papers that Madame de Lusignan would pass the winter at Torquay, and Paradiso sending down her household, set up there the royal establishment. Princess Julia was supposed, therefore, to be living in retirement, when in reality she and her devoted followers, in company with Wilfred and Hilda, were already on their way to Varzo. The spies were thus thrown completely off the scent, and Paradiso hoped before they learned the truth to have bribed Methodios, secured the army, and restored Princess de Lusignan to the throne.

Unfortunately, the face of Julia was so well known in Varzo that there was considerable risk in her returning thither, unless completely disguised. This she achieved by cutting off her fair hair, wearing a black wig, dyeing her face a nut-brown colour, and assuming the dress of a lady's maid. All this was done under the superintendence of Janshah, who was an adept at such things, and when the transmogrification was complete, no one would have recognized the regal-looking Julia in the demure Italian maid of Mrs. Dacre. Madame de Lusignan assumed this special nationality because she spoke Italian like a native, and, despite a certain imperiousness of manner, adapted herself very well to her new position. Paradiso also disguised himself by assuming a long beard and changing his dress, passing himself off as the physician of Wilfred, in which capacity he was but little likely to arouse suspicion. Richborough, being, of course, the guest of his cousin, had no need of disguise, as he was quite a stranger in Varzo. Thus prepared, the little party started on their journey with great hopes of success, and as yet everything promised well for the fulfilment of the project.

Janshah, in conformity with the commands of Wilfred, had gone on ahead with his satellites, to prepare the villa for the reception of the party, and announce their coming to those in Varzo. So skilfully did he do this that the government never for a moment dreamed that a dangerous conspiracy was on foot, but merely thought it was the party of an English milor coming to pass the winter on the shores of the Black Sea. Some Russian agents, indeed, tried to find out the truth from the servants at Villa Tvartko, but Janshah had guarded well against all possible treachery. Owing to his duty to protect the owner of the ring, he had a perfect host of invisible servitors who obeyed him implicitly, and thus the spies of Russia and Busk were met and baffled by the spies of Janshah. The Indian took a certain pride in all this, as his duties in regard to Mr. Lascelle had been of a very mild description; but now this European intrigue was of so important a nature that he was forced to employ all his resources to fulfil his duty to the ring, and was determined that everything should be done in the most thorough manner.

While Janshah, therefore, awaited their arrival in Varzo, the royalist party, consisting of Madame de Lusignan, Mrs. Dacre, Wilfred, Measurby, Richborough, and Paradiso, with a small suite, left London by the club train for Paris. So absolutely in the dark were the spies in the service of the republic that all those present in London had gone down to Torquay to watch the house of the presumed princess Julia, quite oblivious to the fact that she was already on her way to Busk. Paradiso was delighted at his diplomacy, and rubbed his hands with glee as he stood with Measurby on the deck of the Calais-Dover steamer.

"So far, so good, monsieur," he said with a gay laugh; "all is going well."

"A good beginning does not necessarily mean a good ending," observed the major significantly.

"Eh? I do not know. We can only judge the future by the past, and you must admit that if we arrive at the Villa Tvartko without exciting suspicion, it is a great point gained."

"Certainly; but then we shall be in the jaws of the lion."

"So much the better. There is nothing like being on the spot in matters of this kind."

"I quite agree with you," said Measurby, cloaking his distrust in the success of the mission under a false smile. "We can take advantage of every move made by Methodios and his gang. But how are you going to approach him with a view to bribing?"

"That depends upon the position in which we find ourselves," replied Paradiso seriously. "I cannot appear in the matter myself, for the rascal knows me too well, and might penetrate my disguise, in which case it would mean failure and death. No. You, monsieur, and M. Dacre, must treat with him and his crew. Ask them to the Villa Tvartko, and there hint at the possibility of buying their services. If they are willing, you will soon discover the fact; then the rest will be easy."

"That is, if the money can be produced," said Measurby dryly.

Paradiso turned pale.

"Eh, monsieur, — you do not think there is any doubt on that point?"

"Oh, no, no," said the major, hastening to reassure the marquess; "but it is as well to be prepared."

"If the money cannot be produced at the proper time," said Paradiso solemnly, "it means death to us all."

"But we are British subjects."

"That won't count with Methodios. He will hang you all first, and explain matters to the British government afterwards. There is no hesitation about the president of Busk, I can assure you, monsieur."

Measurby made a grimace. He was fully determined to obtain the ring, and did not care if the conspiracy succeeded or failed. This idea of Paradiso's, however, put a decidedly awkward complexion on the affair, and he might gain the ring only to lose his head. Still, he trusted that Janshah would be enabled to save him if he became master of the ring, and, with diabolical coolness, was quite prepared to leave Wilfred and his gallant little party to their fate. At present, therefore, he merely laughed at Paradiso's alarm.

"You need have no fear on the score of the

money, Marquess," he said lightly. "Mr. Dacre will produce the money when it is wanted. If he does not, I will do so myself."

"Can you produce a million?" asked Paradiso ironically.

"Ah! that depends upon circumstances," replied Measurby ambiguously, and closed the conversation. He might have added that it depended upon the ring, but was too cunning to say such a thing to Paradiso lest he should learn too much.

It afforded him food for reflection, however; for, on leaving Paradiso, he withdrew to another part of the deck in order to think over the matter. Major Measurby was a man in whom the moral sense was entirely wanting. So long as he benefited himself he cared not who suffered, and, in this case, in order to gain the ring, was quite prepared to sacrifice the royal cause and its supporters. He had succeeded in luring Wilfred into a wild and lawless land, where he hoped to obtain the ring by force; but, surrounded as Dacre was on all sides by loyal men who looked on him as the saviour of their country, it would be extremely difficult to resort to violence. The major anticipated this before leaving London, and in order to afford himself every chance of gaining by fraud what he could not hope to secure by force, had caused to be made a ring precisely similar to that worn by Wilfred.

The renegade priest who had betrayed the secret of the ring to him in Benares had supplied him with a drawing of the talisman, and this drawing the major had handed to a London jeweller with a request that a precisely similar ring should be made for him. The man had accomplished his work with wonderful skill, and now Measurby carried in his pocket a ring of gold, with a lapis lazuli stone inscribed with Sanscrit characters, similar to the ring commanding the treasure. The only thing wanting was the secret mark, which was known only to Janshah, and Measurby hoped, if all other efforts failed, to seduce Wilfred into letting him have the ring, and then, changing it dexterously for the false one, hand back the latter to his unsuspecting friend, and retain the true one. Dacre would be unable to tell the difference, and the major could fly with his booty, which he intended to do, leaving the royalist party in the lurch. Such treachery might cost them their lives, but Measurby cared nothing for that.

When Wilfred then commanded Janshah to supply the money to the rebel leaders, the slave would refuse to obey, and tell him that he wore the false ring; but by that time Measurby hoped to be beyond the reach of pursuit. Such was the dishonourable plot which the major intended to carry out, and, meanwhile, like the scoundrel he was, affected to be the friend of the man he intended to betray. He was always on the watch to change the jewels, and had several times hinted to Wilfred that he would like to look at the ring; but Dacre, unsuspecting as he was of Measurby's proposed treachery, would never remove it from his finger. The major, therefore, carried the false ring in his pocket, and bided his time.

"If I do get the ring," he soliloquized, after his conversation with Paradiso, "I may help to carry on the plot, but the princess will have to pay for my help. Not with money, but with her hand. If she agrees to marry me and make me king, I will help her; if not, I will fly the country and leave them all in the lurch;" from which speech it will be seen that the major's aspirations were anything but modest.

All these visions, however, were yet to be fulfilled, and Measurby, though he did not look at the matter in that light, was uncommonly like Alnaschar in the Arabian Nights, building up castles in the air which at any time might fall into ruins. But the strange part of the whole affair was that Measurby could not see that he was acting dishonourably, as he argued himself to be in the right. Dacre had secured the ring by fraud, according to the major's opinion, and it would be only justice that it should be taken from him in the same way. This was all very well, but Measurby never thought that the loss of the ring and his subsequent flight might cost the lives of the whole party with whom he was now travelling. After all, if his conditions were complied with, he could save them from such a fate. But there was one thing on which Measurby did not count, and that was that Julia de Lusignan was as artful as himself, and would promise him anything till she was seated on her throne; then Measurby would find himself in Queer Street.

The princess Julia and Hilda got on very well together, despite the entire difference in their dispositions. Hilda could not help admiring the heroic character of the royal lady, though she did not care for her in many ways; and on her part, Julia de Lusignan was grateful to Mrs. Dacre for thus risking her life in doing her a service. From the first, not one of the party disguised the danger of the whole affair. In an uncivilized country like Busk, governed by a parcel of scoundrels, international law had but little chance of being respected, and Wilfred knew that if the conspiracy were discovered, the status of a British subject would not protect either himself or his wife from the vengeance of Methodios. In order to neutralize the danger, he had ordered Janshah to have a yacht sent round to the Black Sea, where it could lie off the Villa Tvartko and thus afford means of flight if matters became desperate.

Then, again, the villa was within twenty miles of the Bulgarian frontier, and horses ready saddled were always to be waiting day and night in the stables. If they failed to escape by the yacht, they could ride into Bulgaria, and once across the frontier, they would be comparatively safe. During their journey, Wilfred explained all these matters to Princess Julia; but though she highly approved of these precautions for himself and his wife, she declined to take advantage of them for her own safety.

"No, M. Dacre," she said decisively, "once I am in Varzo I will not leave it again. They dare not put me to death, for even Methodios would shrink from such a crime. I have at least a certain number of the populace in my favour, and at the worst I can take refuge with the archbishop."

"But can he protect you?"

"Yes. We are of the Catholic church, you know, and that body has no sympathy with republics. It is as necessary to Catholicism to have the monarchy as the popedom."

"But the archbishop does not acknowledge the power of the pope."

"Yes, he does. We are of the Latin, not the Greek church. My forefathers, as you know, were crusaders, and though compelled for centuries to conform to the precepts of Mahomet, yet we were always Catholics at heart, and on the first opportunity restored the Christian religion to Busk. The present archbishop of Varzo is Cardinal Gregory, one of the cleverest and most astute prelates in Europe. Indeed, he is looked upon as a possible candidate for the tiara, and if personal ambition goes for anything, he will obtain it. My support in such a matter would be of some service to him; so he will do all in his power to aid me to the throne."

"What is his name, madame, did you say?"

"Gregory. He's a cardinal, and owes his red hat to my father's influence; so he has every right to be devoted to our family."

"Gratitude is not an ordinary quality, Princess."

"It is when bound up with personal interests. Under the republic, Cardinal Gregory has no power, but when I am restored to my throne the church will regain all its former influence in Busk."

"That certainly is a powerful reason for him to remain faithful to your house; but have you seen anything to lead you to suppose that such is the case?"

"You can tell by straws which way the wind blows, M. Dacre," replied the princess serenely. "Cardinal Gregory has possession of the regalia of Busk. The rebels wanted it in order to melt down the gold for money, and the cardinal refused to give it up. He would not have done that unless he cherished a hope of seeing the Lusignans once more on the throne."

"And will he give you the crown?"

"So the marquess says, and I have little doubt that such will be the case. I will appear before all those faithful to me, with the crown of my ancestors on my head. Then," added the princess, with a dark smile, "I will remain and face the worst. A crowned queen, I cannot, I will not fly."

"Yet it may cost you your life."

"I do not mind. Life is nothing to me without a throne. I am playing for a bold stake, monsieur, and with my head. If I fail I lose it; if I win, woe to those who have put such indignities on their rightful queen."

She dismissed Wilfred with an imperious gesture, quite out of keeping with her assumed character of a servant, and he withdrew with a bow.

"I am glad that woman is not my wife," he said to Hilda afterwards; "she is the kind of female who would behead a husband a day, like a she-sultan of the Arabian Nights."

"She is heroic."

"Heroic characters, my dear, are like oil paintings, — best at a distance."

"Still, Wilfred, you cannot help admiring a woman who dares her life for a throne."

"As for that, we dare ours without a chance of reward."

"Do you think, then, this expedition is so very dangerous?"

"Yes, we carry our lives in our hands. But don't be alarmed, Hilda," he added, taking her hand; "while Janshah is with us you need not be afraid."

"But how can Janshah, a servant, protect us?"

"Janshah is not an ordinary servant," replied Wilfred with a smile; "he possesses more power than you think."

"There is some mystery about him, and you know it."

"My dear Hilda," said Wilfred gravely, "when we arrive at Varzo, you shall know all things."

"Why not tell it now?"

"There is no necessity. It is not a secret likely to alarm you. On the contrary, it will give you a great deal of pleasure."

Hilda, devoured by curiosity, would have liked to have demanded an explanation, but stifling her desire, she took his hand affectionately.

"I have every confidence in you, Wilfred," she said, kissing him, "and know you would not keep the secret from me without just cause. I will wait your pleasure to reveal it."

"At Varzo you will know all," answered Wilfred, smiling, "and then you will see how important Janshah is to us both. But apart from the Indian, do not be alarmed, Hilda. In the event of danger, there is the yacht, and also horses in the stables. In some way we will escape; but to tell you the truth, I have a presentiment that all will turn out as we desire. The queen will have her crown again, and we shall be hailed by the people of Busk as the saviours of their country."

"I hope so," replied Hilda, with a sigh, "but I am not so sanguine as you are. I fear for my cousin."

"Yes. I do not think he will prosper in his wooing; and as a matter of fact, I would not care to see him married to Princess Julia. She is a most implacable woman."

"Well," said his wife hopefully. "We must do the best we can."

They had a very pleasant journey to Varzo, for the Oriental Express is a very comfortable train. On leaving Paris they went via Munich to Vienna, thence through Buda-Pesth to Belgrade. There the line branches off to Constantinople, which they desired to avoid; so leaving the train, they went on board a steamer, and dropped down the Danube as far as Rustchuk. From that town they took the train to Varna, on the Black Sea, and then travelled by diligence to Varzo, which was a comparatively short distance away. Fortunately the passports of the whole party were in good order, so on satisfying the authorities that they were merely travelling for pleasure, they left Varzo and proceeded to the Villa Tvartko, four miles from the capital.

Both Wilfred and Paradiso heaved a sigh of relief when they found themselves once more in safety, the former especially deriving great comfort from the presence of Janshah, whom they found installed at the villa. Princess Julia was much moved at finding herself again among her own people, but, thanks to her powerful nature, suppressed all outward show of emotion, and as the maid of Hilda passed the ordeal of Varzo quite unsuspected.

"At last!" she cried, when within the walls of Villa Tvartko. "I will find here a crown or a grave!"

CHAPTER XVII.

VILLA TVARTKO.

Busk is one of the most picturesque places in Europe, and though as yet but little known to the tourist, promises to become a favourite place of resort in the near future. Increased railway communication with the West, a gradual civilizing of the inhabitants, and the eager desire of the people to participate in the luxuries of the Occident,—all these are powerful causes in making Busk known to the civilized world. Protected on the west by lofty mountains, on the east by the wide waste of the Black Sea, this gallant little kingdom has preserved its liberty and political integrity for many years. The conquest by the Turks was merely one in name, owing to the successful diplomacy of the Lusignans; and nominally a pashalic of the Ottoman empire, Busk has in reality been perfectly free.

The inhabitants, belonging to the Slav race, are a hardy people, jealous of their liberty and bold in defense of their cherished institutions. Had it rested with the majority of the people, Busk would never have driven forth her ancient sovereigns; but Varzo, the capital of the country, bears the same relation to the kingdom as does Paris to France. In Varzo alone have risen all the revolutions which have shaken the throne of the Lusignans, and the republic once established by the last successful attempt, the rest of the country accepted the inevitable with grudging submission. Yet a strong feeling existed in favour of the restoration of the royal house, and had they possessed a skillful leader, it would certainly have followed that Julia de Lusignan would have been recalled in a few months, to reoccupy the throne of her native land.

Circumstances, however, were against this revolt in her favour, as there was no man daring enough to defy the government at Varzo, and Princess Julia, with all her partisans, was in exile. Varzo, held by a handful of adventurers headed by Methodios, had the public treasures, the fidelity of the army, and the citadel of the power, and against this powerful combination the scattered cities could not coalesce sufficiently to make any strong show of resistance. So long as Varzo was in the possession of Methodios, so long would the republic endure; but once a revolt began there in favour of Princess Julia, there was but little doubt that the country people flocking to her standard would speedily restore the ancient monarchy.

Methodios knew this, and therefore tampered with Russia in the hope that the Muscovites would help the republic; but his colleagues, more patriotic than the adventurous Greek, mistrusted the good faith of the St. Petersburg cabinet, and had no wish to see their country become a Russian province. This, then, was the situation when Princess Julia arrived at Villa Tvartko, and it needed but her arrival to be known for the whole country to revolt against the established government.

The Villa Tvartko, a former royal palace, took its name from one of the ancient rulers of Busk before the advent of the Lusignans. Situated about four miles from the capital, on the shores of the Black Sea, it was a most delightful summer residence and a favourite resort of the kings of Busk. Wearied of the tumult of Varzo, which is the Paris of the East, and one of the most restless cities in existence, they would retire to this enchanting villa for peace and rest. A more charming spot could scarcely be imagined, and, adorned by the taste of an artistic race, all that nature had failed to do art accomplished.

On the proclamation of the republic of Busk, the president had used the villa occasionally in the old royal style, but as time went on, the new government wanted money; so it was decided to sell the place at a good round sum. About this time Janshah was searching for a summer residence for Wilfred, and, hearing from one of his underlings that the Villa Tvartko was in the market, he purchased it at once for the sum demanded by the government of Busk; and so it became the property of the Englishman. Having parted with it on these terms, the republican government, to maintain their reputation for fair dealing, were obliged to do all in their power to protect the inmates, and render the country pleasant to them; therefore, by the irony of fate, those in power were aiding their deadliest enemies.

Built in the Saracenic style, Villa Tvartko presented a bizarre combination of cupolas, slender minarets, graceful horseshoe arches, and lofty, airy halls. In the centre of the house was a large court of white stone, wherein appeared a fountain springing like a silver rod from the quiet surface of a pool, filling the circumference of a marble basin. All around was an arcade deep and cool, which divided the courtyard from the habitable apartments of the palace. The interior was decorated in the Moorish style, similar to the arabesque fantasies of the Alhambra, and through painted windows the ardent light of the East filtered in to create a mysterious twilight. The eye was bewildered by the profuse traceries of the arched roofs gilded and coloured in the most brilliant manner, and from floor to ceiling sprang slender pillars of costly marbles. It was like a vision of the Arabian Nights, and glowed with the rich imagination of the desert race.

Throughout, it was furnished in the Eastern fashion, for in that warm climate the presence of tables and chairs is incongruous. It is true that in many of the chambers, European fashions were adopted, but in the courtyard, throughout the long ranges of galleries and lofty halls, there was nothing but the richly tinted mats, divans, and other simple requisites of the Eastern race. To add to the Oriental look Janshah had placed therein as servants a considerable number of black slaves, and these, seen gliding about amid the dim splendors of the halls, made them look like the chambers of the caliph.

Without, the villa was scarcely less splendid, for the walls were frescoed in Italian fashion, and in the warm, balmy air had kept their vivid tints wonderfully. Set amid the luxurious green of the vegetation around, Villa Tvartko sparkled like a jewel; and high above its medley of turrets, towers, minarets, arose the enormous gilt swelling of the central dome, surmounted by the golden crescent of Mahomet. The grounds, laid out with great care and taste, sloped down through green lawns and verdurous paths to the white marble terrace which bordered the blue waters. Throughout this pleasance arose numerous statues of marble gods, amber tinted by the ardent rays of the sun; and the whole place represented a mixture of East and West, a mingling of Arab fantasy with antique art, and the graceful incongruities of the Renaissance. In effect, it represented the history of Busk, for there were evidences of the Slavonic genius in the designs; the Turkish fantasies hinted at the influence of Ottoman occupation; and the Italian mediævalisms spoke of the Western taste of the Lusignan kings. As in the Hautville edifices of Palermo, the ascetic spirit of the West had impressed itself on the glowing imagination of the Orient, and the result was a fantastic blending of alien races, of contrasted climes.

Princess Julia was much moved when she found herself once more in this palace of her ancestors. Every nook and corner was perfectly familiar to her. In these brilliant halls had she played as a child; in that delightful garden had she wandered in girlhood; and her youthful imagination had often seen visions in the glowing sky beyond the glittering waters of the Black Sea.

"It was a fair heritage to lose," she said to Lady Hilda, the morning after their arrival. "It was from this villa that I fled when the rebels came from Varzo. The marquess, anticipating trouble, had a boat ready for me to fly, and, standing on its deck, I felt like Boabdil when he took his last look at the towers of the Alhambra."

"But you have returned, and Boabdil did not."

"The craven!" cried Madame de Lusignan, in a fiery voice; "had I possessed Granada, I would have died sooner than have yielded it to Ferdinand. Better to perish sword in hand than to live in exile."

"Yet you can scarcely blame Boabdil. Like yourself, he yielded to force."

"I did not yield of my own free will," retorted the princess indignantly. "I wished to stay and face the rebels, but Paradiso persuaded me to seek safety in flight. Oh, the humiliation of that moment! I was wrong to fly. Had I stayed, I might have held my throne."

"And possibly have lost your head."

"At least, I would have died like a queen, instead of eating my heart out in exile. Ah, how often have I sighed for these breezes! How often, in the gray London clime, have I longed for the blue skies of Busk! Believe me, madame, there is nothing so bitter as exile."

"Still, your Majesty has returned."

"In secret, like a thief in the night," said Julia, clenching her hand. "Oh! how bitterly will I be revenged on those who have forced me to such humiliation! To-day to them, to-morrow to me. They drove me forth once, but they will not do so again."

"Pray be calm," said Hilda, alarmed lest her furious gestures should betray her. "Even here we may not be safe. The least suspicion may cost us our heads."

"I forgot I was a servant," replied the princess disdainfully. "Yes, you are right, madame. I must be careful; but not for long will this humiliation endure."

"You stoop to conquer, madame."

"And when I conquer," hissed Julia through her clenched teeth, — "ah! how bitterly will I be revenged!"

"Pray be merciful," urged Hilda, in a pleading tone.

"Merciful! Yes, I will be so when I have cut off the heads of Methodios and his crew of traitors. Oh, never fear, madame; I shall be no Semiramis of the North. The kingdom of Busk never consented to my exile. It is the city there," she added, shaking her fist in the direction of Varzo, — "it is the city that I will punish. They will learn then, those fat and comfortable citizens, what it is to dare a Lusignan."

Certainly Hilda did not envy Richborough as she saw how tiger-like was the nature of this woman. In her character there was no touch of feminine softness. She was like a diamond, as brilliant and as hard. Such women make admirable rulers, because they never let the weakness of their sex interfere with their administrative powers. As sovereigns they are perfect. They are admired, feared, dreaded, but never loved. Richborough adored the woman, not the queen; and the woman was feigning a passion she did not feel. Alas for the young man when he discovered the truth!

As these thoughts were passing through the mind of Hilda, her cousin came down the steps towards the terrace where she was seated with the princess. He looked gallant and handsome as he came towards the two women, but Julia, much as she loved a goodly man, had no eye for his masculine perfections at this moment.

"Well, Monsieur le duc," she demanded imperiously, as he approached, hat in hand, "has the marquess returned?"

"Not yet, your Majesty," replied Richborough punctiliously, "nor has Monsieur Dacre. I presume they are still with the cardinal."

"They are a long time," said Hilda uneasily. "I trust nothing has happened, Gerald."

"Never fear, madame," interposed the princess hastily; "the marquess is too well disguised to excite suspicion, and your husband is simply paying a visit of ceremony to Monsieur le cardinal. He is devoted to my interests, and once they make themselves known to him, they are quite safe."

"I should rather think *that* the first dangerous step," submitted the duke, with a deferential smile.

"Not with Cardinal Gregory, monseigneur. He would be no prince of the church did he not exact implicit obedience from his household. Not one of his servants would dare to betray his secrets. They dread the law of the republic against harbouring so-called traitors, but they dread the thunders of the Vatican still more."

"I thought that the thunders of the Vatican were harmless now."

"In the West they are, in a great measure; but here we move slowly, and our people are as faithfully devoted to the church as they were hundreds of years ago. Here the church is more than a name. It is a power, and one which I intend to use through Cardinal Gregory."

"Will he submit to be an instrument?" asked Richborough doubtfully.

"Monseigneur," said the princess, with great dignity, "it is not my desire to make use of his Eminence merely as an instrument. It is my firm conviction that to govern a kingdom the church and the monarchy should be in perfect concord. The crown controls the temporal needs of men; it preserves the liberty of the country, the framework of society. On the other hand, the church has supreme control of the minds of its children. It can, by influencing them, achieve results which can be arrived at by no other means. Church and state must, therefore, be allies to control the society over which they rule. They should be one, like a husband and wife, for their interests are or should be undivided. Cardinal Gregory is a servant of the church, but he is also my subject, and as such is bound in all honour to forward the interests of his sovereign."

"Where they do not clash with those of the church."

"I have no wish to go contrary to the power of the pope," replied Julia coldly. "Rather do I desire to use his influence as delegated to the cardinal for the improvement of my country. Monarchy is the institution of most service to Catholicism, not republicanism. Cardinal Gregory has always seen that the interests of the Vatican and the Lusignans are identical in all respects. In two years he can scarcely have changed so much as to have thrown over his sovereign for a parcel of adventurers. He is true to me, and he is ambitious. Without my aid as the queen of Busk, he cannot obtain his ambition; therefore, he is bound to me by personal interests as well as political."

"You have, I see, every confidence in him," said Hilda, after a pause.

"Every confidence," answered Julia, with emphasis. "Still, I am on my guard against all men. Circumstances may turn the firmest friend into the bitterest enemy. The cardinal has all to gain by my restoration, yet — who knows?"

"Then you have not any confidence in him," observed Richborough ironically.

"I have so far as I can judge," replied the princess, impatiently qualifying her former statements. "To all appearances he is thoroughly trustworthy; and if I know anything of the man, he is so assuredly. Of one thing I am certain, that whatever may be his views, he will not betray me."

"Have you instructed Paradiso to tell him you are here?"

"No, not until I see his attitude towards me. But I have left much to the discretion of the marquess. In him I have great confidence."

"Here is the marquess," said Hilda suddenly, looking up; "and my husband with him."

Julia de Lusignan turned pale as she saw the two men coming towards her. Much as she professed to trust in the cardinal, yet she was of too pessimistic a nature to believe wholly in his sincerity, and dreaded lest Paradiso should have failed in his mission. She was reassured, however, by the face of the marquess, which expressed nothing but hope and contentment.

"Your Majesty," he said joyously, coming towards his mistress, "I have to announce to you that Cardinal Gregory is devoted to your interests."

"Ah!" cried the princess, with a flush of joy overspreading her face. "I knew I was not mistaken. Tell me what he said, monsieur."

"Can we speak here?" said Paradiso, glancing apprehensively around.

"Assuredly," interposed Wilfred promptly. "You may be certain, Marquess, that there is no traitor within these walls. Janshah is utterly devoted to my interests, and all those whom he has selected are as secret as the grave."

"Still, there may be some one from without," said Richborough.

"Impossible. See, we are in the terrace, far removed from any trees which may afford a lurking-place for a spy. There are no boats on the water. If we talk in a moderately low tone we are safe."

"Come, Marquess, tell me all," said Julia, impatiently, taking no notice of this discussion. "You saw the cardinal?"

"Yes, madame. On the application of Monsieur Dacre, we were admitted at once. Monsieur Dacre paid his respects to the cardinal as a travelling Englishman, and his Eminence had no suspicion as to the political nature of our errand."

"He did not recognize you, then."

"No. I was too well disguised for that, and, moreover, kept in the background, while Monsieur Dacre talked to the cardinal about the disturbed state of Busk. I wished to hear the cardinal's views before revealing myself."

"A useless precaution," said the princess disdainfully. "You might be certain, Marquess, that the cardinal would not give his real views to a stranger like Monsieur Dacre."

"That is very true," said Wilfred, smiling, "for he certainly did not."

"I can guess exactly what he said," pursued Madame de Lusignan vivaciously: "he praised the republic, — assured Monsieur Dacre that the country was at peace, and that he need have no fear of the possibility of a revolution."

"Your Majesty is entirely in the right," answered Paradiso, somewhat astonished at her penetration. "While talking to Monsieur Dacre the cardinal was too diplomatic to commit himself to any expression hostile to the existing government. But when I revealed myself, he threw off the mask."

"As I thought," said Julia in a satisfied tone.

"Well, and what did Monsieur le cardinal say at your sudden appearance?"

"He was much astonished, and seemed rather doubtful of the policy of Monsieur Dacre; but when I explained the whole of the circumstances to him, he approved of all that had been done."

"He knows, then, of this villa being tenanted in my interest?"

"Yes, your Majesty, but he does not know that your Majesty is here."

"Why did you not tell him so?"

"I did not think it politic to reveal all."

"You have revealed quite enough to ruin all things should his Eminence prove a traitor."

"He will not prove a traitor," said Paradiso with conviction; "he is quite on the side of your Majesty. Methodios, who, as you know, belongs to the Greek church, has been despoiling the Latins for the sake of currying favour with the patriarch at Constantinople."

"As if that would do him any good," observed the princess ironically.

"They say the patriarch has influence with the sultan," whispered Dacre significantly.

"The sultan is a cipher. He can do nothing. If Methodios had tried to curry favour with the patriarch at Moscow and thus gained the good will of the Czar, I could understand his statecraft. But Methodios is no politician. Well, Marquess, I suppose the cardinal is furious against the republic."

"Can you wonder at it? Devoted as he is to the church to which the Lusignans have always contributed largely, he wishes to bring the dynasty back into power and thus be saved from further spoliations."

"Then he will do his best to forward the cause."

"I am sure he will. But your Majesty must see him for yourself."

"But I understood you to say that he was ignorant of my presence in Varzo."

"So he is, madame," said Wilfred quickly; "but when the marquess and myself found that he was on your side, I asked permission of him for my wife to visit his place to-morrow. He graciously granted it, and so my wife can go there with you, and then —"

"And then," cried the princess impetuously, "I will assure myself of his fidelity and get him to aid me by all the means in his power."

"You need have no fear on that score, madame."

"Then I am to see the cardinal to-morrow?" said Hilda with vivacity.

"Yes, and her Majesty will accompany you. The rest will be easy."

"What is the temper of the country according to the cardinal?" asked Julia quickly.

"It is in a state of suppressed revolt," replied Paradiso with satisfaction. "Methodios is not at all popular, and may be unseated from his presidential chair at any moment."

"Then they will recall their queen," said Richborough.

"No," answered Paradiso, slowly shaking his head, "they will elect Upravado."

"What!" exclaimed Julia in a fiery tone, "does the country still incline to the republic?"

"The country at large does not, but Varzo is in possession of the army, and all the power is centralized therein. The army is devoted to Upravado, and if he desires to be president, the army will make him so."

"Can we not gain him to our side?"

"There is every chance of our doing so, according to the cardinal," replied Dacre hopefully, "but your Majesty will hear all to-morrow."

"I will go!" cried the princess decisively. "Madame, you will accompany me, and when I am face to face with Gregory, we can concoct some measure by which to gain Upravado to our side."

"If your Majesty can do that, all will be in our favour. Methodios cannot stand against the power of the army. But if you fail?"

"Fail?" echoed Julia with a laugh of scorn. "I did not risk my life and liberty in Varzo to fail at the last moment."

CHAPTER XVIII.

THE KEYS OF ST. PETER.

There are few ecclesiastics more celebrated in Eastern Europe than Stephen Gregory, archbishop of Varzo and a cardinal of the Romish church. Born at Ragusa, he traced his descent from a former rector of that unique republic; but after the earthquake of 1667, which reduced the town to ruins, the family of Gregory lost their former rank and opulence. So low did they sink in the social scale that they were classed as mere peasants, and it was not until the beginning of the nineteenth century that they arose again from this state of degradation. It was reserved for Stephen to revive the ancient glories of his house, of which he is now the last surviving representative.

Always ambitious, he entered the church of Rome when a boy, with the resolution to battle his way to the chair of St. Peter. Having Eastern blood in his veins, derived from an Arabian princess who married one of his ancestors, young Stephen possessed all the keen intellect of the Semitic race, and speedily commended himself to his superiors by his clear-headed sagacity and unerring tact. A man with such a character could not remain long in obscurity, and he rapidly rose through different grades, until, in middle age, he attained the high rank of a bishop. This, however, did not satisfy his ambition, and, foreseeing a field for his abilities in Busk, which then promised to become an important factor in European politics, he made up his mind to become archbishop of Varzo. The troubles in the Balkan states, of 1876, afforded him his opportunity; for, owing to the war and the enfeebled authority of the then archbishop, the affairs of the diocese were in a deplorable condition. Gregory was recommended to the notice of the pope as a skillful prelate, able to cope with these ecclesiastical troubles, and an interview with the holy father resulted in his being appointed archbishop of Varzo.

He set out at once for his diocese, and, finding an able coöperator in the king, Pierre II., speedily reduced the affairs of the kingdom to thorough order. He became the right hand of the king, restored the prestige of the church in Busk, and conducted the whole of his difficult task with such tact and prudence that, at the solicitation of Pierre, he was rewarded with the red hat. Now, he was archbishop of Varzo and a prince of the church; but, not even satisfied with these honours, this insatiable prelate was already in imagination seated on the pontifical throne. With a view to securing the interest of the Lusignans, he made himself indispensable to the king, and for many years acted as the Richelieu of this little-known state.

All seemed to be going well, and he confidently expected to some day realize his ambition, when the unexpected death of the king upset the whole of his calculations. The intrigues of Methodios, a man whom the cardinal had always dreaded, drove out the princess Julia, heiress to the throne, before she could be proclaimed queen, and the republic was established. It seemed as though the church would be swamped in the tempest, but Gregory was a valiant and crafty man. What he could not gain by force, he resolved to obtain by fraud, and, by making apparent submissions to the new president, managed to maintain his position in Varzo. He made good use of the time thus gained, and intrigued so actively that in a very short space of time, though apparently deferential to Methodios, he was in a strong enough position to defy the republic.

Such daring, however, was not his desire, as he did not wish to reassert his position until, with the return of Julia to the throne, he could regain his former authority. As soon as he had firmly established his position, he set to work to intrigue for the restoration of the Lusignans, and so successful was he that at the time Julia arrived at the Villa Tvartko, he was almost on the point of sending for her to England and urging her to display the royal standard. The sudden appearance of Paradiso, whom he knew to be a devoted adherent of the exiled princess, had somewhat startled him; but on thinking over the matter, he was glad that the marquess was on the spot, as he required assistance in his plans.

As yet the cardinal knew not that Julia was at the Villa Tvartko, and was seated in his room musing as to the advisability of asking Paradiso to bring her over from England. His secretary, Nicolas, a demure, cunning-looking man, was present, and they were conferring as to the advisability of precipitating matters. In front of the secretary were a few sheets of paper which would have cost the cardinal his head, had they been seen by Methodios. They contained a list of all those ready to join the standard of the princess Julia, of the number of men that could be called into the field, the amount of money promised, and other important matters which proclaimed the existence of a wide-spreading conspiracy against the government.

The man who held the innumerable threads of this intrigue in his hand was a stately and dignified-looking prelate. His powerful face was something of the Napoleonic type, and in the voluminous robes of his rank as cardinal, he looked a singularly majestic figure. The most careless observer could have told by his glittering eye, his decisive way of speaking, and immobile face, that this priest was a dangerous adversary. As archbishop of Varzo he possessed great power, and that power he desired to use for the good of the church as well as for his own aggrandizement. At present, however, owing to the republican form of government, he was ostensibly a cipher, and only with the advent of Julia would he regain the authority necessary to forward his schemes for the keys of St. Peter.

It was a small apartment in which these two men were seated, being a private cabinet situate at the top of the palace, quite free from any danger of lurking spies. The highest floor of an octagonal tower, it was lighted on all eight sides by windows; above was the roof, on which nothing but a cat could hope to keep its footing, and below an empty room securely locked up. Thus protected on all sides from listeners, Gregory could speak freely without the danger of having his words carried to the ever-open ears of Methodios. Nicolas, his secretary, was a man absolutely devoted to his archbishop, in whose star he had implicit faith, and hoped when Gregory became pope that he might in turn assume the purple of the Sacred College. He was as ambitious as the cardinal, more crafty and unscrupulous; but lacked the commanding intellect, which alone gains the highest posts of the church. Nicolas knew this, and, as he could not climb aloft by himself, clung to the skirts of his master in order to be carried up. Influenced by these feelings, he was a blind instrument in the hand of the cardinal, and though unscrupulous enough to betray any one for his own ends, he yet remained faithful to Gregory, simply because his falsity would lose him all and gain him nothing.

At present he was reading out to the cardinal the number of men that could be counted on in the case of a revolt, and every now and then stole a look at his master to see how he received the news. The cardinal, however, was not for the moment listening to his speech, as he was musing over the sudden arrival of Paradiso on the scene. All at once, rising from his seat, he began to pace to and fro in the narrow confines of the room. Nicolas stopped his reading and respectfully waited for the cardinal to speak, which he did shortly. He was, however, not conversing with Nicolas, but soliloquizing aloud.

"This arrival of the marquess," he murmured, as he walked slowly up and down, "is not unpremeditated, and I question much whether Julia de Lusignan would let him embark alone on this enterprise. They have been in ignorance of my conspiracy here, but, notwithstanding that they expected to find difficulties, she is not the woman to remain in the background. I know these Lusignans. Daring to the verge of recklessness, they often achieve unexpected results. Backed by the money of this Englishman, and knowing she could depend on me as a faithful servant of her house, I feel certain that she is at present in Varzo and ready to take the field at once. If so, why did Paradiso conceal the information from me? He knows I am devoted to the Lusignans, that I desire for my own ends and those of the church to restore the princess to the throne; yet he has not told me all. I may be mistaken, certainly, but I feel sure that Julia is in Varzo."

"The princess here!" said Nicolas, breaking in on his master's reverie with the assurance of a privileged favourite.

"Hah!" ejaculated the cardinal, fixing his keen eye on the secretary, "I forgot for the moment that you were present. Yes, I feel certain that the princess is here. You know what the marquess Paradiso said yesterday!"

"About the occupation of the Villa Tvartko by this M. Dacre? his intention to supply the princess with money, and the conspiracy formed in London? Yes, your Eminence, I heard all this, but it does not say that Princess Julia is here."

"To me it does," replied Gregory emphatically; "do you think that they would leave behind them such a necessary adjunct to the plot as Princess de Lusignan? I tell you no. With her on the spot they can do everything; in her absence, notwithstanding all their craft and conspiracy, the result will be nothing. And again, Julia is not the woman to be left behind."

"If this is so, why did not the marquess tell your Eminence?"

"That is what I do not know. Perhaps the princess chooses to reveal herself at her own time."

"The wife of the Englishman comes to-day?"

"Yes; she is due now. She comes, Nicolas, to see a poor prelate of the church, but not alone."

The cardinal uttered this sentence with such irony that the secretary looked up quickly and then dropped his eyes again in a demure manner.

"I do not understand your Eminence."

"This Madame Dacre," said the cardinal slowly, "has requested permission to bring with her a female companion. Why so? There can be no risk in visiting a priest like myself. If so, this female companion is useless."

"Then your Eminence thinks — "

"I do not think," said Gregory emphatically, "I am sure, that this companion is the princess Julia."

At this moment an electric bell sounded, which announced to the prelate that his guests had arrived.

He walked towards the door with the intention of going downstairs, but paused abruptly, as though he had changed his mind.

"No. I will not leave this room," he said, turning towards Nicolas; "if it is, as I suspect, the princess Julia, she will prefer that I should receive her here. Go you down, Nicolas, and request the English lady and her attendant to come here."

Nicolas bowed deferentially and left the room, while the cardinal, going over to his desk, quickly locked away all the papers pertaining to the conspiracy. Having done this, he glanced round the room to see that there was nothing else he wished to conceal from the sharp eyes of the princess, and finally seated himself in an armchair. He was firmly convinced that this mysterious attendant of the English lady was the princess Julia, as he was too well acquainted with the resolute character of that royal person to think she would remain in the background while her fate was in the balance.

Well versed in the way of creating an impression, Cardinal Gregory arose from his chair as Hilda entered, and moved majestically across the room to greet her. While apparently looking straight at the foremost lady, he was quick enough to glance at the figure in the background, and congratulated himself on his prescience. Disguised as was the princess, he knew her bearing too well to be deceived by dark hair or stained face. Convinced that she thought herself undiscovered, and always ready to seize the advantage, Gregory resolved to receive the disguised queen as though she were expected.

"I am glad to see you, madame," he said in French, giving his hand to Hilda. "I must pray you to excuse me, asking you up to my eyrie, but my age must be my apology for not descending the stairs. Monsieur, your husband, told me to expect you; but he did not announce the visit of the illustrious lady I see by your side."

"My attendant!" said Hilda, with a blush, while Julia hung back, doubtful as to whether the astute prelate had discovered her real rank.

"Pardon me, madame," replied the cardinal with a slight smile, "it pleases the queen to masquerade as an attendant, but no eye can mistake the face of a Lusignan."

"I am discovered, I see, Cardinal," said Julia, coming forward with an air of chagrin. "You are to be congratulated, monseigneur, on your penetration."

"It is necessary in the present crisis," answered his Eminence, as the princess kissed his hand. "I am glad to see your Majesty once more in your faithful city of Varzo."

"My faithful city!" echoed Julia, seating herself in the cardinal's chair. "That is a remark which admits of much argument. I have few faithful to me now, but among those few I count your Eminence, and also this lady, who is the wife of M. Dacre, whom you saw yesterday."

"Madame is very welcome," said the cardinal with a courtly bow, "particularly as she brings me the gift of a queen. I am playing a game of chess with Methodios," added his Eminence with a smile, "and to checkmate him I required a queen, which I had not. Now I think the game will end in my favour."

"That is, if Methodios does not think of some new combination."

"He will exhaust all combinations in the end," replied the cardinal quietly. "The fox has many tricks, but he is run to earth at last."

"How did your Eminence guess that I would bring her Majesty with me?" asked Hilda, who could not help marvelling at the prompt manner in which the prelate had recognized Julia. "Did my husband tell you, or the marquess?"

"Neither, madame. I know the Lusignans' temper too well to think that one of them would remain in the background. When I saw the marquess yesterday I knew that her Majesty could not be far off. To-day you visit me with a female attendant; I know you, madame, as Madame Dacre; so it needed but little thinking on my part to guess that you were accompanied by her Majesty."

"All the same, I think your Eminence is to be congratulated on your acumen," said Julia, smiling; "but I might have known no disguise could baffle your eye. I only hope Methodios will not discover the truth also."

"You must keep out of his sight," said the cardinal hastily; "these Phanariot Greeks are very keen and very suspicious. It was unwise of you to come hither."

"Her Majesty was anxious to see your Eminence personally."

"Then her Majesty should have sent for me to the Villa Tvartko."

"My dear Cardinal," broke in Julia impatiently, "I was too anxious to know what position you intended to take up to await your arrival."

"What position could I take up, but that of your friend?" said the cardinal in a reproachful tone. "You forget that our interests are identical. But, apart from all worldly considerations, I should indeed be base to desert the daughter of a monarch to whom I owe so much."

"Forgive me, Cardinal, I know you are devoted to my interest," replied Julia, taking his hand; "but you know the fallen are ever suspicious."

"Your Majesty —"

"Why address me by that mockery of a title? A queen without subjects, without lands; I have not even been crowned."

"But you shall be," said Gregory determinedly, "and by my hands in the cathedral of Varzo."

"But the crown of Busk? Is that in the possession of Methodios?"

"No; it is yet in the treasure-vault of the cathedral, where it has ever been. Methodios wished to seize it, and I had to threaten him with excommunication before he would desist from his sacrilegious purpose."

"Still, if he is not of your church he would not care for that," observed Hilda thoughtfully.

"Not in himself, perhaps. But if he was excommunicated he would lose his position as president of the Republic; and he fought too hard to risk such a loss."

"What think you of our plans, monseigneur?" asked Julia anxiously.

"I think they are excellent. We are greatly beholden to your husband, madame," continued the cardinal, bowing graciously to Hilda, "both for his proposed loan of money to the cause, and his suggestion regarding the Villa Tvartko being the headquarters of the queen's partisans."

"My husband will do all in his power to replace the queen on her throne. But in the event of war, do you think the cause will be well supported?"

The cardinal smiled, and, going over to the desk, took from thence the papers concerning the conspiracy and placed them in the hands of Julia.

"Look at these, your Majesty," he said significantly, "and you will see that I have not been idle."

The princess eagerly examined the lists, while the prelate addressed himself with suave courtesy to Hilda, whose beauty had made a great impression on him.

"M. Dacre must indeed be a prince, madame, when he can afford to raise a million of money in the cause of fallen royalty!"

"It is a good use to make of the money," replied Hilda politely. "Wilfred — my — husband is only too delighted to have some object in life."

"Ah!" said his Eminence in a significant tone. "He felt, then, that life was made for more than play?"

"I think we all feel that, monseigneur!"

"No, my daughter. There are those so frivolous that they care for nothing but gaiety and idle pleasures. You are not of our communion, I believe?"

"No: we are of the Anglican church."

The cardinal sighed, for he would have dearly liked to convert a portion of this Englishman's apparently inexhaustible wealth into the coffers of the church of Peter. He was too great a courtier, however, to make any further remarks touching religion, but privately determined to do his best to convert this young couple to the true faith during their stay in Varzo.

"How long, madame, do you intend to remain at Villa Tvartko?"

"If we are permitted, all the winter."

"You will certainly not be permitted by me to leave Varzo," said Julia, looking up with a bright smile. "We shall succeed, and you must stay to assist at my coronation."

"And at your marriage, too, I trust, my daughter," hinted the cardinal, who had views for his mistress in the direction of matrimony.

Julia sighed.

"Alas! I know not when that will take place. If I marry, it must be for political reasons."

"Assuredly," said the cardinal emphatically. "When you regain the throne you will have to strengthen it by all the means in your power. You must marry to consolidate the kingdom."

"Then there will be no love in the matter," observed Hilda mournfully, thinking of her cousin.

Julia followed her meaning, and flushed even through the dark stain of her skin. Afraid lest Hilda should say something to her cousin which would reveal the truth, she veiled her real feelings with an uneasy laugh, and avoided the dangerous topic.

"I am not so sure about that," she answered, smiling. "Who knows! I may marry for love after all."

"And by doing so, lose your kingdom," hinted the cardinal darkly.

"M. le cardinal, we will leave the discussion of this question till another time. Meanwhile, more important matters await our consideration. Can you rely on these nobles mentioned in this list?"

"To the death. They are all devoted to your Majesty."

"Their devotion did not save me from exile," retorted the princess dryly. "However, better late than never. They will rise when you give the signal?"

"Yes! And if your Majesty's presence becomes known, they will flock without a signal to the Villa Tvartko."

"No! No! I do not wish that," said Julia hastily. "In that case there would be a civil war."

"In which I think we should conquer," replied Gregory, with great satisfaction. "Still, I am of your Majesty's opinion. War must be avoided at any cost; for, besides the loss of men, it would afford Russia a pretext for interfering."

"Ah, the Russian bear still watches the Lusignan lion."

"Of course! Through Busk lies the road to Stamboul. Russia will never be satisfied till she possesses the Bosphorus."

"Shall I tell you, monseigneur, what I heard an English statesman suggest?" said Hilda at this moment.

"Pray do, madame.'

"That, to preserve the balance of power in Europe, Constantinople should be taken from the Turks, made a neutral city, and given over to the temporal authority of the pope."

Gregory started, and looked at her keenly.

"English statesmen are not alone in that opinion, madame," he said significantly. "Who knows what may happen in the near future?"

Julia smiled. She knew the ambition of the cardinal, and, while quite ready to aid him to sit in the chair of St. Peter, wished to reserve the golden throne of the Cæsars to herself.

"That will never occur," she said decisively; "the only chance of safety to Europe, from Russia, is the reconstruction of the Byzantine empire."

This time the cardinal smiled. He also knew the ambitions of Julia de Lusignan, and was afraid that when she became queen their interests would clash. She was too imperious for him, and he could not mould her to his will as he had moulded her weak-minded father. Too diplomatic, however, to betray his thoughts, and quite willing to assist a possible adversary in order to benefit himself in the end, he smiled blandly, and addressed himself to the subject in hand.

"Who knows what aspect affairs may assume, when you regain your throne?" he said, waving his hand gracefully. "Remember, it does not concern

Busk alone, but all Europe. As you say, it is best to accomplish your restoration without war, but if war must be, it must. Still, if we can secure Upravado and the army, you will have no one to oppose your reëntry into Varzo."

"Methodios?" queried Hilda, curiously.

"Can do nothing. The country is with her Majesty, and it is only in Varzo that the republicans have partisans. Upravado has gained the devotion of the army, and they will follow where he leads. If we can bribe him over to our cause, Methodios will be left without a supporter, and will have to fly the country."

"Who is to approach him on such a delicate mission?" demanded the princess.

"Ah, madame, that requires some consideration," answered the courtly archbishop; "not Paradiso, — not myself, — he will commit himself with neither of us: it must be some stranger."

"M. Dacre!" suggested Julia promptly, "or M. le duc."

"No!" said Hilda, with a sudden inspiration. "Major Measurby is the only one who can successfully conduct such a delicate business."

The archbishop shook his head.

"Upravado speaks no English," he said doubtfully. "I am afraid it will be useless to employ this M. Measurby, unless he is conversant with French."

"Oh, he is an excellent French scholar."

"In that case, he may be a useful envoy. But we must not decide on this question suddenly. Madame," he added, bowing to Julia, "I will call next week at the Villa Tvartko, in order to return the visit of Madame Dacre. When I am there, we can have a meeting, and decide finally on our plan of operation."

"Can I take these lists with me?" asked the princess, eagerly.

The archbishop held out his hand, with a smile, for the papers.

"By no means. If, by chance, they fell into the hands of Methodios, it would cost the heads of many of your partisans, including my own."

"Methodios would not dare to harm you," said Julia, giving back the papers with great reluctance.

"Methodios will shortly be like a caged rat, and therefore capable of any crime."

"Well, will you bring those papers to Villa Tvartko when you come?"

"Yes, your Majesty! Next week, call a meeting of those devoted to you, and I will be there."

"Adieu, your Eminence," said Hilda as she took her leave. "If we are successful, it means much to us all."

"To me the throne," said Julia, proudly.

"And to me a chance of holding St. Peter's keys," thought Gregory, but he was too wise to say so.

CHAPTER XIX.

A MODERN PATRIOT.

It was not unintentional on Hilda's part that she had mentioned the name of Major Measurby. Personally, she did not care for him in the least, and, with the quick intuition of her sex, she saw that his friendship for her husband was unreal. Several times she had hinted to Wilfred that Measurby was not a man on whom could be placed any dependence, but he had always turned the conversation aside when it came to a discussion of this delicate topic. Wilfred could not reveal the cause of his friendship with Measurby without exposing the secret of the ring, and although he had made up his mind to tell Hilda everything, yet, owing to the constant occurrence of exciting events in connection with the conspiracy, the opportunity of so doing never took place.

It was therefore Hilda's firm resolve that Measurby should undertake the dangerous mission of gaining Upravado to the royalist cause. She was unwilling that either her husband or her cousin should risk his life by thrusting his head so far into the lion's mouth, and if any one could be spared, it was Major Measurby. If he succeeded in bribing Upravado, all would be well; but if on the other hand the republican leader proved incorruptible and had him arrested, the whole conspiracy would be revealed to the authorities, and the inmates of Villa Tvartko would have to seek safety in flight. Hilda then wished to save her husband and cousin at the expense of the major, and she could hardly be blamed for such a desire. Besides, Measurby, who talked a great deal about the dangers they were incurring, had hitherto kept in the background, and pushed forward his friends to take the risk. This, in Hilda's opinion, was scarcely fair; and she was determined that if he shared in the glory, he should also share in the danger.

On her return from the visit to Archbishop Gregory, a meeting was called by Julia, to consider the suggestion of the cardinal that some one should be sent to bribe Upravado. Paradiso of course wanted to go, but was overruled by the others, who did not think it wise that such a well-known royalist should visit Upravado, and perhaps be arrested before he could offer terms. As the cardinal said, it was wiser that a stranger should be the delegate, and although both Wilfred and Richborough offered their services in this capacity, the princess, at the suggestion of Hilda, fixed on Major Measurby as the best person to perform the task. He was a soldier; in India he had been accustomed to conduct delicate negotiations with native princes; he was an admirable French scholar, and to all appearances devoted to the cause; so with all these qualifications the royalists decided that they could not have a better man. Measurby was offered the dangerous honor of bearding the lion in his den, and not lacking physical courage, accepted with the utmost promptitude. This important question having thus been decided, the council broke up, and Julia retired with Paradiso to confer with him regarding the plans of the cardinal.

Measurby was by no means pleased to have greatness thus thrust upon him. Had he come to Busk purely as an adventurer to replace the princess on her throne, he would have been delighted; but as his sole object in planning and pushing forward the conspiracy was to wrest the ring from the possession of Wilfred, he did not care about risking his life and possibly losing it before achieving his desire. As yet no opportunity had been offered to him of securing the ring by fraud, for Wilfred never took the precious talisman from his finger, and it was useless to think of force, seeing how vigilant was Janshah in guarding his master. The Indian suspected Measurby's designs, and though personally he did not care who held the ring, yet, bound by its laws, he had to defend him who was its present possessor. Had Measurby been the master of the ring, Janshah would have been as devoted to him as he was now to Wilfred. The man was a mere machine, who obeyed no one but him who possessed the talisman, and Measurby, knowing this, was quite satisfied that if the ring was once on his finger, Janshah would take all precautions that Wilfred should not get it again. Force was therefore quite out of the question; no opportunity offered for the practice of fraud, so Measurby, with inward reluctance, was forced to accept the dangerous mission of treating with Upravado, and leave the rape of the ring till a more convenient occasion.

The meeting with the rebel leader could not take place at once, for he was a difficult person to see in private, owing to the incessant suspicions of Methodios. The wily Greek was a traitor himself, and, surrounded by other traitors, distrusted them all, particularly Upravado, whom he suspected of having an eye to the presidential chair. Next to Methodios himself, with whom possession of the supreme power was nine points of the law, he was the strongest person in the government, as he had the devotion of the army, and with such a recourse at command, could overturn the rule of the Greek at any moment. Several times Methodios had been on the point of throwing Upravado into prison, and slaying him secretly, but had always dreaded lest this extreme course should lead to a revolt of the soldiers. In default of this, however, he had his rival constantly watched by spies, so any meeting between Upravado and a stranger would at once be reported to the president, and arouse his suspicions. If such an event happened, the Villa Tvartko would be at once subjected to the espionage of the republican spies, and at any moment all might be discovered.

Under these circumstances, it can easily be seen that Measurby was forced to act in a very circumspect manner. The task was so difficult that for fully a week no definite conclusion could be arrived at as to how a meeting could be arranged, and finally it was the cardinal who hit upon a feasible plan of operation. At first Measurby had thought of calling on Upravado as an old soldier interested in the Busk army, and requesting a review of the troops; but both at the interview and the review they would be surrounded by the spies of Methodios. His second idea was to invite Upravado to inspect the Villa Tvartko; but to do so openly, he would be forced to be accompanied by his suite, none of whom he could trust. At last the archbishop proposed that Measurby should stay with him in concealment for a few days, and during that time Upravado might be lured to the palace, where the interview could take place in secrecy.

This appeared to be the only chance of securing a meeting without the knowledge of Methodios; so the major went one night to the palace of the cardinal, and was concealed by its master in the upper chamber of the octagon tower. Thanks to the precautions which had been taken, his presence there was quite unsuspected by the spies of the republic, despite the fact that they constantly watched the palace. Methodios hated and dreaded the cardinal, but the latter had so secured his safety that the president was unable to do him any harm.

If he had discovered the archbishop to be concerned in any plot against the republic, he certainly could have had him arrested and thrown into prison with some show of reason, but otherwise the people of Busk would not permit so famous a man as their cardinal to be arrested if innocent. Methodios therefore watched the palace for any appearance of treason, and bided his time to get the better of the archbishop, — a thing which was very doubtful, seeing how wily was the prelate. Gregory delighted in intrigues and was never so happy as when engaged in them; so this meeting of Upravado and the major was an affair which, owing to his diplomatic dexterity, he managed in the most admirable manner. Measurby came to the palace and was comfortably lodged there, without exciting the least suspicion on the part of Methodios, and the next thing to be done was to get Upravado to visit his Eminence on some trivial pretext.

This would have been impossible had not Upravado been inclined to the royal cause, but owing to the machinations of Methodios, who desired his overthrow, that general was beginning to find his position anything but pleasant. He saw that sooner or later the petty disturbances between himself and Methodios would break out into open war, and as he was the stronger, Methodios would undoubtedly call in the aid of the Russians to crush his rival. Upravado was a perfectly selfish man, who did not care in the least about his country so long as he himself was safe, and he began to question whether it would not be best for him to embrace the royal cause, replace the Lusignans on the throne, and thus secure his own position.

While in a state of indecision regarding this matter, he received a letter from Cardinal Gregory, written in a religious spirit and hinting that he had not lately been to confession. The spies of Methodios saw this letter and reported on its contents to their master, who simply saw in it a desire of the cardinal to maintain his spiritual power, now that he had lost all temporal authority. Upravado, however, guessed that it meant more than a mere visit to confess his sins. He knew that the cardinal was inclined to the royalist side, and hoping that in an interview with the astute prelate he might glean some information likely to decide his future course, he went to the palace. As he was bent on a purely religious errand he went alone, and thus, for the time being, was relieved from having his actions spied on by the emissaries of Methodios.

When he arrived at the palace he was informed that the cardinal would receive him in his private oratory, and therein found his Eminence prepared to receive his confession. By a strange anomaly Upravado was a devout Catholic, and in his confession concealed nothing from the priest, whereby the archbishop was enabled to forecast at once the success of Measurby's errand. Upravado was not so devoted to the republicans as he had thought; he was in a state of indecision. He was an avaricious man and fond of his own pleasure; so if the matter could be settled by an offer of gold, of a title, and of position under the queen, there was no doubt that he would cast in his fortunes with the royalist cause.

"My son," said Gregory, when the confession was over, and the penitent had received absolution, "you seem to be uneasy in your mind regarding your worldly affairs."

"Your Eminence is perfectly right," replied

Upravado with a sigh. "I know not what is best to be done for the good of Busk."

"Rather for the good of yourself," thought the prelate contemptuously.

"The president," continued Upravado, in an irritated tone, "does not trust me."

"Not trust General Upravado?" said Gregory, raising his eyebrows. "Truly, my son, you must be making some strange mistake. You are the mainstay of the republic."

"Methodios does not think so."

"He does think so, although he does not say so," replied the archbishop suavely. "You know well, Upravado, that Busk does not love the republic. Varzo alone adheres to the existing government, and were it not for the army, Methodios would fall."

"And on whom does the fidelity of the army depend?" cried Upravado impetuously. "On me! I alone have any influence with the soldiers. They are all devoted to me personally, not to Methodios. If I gave the word they would unseat Methodios to-morrow from the chair of the president, and place me therein."

"Hush!" said the cardinal, affecting alarm; "you are talking treason."

"Am I? Well, I hope I am safe with your Eminence," retorted Upravado, fixing his keen eye on the prelate. "If report speaks truly, you lean rather to the royalists than to the republic."

"I have ever been a faithful servant to Busk," said the cardinal, with emphasis on the last word.

"Well, Busk at present is a republic; so you must be faithful to Methodios."

"Methodios is not the republic."

"He seems to regard himself as such. I am not in his confidence, — I who, as you say, alone control the army. Methodios lavishes all his favours on Culin, Geiza, and such like minions. When I supported the republic, I believed that it would benefit the country, but now it would be better to have the Lusignans back again."

"Do you really think so?" asked the cardinal, with affected simplicity.

"Yes. The Lusignans at least are more scrupulous than Methodios."

"You say the Lusignans," repeated the archbishop, in a melancholy tone. "Remember, there is now only one representative of that famous family, and that one a woman."

"True. She can never rule Busk."

"There you are wrong," retorted Gregory, for the first time giving a hint of his true feelings. "Julia de Lusignan will rule with a rod of iron. She has the genius of Catherine of Russia."

"If I thought so I might be inclined to restore the monarchy," said Upravado in a musing tone. "Oh, I speak treason against Methodios, I know," he continued, in answer to an inquiring look from the cardinal, "but I am weary of his tyranny. It is true I am not now speaking under the seal of the confessional, and you can betray me if you like. But you will not do so. Republican as you pretend to be, you are a royalist at heart."

"It is true. I am a royalist," replied Gregory, throwing off the mask. "I owe everything to the Lusignans, nothing to Methodios. The church can gain nothing from one who professes the heresy of the Greek. You, Upravado, are a Catholic, he a member of the Greek church; you a true-born son of Busk, he a foreigner, who would sell us to the Russian. For the sake of your religion, for the sake of your country, drive this man out of Busk, and replace Julia de Lusignan on the throne."

"Why not myself?" asked Upravado, bending his brows. "I have the army at my back. I could seize and hold Varzo —"

"But not against the Russians," interrupted the cardinal imperiously. "If you made yourself king, it would afford a pretext to the Russians to interfere, and they would reduce Busk to an appanage of the Czar. No! I tell you, my son, there is no safety for you and none for Busk in such a course. The only thing to be done is to place Julia on the throne."

"And what would I gain by that?"

"Her gratitude, wealth, titles, honours."

"Doubtless all these would be promised," said Upravado cunningly. "But once she is on the throne, I may whistle down the wind for fulfilment. No, if I support the cause of Julia I must have some guarantee."

"In what way?"

"Say a sum of money, — a large amount. Then, if she proves ungrateful, I can leave Busk and live on what I have earned. Otherwise, if I commit myself blindly to the cause, she may take all and give nothing."

"In the event of a sum of money being given to you," said the cardinal slowly, "would you be inclined to assist Julia to the throne?"

"I would."

It was the reply expected by the cardinal, but he did not accept the offer at once. By degrees he had lured Upravado into a confession of his real sentiments, but if he closed with him at once, he might draw back through fear.

"I hardly see how a large sum of money could be obtained," he said, as if doubtful. "Julia de Lusignan is poor, and so are all those who still cling to the monarchy."

"If, as you say, all Busk, saving Varzo, support her claim to the throne, a sum such as I require can easily be raised."

"Well, supposing it is raised and paid to you, what then?"

"What then?" said Upravado haughtily. "I will send to England for Paradiso, who, I know, is an accomplished statesman, devoted to Julia. Send also for the queen, and with the army at my back, I will seize Varzo, put Methodios into prison, and, before the Russians can interfere, I will place Julia on the throne. Once she is there the great powers will support her pretensions and prevent the interference of Russia."

"How much money do you desire?" asked the cardinal, ignoring this brilliant prophecy.

"Two hundred thousand francs," replied Upradavo promptly.

"Ah," said the cardinal sarcastically, "I see you have already made up your mind on the subject."

Upravado laughed, not having the face to blush at the shameless way in which he was betraying the government to which he had vowed fidelity.

"Methodios looks after himself, so why should not I do the same?" he said defiantly. "Besides, a monarch is better than a despot, and with Methodios as president, Busk is as despotic as Russia. I am weary of his tyranny, and I know not the moment when he may work my downfall. Had I not command of the army I should have been dead long ago. I desire to end this state of suspense and seek safety, either in exile or under Queen Julia. Let her or you, monseigneur, give me two hundred thousand francs in gold, and next week I will proclaim the republic at an end and the monarchy restored. It is a desperate game, but it is worth two hundred thousand francs — to me."

"Since you are quite ready to aid the queen on those terms," said the cardinal slowly, "the money will be paid as you desire."

"Two hundred thousand francs?"

"Two hundred thousand francs."

"Good!" said Upravado, with an expression of satisfaction. "I am yours and the queen's."

Cardinal Gregory took a black ebony crucifix from the oratory altar and held it out towards the republican leader.

"This sacred emblem contains a lock of the hair of the blessed St. Hilarion, patron saint of Busk. I know you to be a true son of the church. Swear on this crucifix that on payment of this money you will support the cause of Queen Julia, that you will sever yourself utterly from the cause of Methodios, and that, henceforth, such things as are said, done, and seen in this house you will keep secret from all."

"I swear!" replied Upravado, laying his hand on the crucifix with an irrepressible shudder; "by the salvation of my soul, I swear that on payment of this money, I am with you, and that from this moment I will reveal nothing to your enemies."

The archbishop heaved a sigh of relief at seeing Upravado commit himself thus irrevocably to the royal cause, and replaced the crucifix on the altar.

"My son, you are now one of us, and to you I can reveal our secrets."

"Have you any to reveal?" said Upravado doubtfully.

"A great many. The princess Julia is at present in Varzo."

"Impossible!"

"She is at the Villa Tvartko in company with Paradiso."

"The Villa Tvartko," muttered Upravado, turning pale; "then that Englishman is a partisan of the queen?"

"He is. Does Methodios suspect him?"

"Not in the least," replied the other frankly. "Neither did I. Your plans have been well laid. But the money?"

"The Englishman will pay you the amount you require," said the cardinal, going towards the door.

"Come with me, my son, and I shall lead you to his representative, who will arrange the matter."

"In this house?" said Upravado, hanging back. "Truly this conspiracy is ripe for the outburst. Would you betray me, Cardinal?"

Gregory looked at him with an air of reproach.

"My son, I am a man of peace, not of war. You have sworn on the crucifix that you will favour our cause. This being the case, I should indeed be foolish to destroy one whom I have gained with such trouble."

"Lead on," said Upravado, advancing boldly. "I will follow. I have gone too far to draw back. If I did—"

"It would mean destruction in this world and the next, my son."

Upravado shuddered again, for, superstitious as he was, the oath he had taken bound him to his word. Even did he not receive the money, he would have hesitated to draw back now at the peril of his salvation. Still, the oath was contingent on the money being paid, and he resolved to keep his promise, provided the cardinal did not deceive him.

With these thoughts in his mind he mounted the stairs, up which he was preceded by the cardinal. On arriving at the octagonal chamber Measurby advanced to meet them, and Gregory introduced the two men.

"Major Measurby," he said in his firm voice, "this is General Upravado, who has consented to join our cause on conditions which you alone can carry out. Upravado, behold this English soldier, who is trusted in all things by our sovereign and who will give you that which you desire."

The two soldiers, scoundrels both, eyed one another keenly, and then sat down to talk over the conditions of the treaty, while the cardinal, withdrawing to his table, pretended to be busy writing, though in reality he was drinking in every word.

"What are your conditions, monsieur?" asked Measurby in a courteous tone.

"I am ready to join the royal cause and bring over the army, on condition that the sum of two hundred thousand francs is paid to me in gold before I declare myself an enemy of the republic."

"Good. It shall be paid as you desire."

"At once?"

"Oh, no," answered Measurby with a cunning smile. "We also must have some guarantee of good faith."

Upravado reddened, but as it was a business in which no moral or honourable principles were involved, he could hardly assume a virtuous indignation. He therefore swallowed his chagrin, and professed himself willing to give whatever guarantee was required.

"You know, monsieur, that the princess Julia is at the Villa Tvartko?"

"Yes, so his Eminence informed me."

"My friend, M. Dacre, will be responsible for this money, and it will be paid over to you on the day on which the restoration of the queen is proclaimed."

"Before that occurs I must have the money."

"Certainly, that is but fair, monsieur."

"Then how do you propose to carry out the matter?" asked Upravado impatiently. "What are your plans?"

"Next week, monsieur," said Measurby rapidly, "M. Dacre gives a ball to which he will ask all the partisans of the queen. When all are assembled, M. Dacre will take you aside, into another room and pay you this money. Then you will enter the ball-room and proclaim the queen, who will at once make her appearance before the guests. As they are all faithful to the royal cause, they will hail her appearance with joy, and you, with your soldiers, can then advance on Varzo, seize Methodios and proclaim the monarchy."

"The plan is a good one," said Upravado musingly, "but I can improve on it. Yes! I will tell all my officers who are in Varzo to be ready with their men for my signal. A body of soldiers I will take with me to Villa Tvartko; so, when the monarchy is proclaimed and we march on the town, the whole place will be in the hands of the army at once. Methodios will fly, and that night the queen shall sleep once more in the palace of her ancestors."

"But will not Methodios be suspicious of your preparations?" asked the cardinal, leaning forward.

"There are no preparations to be made," replied Upravado promptly. "I can tell all my officers secretly, and as they are my devoted adherents, they will not betray me. So in Varzo itself there will be nothing to arouse suspicion. As to the Villa

Tvartko, I am invited there to a ball by M. Dacre, who is an English visitor under the protection of the established government. As a general of the army I have a right to go with an escort of soldiers and a staff of officers. The rest is easy."

"I think it could not be better, monsieur," said Measurby, springing to his feet. "By next week the republic will have ceased to exist."

"Only on condition that M. Dacre pays me this money at the Villa Tvartko," said Upravado emphatically. " I am not going to trust blindly to the gratitude of the queen."

"You shall have the money," said the cardinal soothingly. "M. Dacre will certainly pay you."

"That is, if he has the ring," thought the major; "but if it is mine I am afraid Upravado will get nothing." "Well, monsieur," he added aloud, "are you satisfied?"

"Perfectly."

"In that case," said the cardinal joyously, "we may look on the *coup d'état* as already accomplished."

CHAPTER XX.

THE CALM BEFORE THE STORM.

NEEDLESS to say the princess was delighted with the success of Measurby's mission. As a matter of fact its accomplishment was due more to the cardinal than to the major, but as the latter was the ostensible agent in carrying out the affair, he received all the credit. So far as Julia was concerned it mattered but little to her who secured Upravado so long as he was gained over to her side; but, confident that no ingratitude on her part could alienate the cardinal, she ignored his share in the triumph and lavished all her praise on the major. Conceive the pride with which Measurby heard such compliments from royal lips. He knew perfectly well that Gregory had brought Upravado to him entirely willing to join the royal cause, and that nothing was needed to clinch the matter but the promise that the money would be paid. Yet with this knowledge the major began to believe that he was an uncommonly clever diplomatist, who had conducted a difficult negotiation to a successful termination.

As to the outcome of all this intriguing, Measurby flattered himself that the result rested with him, for he had hit upon a method of securing the ring through the instrumentality of Hilda. The affair was still in embryo, as the major's scheming brain had not yet completed the various details, but it was sufficiently forward to assure him that he would obtain possession of the ring before the money was paid over to Upravado. When this happened, Measurby was not sure whether he would carry out the negotiations or fly the kingdom, leaving the royalists to their fate. If he stayed, he ran a chance of losing the ring again, for Wilfred would do all in his power to recover possession of it; whereas, if he fled, who could tell what horrors might ensue?

Upravado had been promised a sum of money on payment of which he had sworn to assist the royalists. If he were disappointed in payment he would certainly revenge himself by revealing the secrets of the conspiracy to Methodios and arresting all the inmates of Villa Tvartko. Measurby could not make up his mind whether to avert or hasten this catastrophe, but of one thing he was certain, that on the night when the *coup d'état* was to occur he, and not Wilfred, would be the destiny of the affair.

With these ideas in his mind Measurby went about with a very happy expression of face, which those whom he had half decided to betray put down to satisfaction at having been the means of securing the adherence of Upravado. The major did not undeceive them on this point, but chuckled to think how he would shortly hold all their lives in his hand. No touch of compunction for his proposed baseness was in his heart, but as the man was quite lacking in a moral sense this was scarcely to be wondered at. He simply argued that as Wilfred had deceived him by keeping the ring, he had a right to deceive Wilfred by stealing it from him, and as for the contingencies that might happen in the event of his success, he never gave them a thought.

Meanwhile, encouraged by the adherence of Upravado to the royal cause, the partisans of the princess worked hard to unite all the scattered threads of the conspiracy. Cardinal Gregory called at the villa, and brought with him the lists of the nobles in the provinces who had agreed to revolt against the government in support of Julia's pretensions. Each of these nobles could bring hundreds of men into the field, so even though the president made a stand against the soldiers of Upravado at Varzo, in a very short space of time the reinforcements would arrive from far and near, and the republicans would be forced to yield to sheer numerical strength.

The archbishop, in pursuance of his policy, sent out messengers to all the towns, villages, and castles of the kingdom, announcing that the great day was approaching, and so strong was the royalist spirit in the provinces that the news of this disaffection never reached Varzo. The stronghold of the republicans being in that city, they were rather contemptuous of the provinces, assuming that so long as they had the capital the republic would still maintain her ground. Had Upravado remained faithful to Methodios this indeed might have been the case, but now that he and his soldiers had gone over to the royal cause the conspirators of Villa Tvartko looked upon their triumph as certain.

Methodios knew nothing of the danger which was at his very doors; which said but little for his system of espionage. Everywhere men in his pay were watching for signs of discontent and disaffection; but secure in the certainty of their success the royalists made no sign in any way. Seeing, then, this outward content, the spies reported to Methodios that the royalist cause was utterly dead and that never was the government of the republic so stable. It was the calm before the storm, but Methodios did not know it.

The first intimation that there might be a conspiracy on foot came from the Russian agency, where it was hinted that political reasons had brought the master of Villa Tvartko to Varzo. There was no ground for this belief, but the eternal suspicions of Russia made her suspect every one. Owing to the machinations of the nihilists she was well aware that danger might lurk under a seeming innocent exterior, and the Russian agent advised Methodios to personally visit the Villa Tvartko. Once there, he could satisfy himself as to whether the inmates were at all mixed up in politics, and act as he deemed best for the safety of the republic. Thinking over this matter Methodios came to the conclusion that it would be as well to look into it for himself, and asked Upravado's opinion thereon. That cunning soldier laughed at the idea of a dull Englishman mixing himself up in foreign politics, and advised Methodios to call at the villa, by all means, if only to set his suspicions at rest. At the same time he warned Paradiso of the approaching visit of the president, so the consequence was that when Methodios did go to the villa everything was quite ready to deceive him.

Janshah, instructed by his master, kept a strict lookout along the high-road, and one afternoon came down to the terrace where all were seated, to announce that the president and his staff were approaching the house. At once the princess and Paradiso hurried into the house and concealed themselves from view, as it was just possible that the keen eyes of Methodios might recognize them in spite of their disguises. The remaining party, consisting of Hilda, her husband, Richborough and Measurby, seated themselves in careless attitudes on the terrace, engaged in apparently aimless conversation.

Shortly, the president arrived, as he thought unexpectedly, and hearing from Janshah that the master of the villa was on the terrace, proceeded to go there at once, so as to catch the inmates off their guard. Surrounded by a glittering staff of officers he descended the steps towards the water, and Wilfred, springing to his feet in apparent surprise, went forward to receive him.

Methodios was a tall, slim man, not unhandsome in face, though it was utterly spoiled by a crafty expression which at once betrayed the falsity of his nature. He affected considerable state, though but the president of the republic, and, with the innate love of finery possessed by all Greeks, appeared in a rich green uniform braided with gold lace. His officers were also magnificently dressed in uniform, and there was plenty of jingling swords, flashing epaulettes and plumes of feathers. To add to the incongruity of the whole affair, the president had his breast covered with orders, some bestowed on him by the late king before he had proved a traitor. The sight of these would have infuriated the princess beyond all the bounds of endurance, but fortunately she was far distant, watching these jackdaws, disguised in peacocks' feathers, from an upper window of the villa.

"Why did not your Excellency let us know you were coming?" said Wilfred, as he saluted the Greek. "Had I known of your intention to pay me a visit I would have been prepared for you."

"I preferred to come unannounced, Mr. Dacre," replied the president, letting his eyes wander over the group on the terrace.

"You speak English, I see, M. Methodios."

"I lived in London for some time, Mr. Dacre," replied the president with a smile, "and there I learned your tongue. This is the first time I have used it for many years, so you must excuse my deficiencies."

"Allow me to compliment you on your knowledge of it," said Dacre, leading Methodios down the steps to the terrace. "Will your Excellency permit me to introduce my wife?"

"Charmed, madame, to see you at Busk," observed Methodios, with a profound bow. "We have few English lady visitors."

"When your charming climate and country become better known, sir, I think you will have many visits from my countrywomen," replied Hilda, smiling.

"Your Excellency, the Duke of Richborough, Major Measurby."

"Delighted, delighted," said the president, bowing to each in turn, and vainly trying, by scanning their faces, to detect their feelings on the introduction. "You are quite an English colony here, Mr. Dacre."

"It is a pleasant way of passing the winter," said Wilfred, as the president took his seat, and his officers their station behind him. "You know from experience how terrible are the London fogs."

"So you are here on pleasure only, Mr. Dacre?"

"Of course. For what other reason could we be here? We only came to the Black Sea so as to be out of the beaten track of tourists."

"I am afraid you will find it dull."

"By no means, your Excellency," said Hilda indolently. "Varzo is the Paris of the East."

"Almost as restless, I think, madame."

"I hope your Excellency does not hint at another revolution," observed Hilda, in affected alarm. "If I thought so I would leave Varzo at once."

"Have no fear, madame. Busk is now realizing the blessings of a republican government."

"I sympathize with that form, your Excellency," said Wilfred, smiling. "You know we are a monarchy only in name."

"A republican form of government is the best of all," observed the president in a dogmatic tone. "It gives all a chance of rising in the social scale."

"So all the people of Busk, so to speak, are possible presidents."

"Exactly; and hence approve of a government which gives them a chance of political fame."

While Hilda and her husband were thus talking to the president, his officers were fraternizing with Richborough and the major. A number of servants brought down refreshments, of which all partook, and little by little the suspicions of Methodios began to disappear.

"It is only a pleasure party," he thought, scrutinizing the faces of those around. "They could not deceive *me.*"

For once Methodios was wrong, and afterwards, when it was too late, he often bitterly regretted that he had been so easily lulled by the affected carelessness of the party. At present, however, he could not connect these light-hearted English folk with any political designs, and, convinced that the suspicions of the Russian agent were groundless, his face relaxed from the slight frown it had worn when he first came.

"I trust you are pleased with the Villa Tvartko, madame," he said to Hilda, while Wilfred went to converse with the other members of the presidential party.

"I should be indeed hard to please were I not delighted, your Excellency. It is a dream of beauty."

"It was the summer residence of the Lusignan kings."

"They must have been sorry to lose it."

"Their own fault, I assure you, madame. Had

they been less tyrannical, they might still be on the throne. The world now is too enlightened to tolerate the despotism of the Middle Ages."

"But I thought that in the East — "

"This is but Eastern Europe, madame, a vast difference from the east of Asia. The Balkan states have thrown off the yoke of the Turks, and wish to have a voice in European politics. The Ottoman empire is effete, worn out; we are young and fresh, new states which are now starting into being. Islam as a power is at an end."

"Yet Stamboul is still the city of the sultan."

"But for a time," replied Methodios significantly. "Who knows but what the end of the nineteenth century may see the reconstruction of the Greek empire?"

"Or Russia in possession of Constantinople."

"Never!" exclaimed the Greek in a fiery tone. "To arrive there they must pass through Busk, through Servia, and Bulgaria, — all Christian states, which will oppose the grasping ambition of the St. Petersburg cabinet. But I weary you with politics; they are not fit for the ears of ladies. Let us talk of lighter subjects. You have seen Varzo, I trust?"

"Yes, I have visited the town several times. The cathedral is very beautiful."

"And you know his Eminence, Cardinal Gregory?"

"I visited him last week."

"He is a " — "dangerous man," Methodios was going to add, but checked himself with sudden wisdom. Despite the fact that these were merely English tourists bent on pleasure, it would not do to be too foolish.

"Do you intend to stay long here, madame?" he asked in a lighter tone.

"A few months."

"It is dull."

"Oh, not at all. We can amuse ourselves in many ways. For instance, next week I am giving a ball."

"A ball?" echoed Methodios in surprise. "And to whom?"

"Oh, to some of your nobility. We came with introductions, you know, and as I am anxious to see the national costumes and dances of Busk, I have invited several of your famous families to a ball."

"And their names?"

"Let me see," said Hilda, beginning to regret she had mentioned the ball, "your names are so hard to pronounce, — the families of Juda, Sinpian, Nemanja, and others."

"All secret royalists," thought Methodios, his suspicions beginning to revive. "Can it be that Kulsoff is right, after all?"

Meanwhile, Hilda, feeling that she had made a mistake, invited Wilfred to join her, with a look: and that this was a wise proceeding speedily appeared from the next observation of the president.

"I trust, madame, you will ask me to your ball."

Hilda, doubtful what answer to make, shot an inquiring glance at Wilfred, who at once responded to the question.

"We shall feel honoured if your Excellency will come."

"I shall only be too delighted, Mr. Dacre."

"Your Excellency should have had an invitation but that we thought you were too busily engaged in affairs of state. General Upravado is to be present."

"Upravado!" ejaculated Methodios with a start. "He did not tell me so."

"Probably he has not yet had an opportunity," replied Wilfred imperturbably, though he recognized that the suspicions of the Greek were aroused. "At all events, your Excellency will be present."

"Assuredly. I will come with my staff," said the president with emphasis. "I trust, madame, your ball will be successful."

"It cannot fail to be if your Excellency honours it with your presence," she replied with a sinking heart. "I owe you an apology for not having sent an invitation."

"By no means. Better late than never, madame. And now I am afraid I must take my leave. Adieu. I trust to renew our pleasant conversation at your ball. Mr. Dacre, will you attend me to the door?"

When the president and his party had gone, accompanied by the three gentlemen, Hilda, resuming her seat, bitterly reproached herself with having mentioned the ball. With Methodios present, the danger of a conflict would be much increased, and yet, to lull his suspicions, the only thing that could be done was to invite him to attend. She longed to see Julia and Paradiso, in order to ask their opinion about this new complication; but, with the president barely off the premises, she was forced to wait for some more fitting period.

From this reverie she was roused by a light hand on her shoulder, and on looking up saw that Julia was standing beside her in a state of suppressed excitement.

"Well, madame," inquired the princess eagerly, "what was the reason of this visit?"

Hilda arose hastily to her feet, and threw an apprehensive look in the direction of the house.

"You should not have come here so soon, madame," she said reproachfully. "Methodios may return."

"No, he has left the house, and is now on his way to Varzo. Why do you think he will return? Has he suspicions?"

"Not of the true facts of the case. But I fancy he thinks we are here with other designs than those of pleasure."

"So long as he is ignorant of my presence in Busk, it does not matter what he thinks," replied Julia contemptuously. "As things stand now, whatever his suspicions, he can take no steps. Soon it will be too late."

"He is coming to the ball," said Hilda abruptly.

"To the ball?" echoed Julia in alarm. "Surely you did not ask him to be present?"

"I was forced to do so. When he heard that his colleague, General Upravado, was to be present, he insisted on coming. I could not refuse, as his suspicions might have been aroused and he would probably have forbidden me to give the entertainment. Therefore, I had to invite him with apparent eagerness, and he is coming with his officers."

"This will somewhat complicate matters."

"So I think."

"And yet," continued the princess thoughtfully, "he is thrusting his head into the lion's mouth. The room will be filled with our supporters. The villa will be surrounded by the soldiers of Upravado, and Methodios will be caught in a trap. Yes," said Julia in a tone of lively satisfaction, "by coming to the ball he is playing blindly into our hands. As soon as the signal is given, I will order Upravado to arrest the president, and the republic, thus being without a head, will surrender to me at once."

"Do you really think that this can be done, madame?"

"I have every faith in my star," replied Julia proudly. "Methodios, by coming to this ball, is placing himself blindly in my power. The republic is doomed."

CHAPTER XXI.

NEW RINGS FOR OLD.

It would be useless to deny that Methodios was anything but satisfied in his own mind regarding the true reason of the Dacres' visit to Busk. The Russian agent had certainly hinted that they were there for a diplomatic purpose, but Methodios, having, as he thought, caught them off their guard by paying an unexpected visit, was for the moment satisfied that such fears were groundless. In his subsequent conversation with Hilda, however, the mention of the ball had again piqued his curiosity and roused his suspicions. Why should these strangers give a ball to those with whom they were entirely unacquainted? Why should they ask only royalist families to that ball, and why should they be friendly with a notorious monarchist like the cardinal, and a lukewarm republican like Upravado?

Methodios constantly asked himself these questions; but he could obtain no satisfactory answer thereto. He spoke to Upravado, and was told by that wily diplomat that he was going to the ball simply to amuse himself. From the archbishop he could learn absolutely nothing, and the royalist families gave no sign that they took any interest whatsoever in politics. Notwithstanding all this absence of proof, Methodios tortured himself unnecessarily with fancies, and then consoled his mind with the fatal reflection that Julia de Lusignan, without whom they could do nothing, was still in England.

On one point, however, he congratulated himself, and that was that he also would be present at the ball. If it were a political meeting under the guise of a festivity, he could order Upravado at once to arrest all those present, and the conspiracy, if such existed, could at once be nipped in the bud. Unfortunately for this idea, he was quite unaware that Upravado was enacting the part of a political Judas Iscariot, and betraying his country for money; otherwise he would have taken immediate steps to secure his already doubtful position. Thinking thus in this undecided manner, he neglected to assure himself of the truth of the matter, and day after day passed without anything being done, until the night of the famous ball duly arrived.

Owing to the incessant activity of the archbishop and Paradiso, all was prepared for the proclamation of the queen. The prominent nobles were advised of the time when the royal standard would be raised. Upravado had conferred secretly with his officers and found that he could depend on their fidelity, and lastly, Wilfred had been shown by Janshah that the money required for the bribing of the rebel leader was in the villa. All was going excellently, and the success of the conspiracy was looked upon as certain by all the inmates of Villa Tvartko, — with the exception of Major Measurby.

That gentleman had resolved to obtain the ring

from Wilfred on the evening of the ball by fraud, and had already arranged his plan of action. Once he was possessed of the ring, he intended to leave the villa and cross over into Bulgaria, the frontier of which was but twenty-four miles distant from Varzo. Measurby was impelled to this course by the fear that when Wilfred discovered his loss, as he would soon by Janshah refusing to obey him, he might, in a frenzy of fear, betray the secret of the ring to all, in which case, the queen, aided by Paradiso, would have little scruple in making him give it up to her. Thus all his trouble would go for nothing, and having lost the confidence of every one, he would be in a worse plight than before. If, however, he stole the ring and placed himself in safety on the other side of the frontier, he could treat with Julia de Lusignan, and dictate his own terms to that imperious lady.

Unless the money was paid to Upravado, Measurby knew that the conspiracy would fail, and if Wilfred lost the ring, Janshah would certainly refuse to hand over the gold. Things thus being in confusion, the major could step in and offer to settle all, provided the princess acceded to his terms, which, to say the least, were anything but modest. He desired to marry Julia and obtain the title of king, when, with her influence and his wealth, he could hope to make Busk one of the greatest powers of the East.

As yet all these were castles in the air, for Major Measurby was not certain whether his scheme would be entirely successful. It all depended upon Hilda, and if she failed him, the golden opportunity would be lost. The hour had not yet arrived for him to execute his purpose, and, meanwhile, so as to keep up his ordinary character of a careless spectator, he conversed gaily with Richborough.

The duke was in a very restless state of mind, as he was aware that the proclamation of Julia as queen would place her too high for him to dream of becoming her husband. As a political exile she was on an equal footing with him, and he could pay his addresses without appearing unduly presumptuous; but when she became queen of Busk he would be unable to press his suit. It was true that she had encouraged him very much and certainly appeared to love him, but at times the duke had doubts as to the reality of this affection. She might, for all he knew, be using him as a tool, and when she gained her ends would throw him on one side as useless. He had no proof that such would be the case, but yet thought it might happen. Alas! in this instance his instinct was prophetic, for Julia de Lusignan already sure of her throne, had quite forgotten that such a person as the Duke of Richborough existed.

"So the great moment approaches," said Measurby late in the afternoon, as the duke moved restlessly up and down the terrace. "Let us hope success will crown our efforts."

"There can be but little doubt on that point, Major."

"Oh, I don't know so much about that. There is many a slip 'twixt cup and lip."

"No one can be absolutely certain of the future," replied the duke quietly; "but all that human power can do has been done to make the affair a success."

"And yet, if chance intervenes —"

"All our ingenious plans will be frustrated. True; but so far as we can judge, there is absolutely no fear of failure. If we secure Upravado and arrest Methodios, the republic will be at an end."

"True," replied Measurby ironically. "If!"

"You answer as the Spartans answered Philip of Macedon. Hitherto you have been certain that all will go well; now, on the eve of fulfillment, you are doubtful."

"One is never certain till the event happens," said Measurby significantly. "Supposing the sum required by Upravado is not forthcoming."

"Oh, but it will be. I saw it myself. It is in the possession of Wilfred's factotum, Janshah, and he will pay it over to Upravado to-night."

"Let us hope so. If such is the case, of course Julia will be proclaimed queen, and you, Duke —"

"I don't understand you, Major Measurby."

"Pardon! I did not mean to appear rude, but I can hardly fail to see how attentive you are to Madame de Lusignan."

"I admire her for the heroism of her nature."

"So do I," rejoined Measurby promptly. "She will make a good sovereign. Hard, cold, masterful, and crafty, she has all the qualifications of a female ruler."

"Do you, indeed, think she is so lacking in femininity?" asked the duke with a sudden flush.

Major Measurby answered the question indirectly.

"Julia de Lusignan aspires to be a great sovereign, and to be so must be a woman with a man's heart. Those female rulers who have lacked the weaknesses of their sex alone have been great."

"She will sacrifice love to ambition," murmured the duke, half to himself.

"She has already done so," replied Measurby, overhearing the remark. "She will marry for ambition, for political purposes, to perpetuate the dynasty of her house, but not for love."

Richborough did not pursue the subject. He felt in his own heart that the view taken by Measurby was a correct one, and that it was useless for him to expect the princess to return his passion; nevertheless, he did not care about discussing this delicate subject with the major, as he had no particular liking for that gentleman, and looked upon his passion as too sacred a thing to be lightly spoken of. To avoid further remarks on the subject he walked to the other end of the terrace, and when he returned to the major found him talking to Paradiso.

The marquess was in high glee, as everything was going excellently well, and he hoped that Julia de Lusignan would that night sleep in the palace of her ancestors.

"There is absolutely no possibility of failure," he said decisively. "Our plans are too well laid to fail."

"Yet it all depends upon Upravado," hinted the major quietly.

"To a considerable extent it does. But he is faithful. Provided he receives the money as has been arranged, he will support the queen to the end."

"I should not be inclined to put much faith in a traitor who sells his country for money," said the duke bitterly.

Paradiso shot a keen glance at the sombre face of the young man, and answered with apparent lightness, but deep significance, —

"You know the motto of the Jesuits, monseigneur, 'The end justifies the means.' That saying is true, both in the case of Upravado and ourselves. He wishes to make himself safe by getting this money, for, faithless himself, he does not trust others. We see in him the only person who can successfully carry out our plans, because he commands the army of Busk. When the queen is firmly established, however, Upravado will not find himself so high in favour as he anticipates."

"In that case, it seems to me he only did right to assure himself of something by asking for money," said the major, smiling.

"It is on that very account that he will lose all political status," replied Paradiso with emphasis. "He distrusts the gratitude of the queen, and shows it by asking for a certainty. You can hardly wonder that she feels somewhat sore at having to buy his services. By accepting money he has placed himself without the pale. Others will be rewarded for aiding the royal cause, but not Upravado, — he will receive his reward to-night in hard cash."

"Let us hope for his sake and for your own that the money will be paid."

"I have no fear of that," replied Paradiso gaily. "It is now in the villa under the care of Janshah. When M. Dacre bids him pay it over to Upravado, he will do so."

"Where is Mr. Dacre now?" asked the major, rising, with an inquiring look on his crafty face.

"Inside the house completing all arrangements for to-night."

"And his wife?"

"Is with him."

"I think I'll go in and have a talk with them," said Measurby, foreseeing a chance of carrying out his plans. "I wish to know precisely what I am to do to-night."

He walked up the steps, and Paradiso looked after him with a doubtful smile. "I don't like that man," he said abruptly to the duke.

"Why not?"

"He is of the same stamp as Upravado, and would sacrifice us all to obtain his own ends."

"I agree with you there, but, unlike Upravado, he is not important enough to give us any trouble."

"At such a crisis as this the least thing may prove fatal," replied Paradiso with emphasis. "I distrust the tone of Measurby's conversation, and will carefully watch his actions to-night."

"He is quite safe."

"I doubt it."

The object of this conversation had now reached the great hall in which the ball was to take place, and found Wilfred talking in an animated manner to his wife.

"All is ready, Major," called out Wilfred as Measurby advanced towards them. "Not a thing has been neglected."

"Then we can count on a triumph."

"It is certain," said Hilda, confidently. "All our troubles will soon be over, and we, instead of being political conspirators, will be the favoured guests of Queen Julia of Busk."

"Where is the queen now?"

"She is up-stairs, lying down," observed Wilfred quickly. "She has a difficult part to play to-night, and requires all her strength."

"You look a trifle exhausted yourself, Dacre," said Measurby with feigned anxiety.

"I *am* tired," admitted Wilfred frankly. "The incessant strain of the last few weeks is beginning to tell on me. I feel inclined to lie down. But look at Hilda; she feels no fatigue."

"I expect I shall break down when all is over," replied Hilda with a smile. "At present my courage is screwed up to the sticking point, and I am too excited to feel weary. But you, Wilfred, seem to be completely worn out. Go up to your room and lie down."

"Or lie down here," suggested Measurby, pointing to the divan running round the hall.

"A good idea," said Dacre, throwing himself on the cushions. "I will snatch forty winks."

"Wait a minute, before you close your eyes, Dacre. Tell me of the arrangements to-night."

"Well, all those people we have invited are coming, including Upravado, Methodios, and possibly the archbishop. When Upravado arrives, I will take him into another room and make Janshah pay over the money. Then the queen will be proclaimed and Methodios arrested. Afterwards we will march to Varzo, where the soldiers of Upravado will rise in our favour. Holding the city all will go well, and to-morrow the provinces, as arranged, will send in their submission to the monarchy."

"It is a splendid scheme if it comes off," said Measurby quietly. "But in the event of failure?"

"We cannot fail," said Hilda indignantly. "How can you think of such a thing, Major Measurby?"

"It is always best to be prepared for contingencies."

"If we do fail," said Wilfred quickly, "which I don't think for a moment will be the case, there is the yacht yonder ready to start at any moment, and a boat at the terrace steps; in the stables eight horses are already saddled. So that the princess can escape either across the frontier to Bulgaria, or to Constantinople by the yacht. But don't be afraid, Major; neither of these means of escape will be required. We shall succeed."

"I hope so," replied Measurby with emphasis, and turned away with Hilda; while Wilfred, closing his eyes, soon fell into a deep sleep. Having been up late the previous night, and on his feet since early morning, busy with matters political and otherwise, he was fairly worn out. This exhaustion accounted for his profound slumber, from which nothing could rouse him, not even the voices of Hilda and the major as they walked up and down the hall talking of the coming crisis.

"I was quite alarmed when Methodios insisted on coming to the ball," said Hilda vivaciously. "But now I see it is the best thing that could have happened. With the exception of his personal attendants, all present will be devoted to the royal cause. He can easily be arrested, and deprived of its head the republic will fall."

"Unless some one of equal ability can take the place of the president."

"There is no one of equal ability," replied Hilda decisively. "The marquess told me all about it. Culin, Geiza, and the others are born to serve, not to command. Had it not been for Methodios there would have been no republic. He is a master spirit. Without him the present government cannot exist."

"That is bad — for the republicans."

"And excellent — for us. We have with us Paradiso, one of the cleverest men in Europe; Cardinal Gregory, whose diplomatic talents are celebrated; Upravado, who is nearly equal to Methodios in brain power; last, but not least, we have the queen, who is a host in herself."

"A combination of all the talents," said Measurby sarcastically: "yet this galaxy of diplomatic stars can do nothing unless Upravado consents to be bribed."

"He has consented."

"And the money?"

"Is in the possession of Janshah, — two hundred thousand francs in gold."

"By the way, Mrs. Dacre, who is Janshah?" asked the major in an inquiring tone.

"He was the factotum of Wilfred's uncle, and now he looks after all our affairs."

"Does Wilfred trust him?"

"Implicitly. He manages everything. All moneys are in his possession. Personally, I do not like him, but he seems to be a strictly honest man."

While she spoke, they had moved near Wilfred, and the major saw on the hand which hung over the side of the divan the famous ring which he so much desired to possess. Fortune had favoured his plans up to the present, so he slipped the false ring on his own finger and waited for an opportunity to introduce it to the notice of Hilda.

"How weary your husband looks," he said artfully.

"Yes. He is not strong, and has been working very hard."

The major threw a cloak over Wilfred's form, and pretended suddenly to notice the ring.

"That is very strange," he said in a puzzled tone.

"What is strange?" asked Hilda, coming close to the major.

"Your husband possesses a ring similar to the one I wear," replied the major, stretching out his hand.

Hilda looked at the jewel, and also started.

"How very extraordinary!" she said vivaciously. "Why, Wilfred told me that his ring was the only one of its kind in existence. It cannot possibly be the same."

"Let us compare the two rings," observed the major with affected carelessness.

"We might wake Wilfred."

"I don't think so. He seems to sleep very soundly."

"Your ring also has an inscription."

"Yes. I should like to see if his has the same."

"I am afraid Wilfred will not like my taking his ring off his finger," said Hilda, hesitating; "he seems to attach great value to it."

"Well, there is no chance of its getting lost," replied Measurby, smiling; "all you have to do is to take it off and compare it with this, then put it on his finger again."

"I must confess that I am curious to see if the rings *are* alike. Can you read Sanscrit, Major?"

"Yes. I learned somewhat of it in India."

"Well, Wilfred's ring has an inscription on it in that language, and he will never tell me what it means."

"And you would like to know?"

Hilda shrugged her shoulders.

"I am a woman, and therefore curious."

"The inscription on my ring," said the major, taking it off and handing it to her, "means 'Fate will guide thee,' but I don't suppose for a moment that your husband's will be the same."

"Let us see," replied Hilda. And not thinking

for a moment that she was doing wrong, she gently slipped the famous ring off Wilfred's finger. So profoundly did he sleep that he did not feel the movement, the more so as the circle of the ring was slightly large for his finger, and therefore easily removed.

Measurby trembled with delight when he saw the celebrated jewel away from the possession of its master. So far his scheme had succeeded, but all danger would not be past until he had changed the rings and placed the false one on Dacre's finger.

"They seem precisely similar," said Hilda, comparing the two jewels; "both blue stones set in gold, with Sanscrit inscriptions."

"But do they mean the same thing?" asked the major, coming close to her. "Allow me,—" and he took both the rings from her. "No, my ring reads 'Fate will guide thee,' and your husband's 'Brahma wills it.'"

In order to know which was the false ring, Measurby had made a mark on the gold circle of his own; so he was easily able to decide which was the ring to keep. Not so Hilda.

"I declare, they look to me precisely similar," she said, looking intently at both rings in the major's hand.

"To you they appear so," replied Measurby, "because the stones and setting are the same in all respects; but I can tell the difference by the inscription. This one," he added, handing her the false ring, "is your husband's, with the inscription 'Brahma wills it'; the other is mine."

He slipped the real ring, which commanded the treasures, on to his finger, and drew a sigh of relief. The jewel he had so much coveted was at last his own, and nothing now remained to do but to get Hilda to slip the false ring on Wilfred's finger. Only Janshah could tell the real from the false, and Wilfred would never know that he had lost his talisman till informed by the Indian.

"It is a quaint ring," said Hilda, quite unaware of the dexterous change effected by the major. "I suppose I had better put it on Wilfred's finger again, as he seems to value it so highly."

She bent down over her still sleeping husband and slipped the false ring on his finger, quite unaware that her curiosity had cost Wilfred his fortune, and Julia her crown. The major felt inclined to give a shout of joy when this last feat was achieved. He possessed the real ring, Wilfred the false, and before the substitution could be detected he hoped to be safely across the Bulgarian frontier.

"I must tell Wilfred about your ring," observed Hilda, when all this was over; "he will be surprised."

"Wake him now and tell him," said Measurby, with a master stroke of daring.

"No. He is too tired. I will tell him to-morrow, for to-night he will be too busy to think of anything but the success of the conspiracy."

"You look tired yourself, Mrs. Dacre," said the major, in a tender tone. "You also require rest."

"Yes, I think I will lie down for a time. And you, Major?"

"Oh, I will go to the stables to see that the horses are all right in case they are required."

"I have no fear on that score," replied Hilda, laughing, as the major took his leave.

"One never knows what may happen," answered Measurby with a faint sneer, and left the hall with his booty.

At last he was the master of the ring, and commanded twenty millions of money! He felt inclined to proclaim his good fortune aloud, but fortunately restrained himself, and went in search of Janshah. His plans were already formed, and he intended to cross the frontier at once in order to treat with Julia from the safe refuge of Bulgaria. As to the troubles in which Wilfred would be shortly involved, Measurby never gave them a thought. His own safety, his own aggrandizement, was all he sought, and the ring would give him both.

"Janshah," he said in an imperious tone, holding out his hand, "obey the ring!"

The Indian started when he saw the fatal talisman on the hand of Major Measurby, and he examined it closely. By means of the secret mark known only to himself, he saw that the major was now his master; so, bowing low, he professed himself ready to obey his commands. He never asked the major how he had obtained the talisman. Wilfred was now nothing to him, Measurby everything, and in one moment Janshah, influenced by the power of the ring, had transferred his treasure, his fidelity, his genius for intrigue, to his former master's bitterest enemy.

"You will not pay that money to Upravado," said Measurby, in a low voice. "When the time comes for it to be paid, tell Mr. Dacre that I am now the master of the ring. Then leave the Villa Tvartko and all within to their fate, and meet me on the frontier of Bulgaria near the main road. Bring the gold with you."

"My lord will be obeyed," said Janshah, with a profound obeisance.

"I am going to cross the frontier now. Remember, not a word of this until the gold is to be paid: then tell all."

Janshah made another prostration, and the major took his departure. Within ten minutes he was spurring along the main road in the direction of Bulgaria.

And Wilfred?

He awoke without a thought of his loss, and according to his custom looked at the ring. It was still, as he deemed, on his finger, and, not thinking any more about it, he left the hall to dress for the evening.

Had he only known that his kingdom had departed from him and that the cause of Julia was already lost!

CHAPTER XXII.

THE STORM BREAKS.

The Villa Tvartko was ablaze with light, and crowded with the aristocracy of Varzo, many of whom were in the secret of the proposed restoration of the monarchy. The great hall presented a scene of wondrous splendour. Illuminated by innumerable lamps, the honeycombed roof gleamed with decorations of scarlet and gold; the rich curtains draping the walls glowed with vivid colours, and amid the barbaric pomp moved a brilliant throng of dancers. On one side of the hall were narrow windows filled with painted glass, behind which lamps were placed so that fantastic shadows of myriad hues were thrown upon the white marble pavement. On the other, a long range of horseshoe arches supported on slender twisted pillars opened out on to the terrace, which was wreathed with innumerable fairy lamps. Here and there in secluded corners, braziers of fires breathed rich perfumes, and everywhere the sumptuous hall was adorned with flowers and foliage of a tropic brightness.

Within, all was dazzling with light, colour, and fantasy; without, the still cool night, brilliant with stars, chill with moonlight, formed in its immutable serenity a wonderful contrast to the restless festival.

The garden twinkled with many coloured lights which burned like fireflies amid the surrounding trees, and from the verge of the white terrace stretched the still waters glistening like silver under the beams of the moon. A wind laden with perfume was wafted from the shore, and between the bursts of music sounding at intervals from the villa could be heard the sobbing of the waters lapping the marble steps of the terrace. All that unlimited money and perfect taste could do to make the scene splendid had been done by Janshah, and with its mixture of East and West, its strange barbaric pomps and mediæval fantasies, the festival was not unworthy of the palmy days of the caliphate.

All the partisans of the princess were present save the archbishop, who deemed it politic to play a minor part in the revolution until such time as the restoration of the monarchy was an accomplished fact. He had impressed this view of things on Julia, so as to secure her an asylum in his house, should the conspiracy fail. Neither princess nor priest thought for a moment that it would fail; still, as Gregory very sensibly said, it was as well to be prepared for all fortunes, and thus in the event of their plans being upset she could fly to his house, there to be concealed until such time as she could escape across the frontier. Methodios would not for a moment think that the cardinal had been engaged in the plot, as he would have no proof that such was the case; therefore the palace of the wily prelate would be a safe retreat for the fugitives. Under these circumstances the archbishop was not present, but waited with impatience at his palace in Varzo for the shouts that would announce that Queen Julia was entering the capital in triumph.

With the exception of the astute priest, all those concerned in the plot were present. At least such was the opinion of Wilfred, who never noticed the absence of Major Measurby. So crowded was the hall and so busy was he in engaging the attention of Methodios, that he had no time to think of anything else. As yet Janshah had not informed him of the exchange of rings, and he was still ignorant of the loss he had sustained. By this time Measurby was over the frontier awaiting the arrival of Janshah, and at the Villa Tvartko his victims were innocently rushing on to their doom.

Methodios had duly arrived with his brilliant staff and had found the hall filled with the nobility of Busk. Handsome men, beautiful women were present, engaged in harmless pleasure; but Methodios, with all his cleverness, never for an instant guessed that this frivolous mask concealed a design against his safety and that of the republic. Upravado was there, apparently enjoying himself without a thought; but the villa was surrounded by his soldiers, his officers had their orders, and Methodios, in blind security, was caught in a trap. On a given signal, Julia, whom he thought was in England, would appear; he would be arrested by those whom he deemed his supporters, and in the twinkling of an eye the republic would cease to exist. The whole air was full of revolution, of danger, and perhaps of death, but he did not know it.

If, however, Methodios was ignorant of his danger, the royalists were equally in the dark concerning their fate. They knew not that the die was cast, and that the conspiracy was at an end; so both parties, amid the splendours of the festival, went blindly on the path of disaster. It was the irony of Fate that such should be the case, and all the lighthearted guests in that sumptuous hall would have recoiled aghast had they seen how terribly would end the night of pleasure.

Hilda was very much disappointed with the aspect of the dancers. She had expected to see national costumes, national dances: instead of which, the men were all in uniform and the ladies in brilliant Parisian toilets, while the dances were those of the West. None of the provincial supporters of Julia were present, else the scene might have assumed a more national character, but these were the inhabitants of Varzo, and the city prided itself in being an exact copy of Paris. Everything savouring of the East was voted barbarous by the fashionable people of Varzo, and in dress, manners, customs, and social forms they aped Paris as closely as they were able. But for the Saracenic decorations of the hall, and the wonderful scene outside, one would have taken the ball for a fashionable dance of the London season, or a festival on the banks of the Seine. Hilda had seen both, and, desiring to behold something more, was much disappointed at the extremely conventional character of the whole scene.

"You are not at all national," she said to Methodios, as they stood on a dais erected for the president at one end of the hall.

"Publicly, yes; socially, no," replied the Greek, shrugging his shoulders. "Eh, madame, what would you? The fashions of Paris are better suited to our modern life than the antique modes of the Orient. We desire to be equal to the West in all things."

"Still, I think that every nation should retain its national characteristics."

"I agree with you to a considerable extent," replied Methodios quietly. "We should copy the virtues of the West, and not its vices. To my mind it would be much better for our nobility to cling to their national costume; but, as you see, their vanity bids them to copy Paris and London fashions. But then the taste of these cities rules the world. All national costumes are rapidly disappearing, and in a very short space of time the world's inhabitants will resemble one another like peas in a pod."

"It's a great pity, your Excellency," said Hilda pensively. "I love to see the manners and customs of other nations; but as you say, they all copy one another, — at least in Europe. But the East never changes. At least so I have always understood."

"This is not the East," answered Methodios pointedly; "it is Eastern Europe, as I told you before. Cross the Bosphorus and you get into the old-world life; but not here."

"Have you no national dances?"

"Oh, yes. For instance, there is the kardatz, which is very pretty and characteristic of the Croatian nation. But you see the fashionable people of Varzo prefer the cotillion, in which they can deck themselves out with ribbons and jingling ornaments."

"It is a dance about which I do not in the least care," said Hilda, taking the arm of the president. "The figures are so complicated as to be quite confusing. Let us go out on the terrace, your Excellency."

Methodios readily assented, and they passed outside. It was a perfect night, and after the heated atmosphere of the ballroom, the air was wonderfully cool and refreshing. In the east, low on the horizon, burned the round of the moon, throwing a trail of silver across the waters. In the midst of that shaft of light appeared the black outline of the yacht.

"That belongs to Monsieur Dacre, does it not?" asked Methodios abruptly.

"Yes. We often cruise about the Black Sea. Some day we hope that your Excellency will accompany us."

"I am afraid I cannot get away. At the present juncture of affairs, I must be always on the spot."

"Why, is anything likely to occur, dangerous to the republic?" asked Hilda nervously.

"Oh, no. All is quiet, but the ruler of a restless people like that of Busk must always be prepared for the unforeseen. I mistrust Julia de Lusignan and her machinations."

Hilda turned cold with fear, thinking that he must have learned something of the conspiracy, but his next words reassured her.

"Fortunately, however, she is in England; and without her being personally present, the discontented royalists of Busk can do nothing."

Had he only known that the princess was in Busk,

was in that house, that the yacht yonder was waiting to bear her to safety should a daring scheme fail! But he knew none of these things, and, unaware of the danger of the moment, he talked of it as though it were far away, and he yet had time to meet and baffle it.

All this time Paradiso and the princess had remained in their own rooms, preparing for the decisive moment. The latter had taken off her disguise, and was now arrayed in a splendid costume, ready to be presented to her faithful subjects by Upravado. Paradiso, also, had assumed his uniform as captain of the royal guard, which post he had held under the late king. Both of them were in a state of suppressed excitement, for in another hour they would either be rulers of Busk, or fugitives, exposed to the vengeance of Methodios.

Everything was now ready for the proclamation of the queen, save the payment of the money to Upravado; but until that was accomplished, nothing could be deemed certain. It was now nine o'clock, and the great event of the night was arranged to take place at ten; so there was no time to be lost. Wilfred went in search of Upravado to take him into another room and pay him the price of his treachery.

While seeking the general he met Hilda, who had left Methodios, and was now leaning on the arm of her cousin, the duke.

"Wilfred," asked the latter suddenly, "where is Major Measurby?"

"In the room, I suppose."

"No, he is not here. I have searched everywhere for him."

"Have you seen him, Hilda?" asked Wilfred carelessly.

"No, not since five o'clock. We were speaking together when you fell asleep, and afterwards he left me to go to the stables."

"To the stables?" repeated Wilfred, with a start. "Why did he go there?"

"To see that the horses were all saddled and ready in case of need."

"The major seems to quite anticipate failure," observed Richborough disdainfully: "if we were all as chicken-hearted, I am afraid Julia would never get her throne again."

"Hush!" said Wilfred, casting a hurried glance around; "you may be overheard. It is strange the major is absent. I wonder what it means. Did he say anything to you, Hilda, about not being present?"

"Not a word," answered his wife carelessly; "we were talking about your ring."

"My ring!" echoed Wilfred, turning pale. "Good heavens!"

He looked at the ring on his finger, but could see no difference. It seemed to be the one he always wore. Yet the major had spoken of the ring to Hilda while he was asleep, and now the major had vanished. His old distrust of Measurby revived rapidly, and he was so alarmed that he could hardly ask Hilda a question, the answer to which he dreaded.

"What did Measurby say about my ring?"

"Dear me, Wilfred, how disturbed you look!" replied Hilda in an astonished tone. "I assure you there is nothing to be alarmed about. Major Measurby has a ring similar to yours."

"Similar to mine!"

"Yes! Except that the inscription is different."

"How do you know that?" asked Wilfred in a hoarse voice, looking again at the ring.

"Because the major read them both."

"But he could not do so; my ring was on my finger."

"Oh! I took it off for a few minutes," said Hilda smiling.

"Had the major my ring in his hand?"

"For two minutes only. Heavens! Wilfred, don't make such a fuss about the ring. I placed it on your finger again."

"I hope to heavens you did," replied her husband vehemently; "but if the major changed the rings, I am lost, — all is lost."

"What do you mean?" asked Richborough and Hilda in alarm.

"I cannot tell you now. The major is a traitor. If he has acted as I suspect, our lives are not safe. I must make sure. Oh! Hilda, why did you touch my ring?"

"I did not know — " began Hilda, astonished at the vehemence of her husband, when he interrupted her quickly.

"Go back to Methodios and keep him in conversation. Richborough, take her to the president, and then join myself and Upravado in the red chamber. Where is Janshah? I must see him at once."

He rushed away in search of the Indian, with an expression of horror on his face, and Hilda looked at Richborough in surprise. They were both pale, moved by a vague fear of which they knew not the cause.

"What does he mean?" asked Hilda in a low whisper.

"I don't know," answered Richborough, considerably astonished. "However, there is no doubt that something is wrong. Let me take you to the president, Hilda, and then I will go and see what is the matter."

Methodios, who was much impressed by the beauty of Hilda, had missed her greatly, and his mobile face looked sombre as he stood on the dais gazing at the throng of whirling dancers. It brightened, however, as his hostess approached, leaning on the arm of Richborough.

"I have come to ask your Excellency to take me into the supper-room," said Hilda, who was quite unnerved by Wilfred's strange conduct.

"You look pale," said Methodios, giving her his arm.

"The heat of the room," answered Hilda faintly; "but a glass of wine will do me good. Gerald! where are you going?"

"I am going to dance," said Richborough, with an affected laugh, "and will see you again shortly."

Hilda and the president moved off in the direction of the supper-room, and Richborough, trying to control his agitation, slipped out of the hall without being noticed. In a few minutes he gained the red chamber, where he found Upravado, Paradiso, Julia and Wilfred. The latter looked pale and ill, so much so that Richborough walked across to him at once without taking notice of the others.

"Great heavens! man, what is the matter?" he whispered, harshly seizing his arm.

"I fear everything is lost," muttered Wilfred, wiping his pale lips; "but I cannot be certain until I see Janshah."

"He will be here in a moment," said Paradiso, who had caught the name; "then all will be right."

"Or wrong," said Wilfred under his breath. "Good heavens! I am lost! We are all lost!"

He devoured the ring on his finger with his eyes to see if there was any difference in its appearance. But Measurby had obtained an exact facsimile of the ring of Brahma, and no one could tell the difference but Janshah.

"Will all go well?" asked Julia of Upravado in an agitated whisper.

"Yes! The villa is surrounded by my troops. The hall is filled with your supporters, and as soon as this money is found I will proclaim you queen."

"Why can you not trust to my gratitude?" said Julia with a reproachful glance.

"Royal people have short memories," replied Upravado dryly. "Once you are firmly established on the throne, you might forget this moment. In the money I at least have a certainty."

"I will never forget this moment," answered the

princess with terrible emphasis; and indeed Upravado found out to his cost that such was the case.

At this moment Janshah appeared on the threshold of the door, but he did not enter the room. Wilfred, clinging to Richborough's arm, hardly able to stand, stretched out his hand in the direction of Janshah.

"I command you to pay General Upravado the sum of two hundred thousand francs."

"My lord, I cannot do so."

"Hah!" cried Julia fiercely; and her ejaculation was echoed by all present. Richborough looked at Wilfred and saw that a look of despair was stamped on his face.

"By the ring I command you," he said to Janshah, advancing towards the door.

"That is a false ring!"

"I knew it," murmured Wilfred in despair. "We are lost!"

"The real ring of Brahma," said Janshah in a deliberate voice, "is now in the possession of Major Measurby. He is my lord and master. Him do I obey. He is ruler of the treasure, and you are a beggar."

The next moment he had vanished, and all present, thunderstruck with amazement, looked to Wilfred for an explanation of the strange speech of the Indian.

"What does this mean, Monsieur Dacre?" asked Julia imperiously.

"It means that I cannot fulfil my promise," said Wilfred madly. "I have been deceived by a traitor; I can help you no more."

"My money!" cried Upravado, while Julia recoiled in horror from the young man; "pay me my money."

"I cannot! I am a beggar."

"Wilfred! Wilfred! What does this mean?" cried Richborough, advancing towards his friend.

"I cannot tell you now. I will shortly. I have done all I could to help you, but now I am powerless."

Upravado made a step forward, but, waving him back, Wilfred rushed out of the room to seek his wife, and if possible save her in the tumult he knew must ensue.

"Traitor!" cried Julia fiercely. "Traitor! But all is not yet lost. General Upravado, you will still be true to your rightful queen?"

"No!" said the general in a loud tone. "I have been tricked and betrayed. I was right not to trust you. If I placed you on the throne you would give me nothing."

"I swear —"

"No need to promise more, madame," said Upravado contemptuously. "I do not believe you. I agreed to help you if I received a certain sum. It has not been paid, so I am released from the oath I took to the cardinal."

"What would you do?" asked Paradiso, who had turned ghastly pale.

"Arrest Julia de Lusignan as a traitress to the republic."

"No! No! I will die sooner than yield," shrieked the princess, her eyes flashing fire; "all is not yet lost. Within these walls are my supporters."

"And around these walls are my soldiers. Yield, madame!"

Paradiso caught Upravado by the arm, but he broke away and dashed forward to seize the princess. In a second she had wrenched open the door and was running towards the ballroom, shrieking loudly for help.

Paradiso and Richborough both drew their swords, but with a sudden movement Upravado avoided them, and dashed after Julia.

"Treason! Treason!" he cried loudly. "Methodios! Culin! the republic is in danger!"

"We must save the princess," cried Richborough.

"Or die," replied Paradiso with an oath.

The two men sprang out of the room, and hastened to the ballroom, whence shrieks of alarm and the hubbub of a disturbance were already sounding. High above all the tumult sounded the voice of Methodios, sharp with alarm and terror.

"Seize Julia de Lusignan!"

CHAPTER XXIII.

SAUVE QUI PEUT.

The ball-room was a scene of the wildest confusion. Always on the alert, Methodios was the first person to overhear the cry of treason raised by Upravado, and, leaving Hilda in the midst of the dancers, he sprang back to the dais. Astonished at this action, the guests looked at one another in mute amazement, and the whole throng paused in the dance, as though converted by some spell into statues of stone. The musicians themselves, startled by this sudden pause, ceased to play, and at that moment the princess Julia dashed into the room, followed by Upravado. At her appearance the assembled guests burst out into a storm of cheers, which struck terror into the soul of Methodios.

"Treason! Treason!" he cried, shrinking back on the dais. "Arrest Julia de Lusignan!"

"Who love their rightful sovereign, aid her!" cried the princess wildly, and in response to her invitation, a number of the guests rallied to her side. The officers of Methodios formed a ring round their master, and some guests paused irresolutely, not knowing for the moment which side to take. For a second there was silence, and then a tumult began in which all joined. The women, among whom was

Hilda, fled in dismay from that splendid hall, which seemed about to become a shambles. Summoned by the stentorian voice of their leader, the soldiers of Upravado were pouring into the room, not as was arranged, to hail Julia as queen of Busk, but to arrest her as an enemy of the republic. In despair at the failure of the conspiracy, the partisans of Julia drew their swords and prepared to defend their royal mistress.

Methodios, who never pretended to physical courage, was as white as paper, scarcely able to grasp his sword with a trembling hand, and did nothing but cry shrilly that the princess must be arrested.

"The republic is in danger," he cried, frantic with alarm. "Soldiers, do your duty! Beat down their swords! Kill them! Arrest Julia de Lusignan!"

Upravado and his troops obeyed this command at once, but were met by the royalists with undaunted valour. The swords of the combatants clashed together. Cries, oaths, appeals for help, were heard, and then a deadly fusillade was poured into the royalists' ranks by the attacking party.

Richborough and Paradiso had both rushed into the ball-room in order to save the princess if possible. She was standing in the centre of her friends, with a revolver grasped in her hand. If she died, she would die like a queen, but yield, — never.

The fighting was no child's play, but in grim earnest. The ball-room, lately so gay and brilliant, was now misty with gunpowder smoke, and strewn with dead and dying men. The rich hangings were torn from the walls, the floor was slippery with blood, and with grim determination not to yield, the brave little band of royalists were fighting for their queen, their country, their lives.

Frantic with alarm for his wife, Wilfred had hurried at once to the ball-room, on the failure of the interview with Upravado, but in the confusion he was unable to find her. At the first cry of Methodios she had known that all was at an end, and had doubtless gone to find her husband. Surrounded as was the villa by soldiers, she could not possibly escape, and Wilfred hurried from room to room, seeking her, with a sickening feeling of dread lest he should find her a corpse on the floor. Assaulted by some rude soldiers, struck by some spent ball, or arrested by an emissary of Methodios, he feared that she was lost. Careless of his own life, he rushed away in pursuit. Richborough caught his arm.

"Wilfred! Wilfred! Where is Hilda?"

"I am looking for her. Save the princess, Richborough! The yacht! The yacht!"

Before the duke could reply, he had dashed out of the ball-room with a sword which he had snatched from a trophy of arms standing by one of the pillars.

"Hilda! Hilda! Hilda! Where are you?"

There was no answer, and with a cry of despair, he cut down a soldier who opposed his progress, and sprang upstairs. When nearly at the top he met Nicolas, who was there that night in place of his master.

"Madame! — my wife!" gasped Wilfred quickly, — "where is she?"

"In that room. I will save her," rejoined Nicolas rapidly. "She will not come down."

"Hilda!" cried Wilfred, and dashed into the room, only to find his wife standing by the open window.

"If you come near me, I will throw myself down," she cried, distraught with terror, thinking it was some ruffian.

"Hilda, it is I, — Wilfred," he cried, springing forward.

"Oh, you are safe! safe! Thank God! O Wilfred, how terrible this is!"

"Come! Come with me! There is not a minute to lose. Nicolas will save us."

"The princess!"

"Richborough is beside her. They will escape by the yacht. We will go to the stables."

"Whither?"

"To the house of the cardinal. Quick! Quick! But that dress — You will be recognized! Here, put this on."

It was a black cloak, which he picked up off the floor and hastily flung over her shoulders. Then, taking her by the arm, he hurried her from the room.

"Courage, my dear, courage. I will save you yet. Nicolas!"

"Here, monsieur. Come with me, quick, to the palace of the cardinal."

"Can you save madame?"

"And you also, Wilfred."

"For myself I care not," he answered recklessly.

as Nicolas led them down the stairs. "I am lost, dishonoured. I have failed the princess at the eleventh hour."

"Owing to the loss of the ring?"

"Yes. It was as I suspected. Major Measurby exchanged the rings, and instead of commanding twenty millions of money, I am now a pauper, — a dishonoured pauper."

"Oh, why did you not confide the secret to me?" cried Hilda, pressing his arm convulsively. "I would not have touched the ring."

"Hush! this is no time for reproaches. I must save your life."

"Wilfred —"

"Not a word!"

They were escaping to the stables by a back way, not guarded by the troops of the republic. Nicolas wished to save the princess, by taking her to the house of Cardinal Gregory, but when told by Wilfred that she was looked after by Paradiso and Richborough, he professed himself satisfied.

"They will not fail her," he observed in a whisper as they moved stealthily towards the stables. "How will she fly?"

"The yacht," replied Dacre in the same tone. "Once on board and they will be quite safe."

"Thank Heaven! I would never dare to face my master were harm to come to the princess."

They could hear the tumult within, the sound of firing, the ring of steel, and the shouts of the royalists mingling with the cries of the soldiery. The stables were in complete darkness, as, with a view to keep the presence of the saddled steeds secret, the lamps had not been lighted. Wilfred had the key of the door, and immediately opened it. Within, there was a dim light, which enabled them to see the horses already waiting for their riders. Two of them had side-saddles, for, in the event of escape by the yacht being impracticable, Wilfred had been mindful of his wife's safety, as well as that of Julia.

Hilda was trembling convulsively, but, having a brave spirit of her own, bore up wonderfully through the ordeal. An avenue of cypress trees led by a side path to the main road, on to which a gate opened, so that once, outside, they could escape the soldiers of Methodios and make at once for Varzo, four miles away.

Placing his wife on one of the horses, Wilfred led it in silence down the path, followed by Nicolas, who was mounted on another. Notwithstanding Hilda's vehement protestations that she would not go to Varzo without Wilfred, he absolutely refused to seize the chance of escape.

"I am dishonoured in my own eyes and in those of the princess," he said obstinately, as he opened the gate. "I must go back to the villa and see that she is safe. If so, I will join you at the cardinal's palace."

"And if not — "

"If not, I will surrender myself prisoner with her."

"There will be no chance of her being taken prisoner," said Nicolas rapidly. "The queen will never surrender."

"Off! Off!" cried Wilfred impatiently. "There is not a moment to be lost."

"But Wilfred! Wilfred," said Hilda in a tone of anguish, "you will be killed. I shall never see you again."

Wilfred gently released his hands from her grasp, and kissed them as he settled her in the saddle.

"I must stay, Hilda. I would be a coward to leave the princess now. Good-by, darling. I hope to rejoin you soon."

Again Hilda protested, but Nicolas, impatient of delay, and dreading lest they should be surprised by the soldiers, seized the bridle of her horse, and, urging his own to a trot, went away in the darkness. Wilfred stood for a moment watching them disappear, and the last sound borne to his ear was the cry of his unhappy wife. Then he returned to the villa to face disgrace, imprisonment, perhaps death.

All was still and quiet in the stable yard, as, protected by its high cypress trees, it had escaped the notice of the soldiers. He entered by the back passage and rapidly regained the front of the house. Most of the fighting was taking place in the great hall, and as Wilfred forced his way through the passages, he was stopped on all hands by the soldiers of Upravado. Fortunately, however, the royalists were a strong party, and the republicans found themselves equally matched in many ways.

Methodios, to secure his own safety and that of the republic, was now leaving the villa for Varzo, in order to send on reinforcements to the scene of the conflict. Wilfred dreaded lest the president should overtake Hilda and her escort, but as the latter were well mounted, he hoped that they would reach Varzo and be safe in the cardinal's palace before any news of the conspiracy reached the capital.

By this time he trusted that Julia would have escaped in the yacht, with Paradiso and the duke, but to his dismay, on reaching the hall, he saw that she was still there surrounded by her friends. The fact was that Methodios had overheard the allusion to the yacht, and seeing in a moment that the boat was to be used as a means of flight, had sent down a party of soldiers to parade the terrace. Paradiso had cut his way through the crowd and found that there was no chance of escape in that way, so had returned to the hall in the hope that the horses would yet be available.

The princess was leaning against the wall, defended by her party. In her hand she held the now useless revolver, all the chambers of which were empty, and had vainly snatched up a sword from a dead soldier to protect herself from the fiery onslaught of the soldiers. They were determined to take her either dead or alive, and the fiercest of her assailants was Upravado, who was furious at the loss of his money and the way in which he had been tricked.

Richborough was fighting bravely, though one of his arms was hanging benumbed by his side. The ground was cumbered with the slain, and the royalists were greatly outnumbered by the enemy. At first they had been pretty equally matched, but as the republicans possessed guns, and the royalists only swords, the latter were the weaker party and had lost the most men. Still, knowing that the yacht would afford Julia a means of flight, they fought on with reckless despair, striving to cut a passage down to the terrace, from whence, they hoped, she could take a boat to reach the ship.

At the moment Wilfred entered the hall, Paradiso also returned with the news that the terrace was in possession of the enemy, and the royalists gave way to despair.

"All is lost!" cried Paradiso madly. "There is no escape for any of us."

"I will not escape," said Julia with flashing eyes. "I will die here with my heroes."

"The horses!" whispered Richborough to Paradiso.

"We cannot hope to reach the stables," he replied, clenching his teeth; "and probably they also are in the hands of the enemy."

"Richborough! Richborough!" cried Wilfred, at this moment breaking through the crowd and throwing himself into the ring round Julia. "The stables are safe. Come quickly with the princess."

Richborough and Paradiso both gave a cry of joy, as they alone understood the sentence spoken in English, and their cry was echoed by the royalists, who, though they knew not what it meant, yet guessed it was an omen of good.

"Where is Hilda?" asked Richborough.

"Safe! Safe! At the house of the cardinal. Now we must save the queen. Madame —"

"Away!" cried Julia, fiercely, "you traitor!"

"I am no traitor, madame," said Wilfred hurriedly. "I can explain all, but this is not the time. Come, I can save you."

"No! No!"

"I implore you."

"You betrayed me once; you may do so again."

"Paradiso! Richborough! Ask the queen to fly with me!"

"To the stables, madame, — the stables," cried Paradiso, vigorously waving his sword to keep back the soldiers. "It may be too late soon."

"I will die here, Marquess."

"No! No! Your life is too valuable to be thus flung away. Quick! Quick! Dacre, take the queen."

"Do not touch me," said Julia fiercely. "If I fly it will be with an honourable man. Monsieur le duc!"

"I come, madame."

Paradiso hastily told the royalists of the intended retreat of the princess, and that it was to be covered by their swords. With a cry of joy, they began to retreat, keeping Madame de Lusignan in the centre. Wilfred, feeling himself dishonoured by the treachery of Major Measurby, sought death everywhere, but did not find it. In company with Paradiso and his friends, he protected the retreat of the princess, who was holding on to Richborough.

Step by step the little band fell back, to the astonishment of the republicans, who did not know the meaning of this retreat. The general, however, who knew what provision had been made for flight, guessed its meaning.

"They are going to fly. To the stables!" he cried, rushing forward.

His men, however, did not know where the stables were, and fell into confusion, rushing hither and thither in the vain hope of finding some outlet. Paradiso hastily whispered to Richborough, who, without a word, lifted the princess and bore her through the door to the back staircase, at which point they had now arrived. The door closed behind them, and Upravado, furious at seeing his prey escaping, made a terrific dash with his soldiers, to carry the place by assault. The royalists now scarcely numbered a dozen, but managed to do considerable execution, and the republicans recoiled.

At this moment, knowing that there was no use guarding the terrace, as escape by the yacht was impossible, Upravado summoned the soldiers from the garden, and with these reinforcements made another attempt to drive the royalists from the door. Wilfred dashed forward to meet the general himself, who led the party, but in doing so, his foot slipped in the blood on the floor, and he rolled helpless before the advancing men.

"Don't kill him! Take him prisoner!" cried Upravado, striking up the swords of his men. "The republic will punish him."

In a moment Wilfred was bound and helpless in the power of the enemy, and the last thing he saw, as he was borne backward in the crowd, was the royalists overwhelmed by the republicans. Paradiso alone escaped, by slipping into the passage and then closing the door after him. He bolted it rapidly, but such a defence was vain, as a hundred sword hilts and gun butts soon knocked it into splinters.

Still, the respite, though momentary, gave him breathing-time, and he rushed down the staircase into the stable yard. The door of the stable was open, but as six of the horses were gone, he knew that the princess had now a chance of escape. He would have sprung on one of the remaining two horses, but had no time to do so, being hard pressed by the enemy. Fearing to be killed if caught in the stable, he rushed down the cypress avenue, and saw ahead Richborough and the princess flying towards the gate.

The soldiers were after him, and as he ran towards the gate surrounded him with wild cries. Paradiso kept them off for a few minutes, determined to sell his life dearly, but when Upravado came up, he made up his mind to surrender. He had a strong friend in Gregory, and while there was life there was hope, so he flung down his sword.

"Quarter, Upravado! Quarter!" he cried loudly.

"Granted," replied the general fiercely, "for a death on the scaffold."

Paradiso was overpowered and borne to the ground, while Upravado rushed to the gate.

"The princess!" he cried furiously.

"She is saved," retorted Paradiso with a loud laugh. "You have no horses, and in a short time she will be safe in Bulgaria."

He quite forgot the two steeds yet standing saddled in the stables.

CHAPTER XXIV.

BOOT AND SADDLE.

FROM Varzo to the frontier of Bulgaria stretch vast plains of an alluvial character, wonderfully fruitful throughout their whole extent. Of old the waves of the Black Sea covered this tract of land even to the foot of the distant mountains, but during the lapse of ages the waters have receded into their present basin, leaving acres of rich soil for the growing of corn. This is called the granary of Busk, for far as the eye can see, wave fields of yellow grain. It was now the middle of autumn, and under the blazing sun of the East the green ears were rapidly turning to a golden hue, which glinted warmly even under the cold glimmer of the moon.

Through this sea of gold ran a long Roman road from Varzo nearly to the sinuous windings of the Danube. Formed by Trajan for the passage of his legions, it deviated neither to the right nor to the left, but stretched a straight, white line towards the vague line of the horizon. Many times had the Lusignans determined to destroy this highway, seeing it afforded a passage to their foes right into the capital, but, in spite of many attempts made to render it useless, the solidity of the causeway withstood every attempt; so in the end it had been left alone. A causeway it truly was, for when made, the plains must have been little better than marshes, for even now the soil was moist and in many places treacherous. This was the road which led into the heart of Bulgaria, the frontier being only twenty miles away, and along this path of safety Julia and Richborough spurred their swift horses.

The steeds were excellent and quite fresh, else they might have had some difficulty in gaining such an advantage over their pursuers. On leaving the cypress avenue, Hilda and Nicolas, turning to the left, had at once left the Villa Tvartko behind, as they rode to Varzo, four miles distant. Julia and her escort, on the other hand, going to the right, in order to reach the frontier, had to break through some of Upravado's troops stationed in front of the mansion, the principal gates of which opened directly into the main road. Richborough, foreseeing this difficulty, wished to make a détour in order to avoid the dangerous locality, but Julia, who knew every foot of the country, assured him that this was impossible. On all sides the marshy ground was unsafe under the weight of a horse; therefore the only chance of safety was to take the soldiers by surprise, and dash through their midst as they guarded the main road.

With infinite caution they rode along the road from the cypress avenue, keeping in the shadow of the trees, and on arriving at the angle where it turned to the right, stayed their steeds to reconnoitre. Fortunately most of the soldiers were within the grounds of the villa, and a few guarded the gates, which were open. Across the road many others were standing, wrapped in their cloaks, all on the alert for the signal to enter the villa, so that between the fugitives and safety stretched a living barrier of men. Richborough took this in at a glance, and turned towards Julia.

"Their horses are inside," he said in a whisper, "so, if we break through that line, we can gain a start before they can recover from the surprise and follow us."

"Let us make the attempt, at all events," replied Julia rapidly; "it is our only chance of reaching the frontier."

"Are you afraid?"

"Afraid!" she echoed fiercely. "I have lost my crown for the second time, I have barely escaped from the house with my life, and yet you ask me such a foolish question! Let us break through the line at once."

Never suspecting the presence of the fugitives, the soldiers were quite off their guard, as their attention was entirely taken up with the fighting going on in the villa. Richborough sprang off his horse and tightened the girths of both steeds, then remounted and leaned towards Madame de Lusignan, so as to the more conveniently whisper —

"Now!"

The well-trained steeds sprang forward like arrows, and in a moment had burst through the ill-guarded line and were flying rapidly along the highroad. A few soldiers had been knocked down by the rush of the horses, and the others raised a shout of alarm which brought their officers to the gates. On learning what had occurred, these ordered pursuit at once, although they never for a moment thought it was the princess herself who had succeeded in so boldly evading their vigilance.

In spite of all their haste, however, the fugitives, being well mounted, had gained considerable advantage in this start, and the horses of the soldiers, being already somewhat jaded, could hardly hope to come up with them. However, they knew that the fugitives were making for the frontier, and hoping to catch them before they could cover twenty miles, a large body of cavalry started in pursuit.

Luckily for Julia and Richborough, they had a splendid road upon which to travel, and the hoofs of their horses rang sharply on the stones as they galloped along. The moon, shining in a cloudless sky, afforded them plenty of light, and they could see the straight white line stretching for miles ahead. The keen air whistled past their ears as they pressed onward at racing speed, and faintly in the distance they could hear the hue and cry in pursuit.

"We have over half a mile start," said Richborough, turning in his saddle, "and our horses are so fresh that every stride increases the distance. Courage, madame, I will save you yet."

Julia let the reins lie loosely on her horse's neck, and bent forward in order to prevent the sharp air taking away her breath.

"What is the use of being saved?" she replied

impatiently. "I have lost all I value in life since M. Dacre has proved such a traitor."

"Believe me, madame, he is no traitor," answered the duke earnestly. "I am as sure of Dacre's devotion to your cause as I am of my own. There is some strange mystery about all this, connected with that ring of which he was robbed by Major Measurby. When we meet again he will, I am certain, be able to explain."

"When we meet again!" repeated Julia disdainfully. "There is but little chance of that. If he returned to the villa, very likely he is now dead or a prisoner."

"You can see by his so returning that he was no traitor," said Richborough triumphantly. "He could have escaped with his wife to the palace of the cardinal, but he preferred to return and rescue you."

"His conduct is certainly inconsistent, M. le duc. But why did he fail me at the eleventh hour?"

"I cannot tell."

"Had Upravado received the money all would have been well," continued Julia bitterly, "and I would have been now on my way to Varzo, an acknowledged sovereign; instead of which I am flying from my kingdom, a homeless fugitive."

"While there is life there is hope," said Richborough lightly. "I believe in your star."

"Yes, and you believe in M. Dacre."

"I do. I am convinced he will explain all to your satisfaction. If you wish to punish any one it should be Major Measurby. He is the traitor, not Dacre."

The princess did not answer, but hearing the fierce cries of those in pursuit, urged her horse to greater speed. Unable in her flight from the Villa Tvartko to snatch a single wrap, she looked a strange figure, in her rich robes, with bare neck and arms. Her short golden hair was crowned with a small diadem, which she had assumed in order to appear before her people as their queen. On her white neck flashed diamonds, and costly bracelets were on her wrists, while the rich robe of blue velvet, embroidered with gold, looked fantastic and out of place in her present position. With regal robes, flashing gems, and a white, fierce face, this discrowned queen rode through the night, surely the most romantic figure of modern days.

Richborough, in his yeomanry uniform, was better arrayed for riding, and his long boots were armed with spurs, which served to keep his horse at full speed. The steed of the princess, emulating its companion, kept up with it neck and neck, so that Julia had nothing to do but let the reins hang loose and follow her friend.

Behind, the cavalry were still thundering in pursuit, and as he turned in his saddle, Richborough could see them in the distance, a black mass on the white road. The wind of their speed was so fierce and keen that it nearly took away their breath, and the princess, with her uncovered neck and arms, suffered terribly from the lash of the breeze. Richborough saw this, and, without stopping, tied the reins in a knot on the neck of his horse, and slipped off the hussar jacket, edged with fur, which he wore as part of his uniform.

"Put this on, Princess," he said, bringing his horse close to hers; "it will protect you from the cold."

"I am not cold," retorted Julia sullenly.

"Nevertheless, it is dangerous to ride in that dress. I entreat you, madame. Give me your bridle. We need not slacken speed. There! Now take the jacket. Can you put it on without drawing rein?"

"Yes," said Julia, taking the jacket. "I will not fall off. Do not be afraid, monseigneur."

He held the bridle, and snatching the jacket from his grasp she flung it over her shoulders. Without slackening speed they accomplished this, and when it was safely wrapped round her shoulders, the duke let go her horse again, and once more assumed the lead.

"Can the horses hold up, Duke?"

"I think so. They are both fresh and have good blood in them. If we are overtaken I have this."

It was a Colt's revolver which he had snatched up before leaving the villa, and all the chambers were loaded.

"No weapon for me," said Julia in an annoyed tone. "Ah!"

"What's the matter, madame?"

"This saddle has holsters and pistols. Bravo! This will assist us in time of need. Have you pistols also, Duke?"

"Yes, madame. Good! This is Dacre's doing. You see, madame, he has had foresight."

"Hardly a compliment to him. It looks as though he thought we should fail."

"No. I don't believe that. Blame Measurby. Oh, if I meet that traitor, how I will be avenged! I am thankful that you at least are safe."

"I am not safe yet."

"But will be shortly. We are now within ten miles of the frontier. We have four pistols and one revolver, so, if overtaken, we can defend ourselves. But we will not be overtaken, as their horses are not fresh."

"Can we pass the frontier?"

"It will be guarded, of course, madame."

"There is a gate across the road," said Julia anxiously, "and a guard-house on each side."

"A high gate?"

"Five feet or thereabouts."

"We can clear that if it be not open, unless we are stopped by the Bulgarian soldiers."

"They will deliver us up."

"No, I do not think so, madame. We will claim their protection. Besides, from all I have heard, they are not friends with Methodios."

"They hate him," replied the princess quickly. "He is too much in favour with Russia for the prince of Bulgaria to care about him."

"All the better for us. Hark! that cry!"

It was one of triumph, borne on the wind, and Richborough's heart nearly leaped to his mouth as he wondered what it meant. The only thing that he could think was that it betokened a fresh accession of soldiers to their pursuers, which was indeed the case. Upravado, having arrested Wilfred and Paradiso, had sent out a new squadron of cavalry, and these, having fresh horses, were now rapidly gaining on the fugitives.

"I will not be taken alive," cried Julia fiercely, urging her horse onward to its fullest speed. "Shoot me first, Duke."

"I will shoot the traitor Upravado," replied Richborough grimly. "I hope he is with our pursuers."

"Do as I bid you, sir," said the princess in a peremptory manner. "Think not for a moment that I will submit to be taken prisoner and exposed to the scorn of the fat citizens of Varzo. No! I will die a queen, but not on the scaffold like Marie Antoinette."

Richborough was about to reply when he heard a second cry of triumph, and, on looking back, saw two figures riding swiftly ahead of the rest. For the moment a thought crossed his mind that this was Paradiso and Wilfred, who had escaped on the two remaining horses, but he dismissed this thought at once.

He was right to do so, for it was Upravado and one of his officers, who had discovered the two steeds remaining behind, — which had broken loose from the stable, — and were now spurring them far ahead of their companions to catch the fugitives. Their steeds were fresh and of the same quality as those of the princess and her companion, so it looked as though they would be captured in the moment of safety. Owing to the start obtained by the fugitives, those in pursuit were yet far behind, and it was now only three miles to the frontier.

The whole of the seventeen miles they had come had been covered by their horses at full speed, and these now showed signs of exhaustion, which was scarcely to be wondered at. Had they not been thoroughbred, they would have broken down long before, but they had held up bravely. Richborough's was the best, for it still kept steadily at a gallop, while that of Julia had begun to drop behind. In despair the duke seized its bridle and began to urge it forward, but the steed dragged backward and impeded the speed of his own horse. Now it was two miles to the frontier.

"If we can only last the next two miles, we are safe," cried Richborough in agony. "But they are gaining on us in every stride."

The main body of the pursuers had long since given in, but the two in front kept steadily gaining. Upravado had lost no time in starting in pursuit, and his horse and that of his companion, being both fresh, they had raced far ahead of their companions. Now that the steeds of Julia and Richborough showed signs of exhaustion, they spurred their horses on as quickly as possible so as to come up in time. Their steeds responded bravely to the use of whip and spur, but now began to fail like their companions in front, so it seemed as though the whole party would arrive jaded and broken-down at the frontier.

"Princess, Princess," cried Richborough hurriedly, "if you fire, do so at the horses, not at the riders. They offer a better mark, and if they are disabled, we can escape."

"How far is it to Bulgaria now?" asked Julia, desperately grasping a pistol.

"One mile!"

Upravado and his officer gradually gained on them, and they were now almost within pistol-shot.

"We must kill their horses," cried Richborough despairingly, "and then get on as best we can. Our horses cannot do the other mile at this speed."

He turned in his saddle and his revolver rang out sharply in the clear air. Two barrels were emptied, but neither did any damage, and onward like the wind came Upravado.

"I'll take Upravado, you the other," said Richborough between his clenched teeth. "Madame, are you mad?"

Julia suddenly pulled up her horse and put him sideways across the road. The officer with Upravado saw this and uttered a cry of triumph. He tried to check his steed, but the animal could not be stayed, consequently the two horses came together and rolled over, riders and all, a heap on the ground.

Richborough gave a cry of anguish and rode back to check the advance of Upravado, who was almost on the fallen horses. He fired two more barrels and shot the general's horse through the head. As he did so, there was another shot, and then he saw the princess running towards him with a smoking pistol in her hand. Upravado's horse had fallen on him, and he was unable to extricate himself.

"What have you done, Princess?" cried Richborough, as she reached his stirrup.

"Shot that man," she panted, grasping his hand. "Quick, take me on your horse, and away."

She placed her foot on the toe of his boot and, with the assistance of his hand, swung herself on to the saddle in front, while Richborough urged his horse forward with its double burden. Upravado by this time had sprung to his feet, and sent a shot after them. It missed, and to his confusion he found his prey had escaped.

"They have no horses and one of the two men is dead," said Julia triumphantly.

"How did you do it, Princess?"

"While he was tangled in his stirrup I put the pistol to his head and blew out his brains."

Richborough shuddered, and for the first time began to know of what nature this woman was. Julia marked his disgust and laughed.

"What! Would you have me taken because I feared to kill a man?" she said, with flashing eyes. "Not so! He was a traitor and deserved punishment. See, we are now safe. Upravado is alone on the road without a companion or a horse, and yonder are the gates of the guard-house."

The horse, worn out, moved slowly along, and Richborough wondered, if they did reach the gate, how they would get over it. To his surprise it was wide open. They rode across the frontier between the guard-houses, and found themselves in safety. Not a soldier was to be seen.

Julia sprang to the ground, and after her Richborough, while they both put up a prayer of thanks that they were thus far safe.

"Can we not go on further, Duke?"

"No, madame, the horse is worn out."

"Then let us ask hospitality from the guardhouse. Hereditary foes to Busk as they are, they will not refuse shelter to an exiled sovereign."

Richborough fired the remaining barrel of his revolver, and expected that the guard would at once rush out. To his surprise only one man appeared at the door of the house.

That man was Major Measurby.

CHAPTER XXV.

THE POWER OF THE RING.

It would be hard to say which of the two men was the more astonished at this unexpected encounter, — Measurby, who thought that by this time Julia and her partisans were safely bestowed in prison, or Richborough, who had no idea that the major had paused on the frontier. They stared at one another in amazement, and it was the princess who first moved in the matter. Rushing forward she struck Measurby across the face with her glove, furious at thus beholding the cause of all her troubles.

"Traitor and coward!" she cried fiercely, "you, at least, shall meet with the reward of your crime!"

By this time the major had, in a great measure, recovered his effrontery, and, enraged at being struck by a woman, seized the wrist of Madame de Lusignan with an angry gesture.

"Release the princess," said Richborough, bounding forward. "How dare you lay your hand on her!"

"Egad! she laid her hand on me," retorted the major, flinging the princess roughly from him. "So you have escaped?"

"Doubtless you thought we were dead," said

Julia with a sneer, "but we are alive, and can punish your treachery."

"My treachery! What do you mean?"

Both Julia and the duke were taken aback by the effrontery of the man who thus dared them to their faces. Measurby saw that by his feigned indignation he had gained some slight advantage, and at once followed it up.

"There appears to be some slight mistake," he said with elaborate indifference, "but I can doubtless explain it away. Will you be pleased to enter, madame?"

The princess recoiled from the open door of the guard-house with angry suspicion.

"Ah! you would betray me to my enemies."

"Your enemies," said Measurby coolly, "are doubtless at the present time burning Villa Tvartko. Within, there is no one but myself and some dozen drunken Bulgarian soldiers."

"This, then, is the reason the gate stands open," cried Richborough in some doubt.

"There's no question of that, Duke," replied Measurby coolly. "When I arrived here, some hours ago, they proposed to keep me prisoner till the arrival of their comrades from the town two miles away. But as it was important that I should get away from here at once, I waited till Janshah arrived —"

"Is Janshah here?"

"Came over an hour ago. With his assistance I drugged their liquor, so there they lie within, all helpless, not having been able to even shut the gate, which they opened to let Janshah pass through. He has gone on to the nearest town to procure me some conveyance, and will doubtless be here shortly, when we can leave this dangerous locality."

The major made this explanation with the greatest coolness, and the princess looked at him in blank astonishment at his audacity. Richborough, however, was not so speechless, and noting the conclusion of the scoundrel's speech, broke out into angry words.

"We leave!" he repeated furiously. "I wonder at your insolence, sir. You first betray us and ruin all our plans, then offer us a seat in your carriage. We will not accept it."

"Faith, then, you'll have to stay here and be caught," retorted Measurby impudently. "This post is guarded by a dozen soldiers who are relieved every twelve hours by others from the barracks of the town. I have made these within incapable of staying our flight, but the next dozen, who will arrive soon, may prove harder to deal with."

Here was a dilemma. There was no doubt that the major spoke truly, and unless they got away there would be trouble. By this time Upravado was no doubt on his way back to Varzo, from whence he would send an envoy to demand their surrender from the Bulgarians. They might or might not be delivered up to the republic, but in any case their situation was very critical. The offer of the major afforded them a way out of their trouble, as, once having reached the town, they could be able to see the commander of the garrison.

If things were explained to him, he might assist them, and they would at least gain time to form plans of getting on to Stamboul.

This was all very well, but to accept a favour from the scoundrel who had betrayed them was more than Richborough, even at the present juncture of affairs, could make up his mind to do. Not so the princess. Taught from her earliest childhood to dissemble her feelings and make use of every one as an instrument, she at once decided to accept the major's offer. Once in safety, and she could be revenged on the traitor; but, meanwhile, it appeared to her to be only just that he should extricate her from the troubles of which he was the sole cause. She hated this man greatly, and would willingly have shot him where he stood smiling at her. Indeed, her fingers itched to close round the handle of the pistol in the pocket of the jacket, but with wonderful powers of self-control, and to Richborough's amazement, she smiled graciously on the major.

"Can you explain your conduct?" she said in a yielding manner.

"Of course I can," replied Measurby glibly. "I can show you that the fault is Dacre's, not mine."

"How dare you say that?" cried Richborough angrily. "My friend Dacre is a gentleman, a man of honour. You are a scoundrel and a thief."

"A thief?" repeated Measurby, turning white. "That is an unpleasant word, Duke."

He did not lack courage, and stepped forward to

face the duke without flinching, when Julia, dreading lest an encounter between the two men should upset all her plans, hastily flung herself between them.

"It is too unpleasant a word to be true," she said sweetly. "You are too hasty, M. le duc. Monsieur has promised us both an explanation, and I have no doubt will keep his word. Take us into the room, monsieur."

The major bowed, and vanished within, while Richborough looked at Julia in astonishment as she prepared to follow.

"Madame —" he began, when she interrupted him hurriedly.

"Not a word. I know what I am doing. He is a scoundrel — a traitor; but I will accept his aid, and afterward — you need not be afraid he will escape me."

"And you will treat with him?"

"Yes. I will promise him whatever he asks — now. As for you, be silent and let me conduct this affair. You are too honest for intrigue. I am not."

"But, madame —" protested the duke.

"I will be obeyed, monseigneur," she replied imperiously, and vanished into the house.

Richborough stood for a minute in deep thought. He was now beginning to understand the nature of Julia de Lusignan, and did not admire it. This subtle woman, who could adapt herself to any situation, who could make use of the vilest tools to gain her own ends, who called dishonour intrigue, and craft diplomacy, revolted and disgusted him. If she thus was false to all, how could she be true to him? He loved her for her beautiful face, but, alas, he began to think it was but the lying mask of a detestable character, and thus seeing flaws in his idol, his ardent love began to cool.

This was one side of the question. And the other? She was a discrowned queen, a woman flying for her life, a sovereign surrounded by traitors, so he could not help admiring her wonderful tact and judgment. Many a woman would have lost the chance of escaping, by insulting Measurby, but she, with marvellous self-control, twisted him round to suit her own purpose, and would doubtless punish him when she could afford to dispense with his services. Then, again, she had shot that officer in cold blood. It was cruel but needful, and Richborough did not know whether to admire or loathe her for such presence of mind in a moment of danger.

Of one thing he was certain, however, and that was that she needed help, so at the present time he could not in honour leave her. Much, then, as he was beginning to question the delicacy of her feminine qualities, he was pledged in all honour to aid her to the end. She was a woman in trouble, and that was enough for Richborough's chivalrous nature.

"She is a queen, not a woman," he said with a sigh, as he stepped within, "and cannot be judged by the common standard."

The room in which he found himself was a mean, dirty-looking apartment, filled with soldiers, all lying motionless like logs. On the table were cups, some still half full of wine, but no common debauch could explain the utter helplessness of the men. They had been drugged by Janshah, and Richborough shuddered at the horrible subtlety of the Indian.

"Why does that man obey first Wilfred and now Measurby?" he thought, as he proceeded towards a door whence he heard the voice of the princess. "Can the lost ring have anything to do with it? Scarcely; and yet — Oh, this is some horrible mystery. I cannot understand it at all. Poor Wilfred? I hope he escaped, but I doubt it, doubt it very much."

The princess was seated at the table, with a cup of wine in front of her, and the major standing at her elbow in an attitude of respectful attention. Remembering the soldiers, the duke cast a shuddering glance at the wine, but the princess, guessing his thought, laughed ironically.

"This is quite safe, monseigneur," she said with a meaning glance; "our friend here plays no tricks on me. He intends to assist me to the crown of Busk."

"That is easier said than done," replied Richborough coldly. "If Dacre could not do it, I am confident the major will fail."

"I am not so sure of that, Duke," retorted Measurby with a sneer; whereat Richborough turned his back on him in disdain.

"Come, this will never do," observed Julia, frowning, as she noticed the action. "You are wrong, M. le duc, to treat our friend in this way. He has explained everything."

"I have not yet heard his explanation, madame."

"I can repeat it to your Grace," said Measurby with great dignity. "This afternoon Dacre was afraid the conspiracy would fail, and sent me on here with the request that I would make all smooth for the princess should she be forced to fly. She has been forced to fly, and I have obeyed my orders. The post-chaise, or whatever they call it here, will arrive shortly, and Madame de Lusignan can continue her flight. I —"

"I don't believe a word of it," interrupted the duke bluntly. "Dacre told a very different story."

"And may I ask your Grace to repeat that story?"

"He said you had stolen a ring from him, and fled."

"Is it this ring to which your Grace refers?" said Measurby, holding out his hand. "This is my ring, and it is a similar one to that possessed by Mr. Dacre. As to stealing his, why should I do that when I have one of my own?"

"I don't understand it all," retorted Richborough, angrily turning to the princess, "nor will the truth be known until we see Dacre and he tells his own story. But this I am sure of, that he is an honest man and you are not."

"Another time I would take notice of your words," said the major insolently, "but affairs are too critical at the present time to admit of our quarrelling."

"I only quarrel with men of my own rank, sir," retorted the duke haughtily, and turned on his heel. "Madame de Lusignan, act as you think best in this matter. I will obey you in all things until you are in safety. Meanwhile, permit me to withdraw, as I neither believe this man's story nor trust his actions. Should you desire me, I will be at the door."

After making this speech Richborough bowed coldly to the princess, and, without taking the slightest notice of Measurby, left the room. The major looked after him with an expression of rage on his face, but not deeming it diplomatic to quarrel at the moment, held his peace. In her heart the princess approved of the duke's action, and, like him, she believed Measurby's explanation to be all false. Nevertheless, she had a game to play, and played it with consummate skill. For this reason she was rather pleased than otherwise that Richborough had left the room. He was too honourable to understand all her finesse, and might by his honest blundering spoil her game. Honest men are sometimes very troublesome.

The stake was a crown; the players, an exiled queen and an adventurer who possessed some mysterious power of which his opponent was quite ignorant; the scene, a mean room in a frontier guardhouse, illuminated by the dirty yellow flame of an oil lamp; the stake, the scene, the players, surely the strangest combination that had ever come together for such a purpose.

The major prided himself on his clever head, on

his knowledge of character; but in these respects he was a mere child to Julia de Lusignan. She was a female Machiavelli, and could have baffled Cæsar Borgia himself. Nothing was too high for her to dare, no one too mean for her to use as an instrument. Intrigue was the breath of her life, and seated in this mean apartment, playing a dangerous game with a tricky opponent, she was quite in her element. She was too clever, and frequently over-reached herself by foiling her own schemes. But that principally occurred in Russian intrigues, where her antagonists were equal to herself in diplomatic cleverness. Major Measurby, as an opponent, she despised. Still he required some dexterity of handling, and Julia, with a smiling face, proceeded to win the game. The victory she looked upon as a foregone conclusion, while as for the major, — well, he fell blindly into the net.

"You must pardon the duke, Major Measurby," she said in English, with a pretty foreign accent; "he does not understand these matters. To me your explanation is quite satisfactory, and I can only thank you for having carried out your plans so well. By the way, did you not take two horses from the stables?"

"Yes, madame. I wished to get here as speedily as possible."

"That only required one horse."

"Janshah took the other."

"Ah," said the princess reflectively; "now the whole eight are accounted for."

"In what way, madame?"

"Madame Dacre and Nicolas took a pair to escape to the cardinal's palace—"

"Then she is safe," interrupted the major quickly. "I am glad of that."

The princess, still wroth against Wilfred, of whose honesty she was not yet assured, had her own opinion as to the advisability of Hilda's flight, but said nothing at the time.

"The duke and myself took another pair, you and your servant a third, and the fourth pair were used by Upravado and one of his officers."

"Upravado!" cried the major in astonishment. "Did he follow you?"

"Nearly to the frontier," replied Julia quietly. "A body of cavalry pursued us at first, but, as our horses were fresh and theirs were not, they soon gave in and rode back. Upravado and his aide-de-camp were mounted on our own horses and overtook us. The duke shot Upravado's horse, and I killed his aide-de-camp."

"Killed his aide-de-camp?" echoed the major, taken aback by her coolness.

"Yes, I blew his brains out," replied the princess quietly. "It was disagreeable but necessary. Then Upravado went back, and we came on. I am sorry, now," continued Julia reflectively, "that we did not kill him also."

Measurby, in spite of all his villainy, was a humane man, and hated to hear a woman talk so cruelly. It did not suit his purpose, however, to express his real feelings; so he simply shook his head and smiled.

"It would never have done to have killed Upravado."

"Why not?"

"Because we must make use of him."

"Unless you can pay him two hundred thousand francs, we can do nothing. In fact, I don't know whether he will accept money now."

"Oh, yes, he will," replied Measurby confidently. "I will double the amount. If he places you on the throne, I will give him four hundred thousand francs."

"But you have not so much money."

"I have, — and more."

"So M. Dacre said," observed the princess scornfully; "but I will not believe it until I see it in gold."

"As soon as Janshah returns you will see it," answered the major coolly. "He has in his possession two hundred thousand francs belonging to me, and can obtain the rest at Varzo."

"That is, if you can go back to Varzo."

"Of course I can go back, and so will you, madame, — in disguise."

"What! trust my head in the lion's mouth? Do you take me for a fool, monsieur?"

"If you go to the cardinal's palace in disguise, he will not betray you to Methodios. There you can obtain an interview with Upravado, and if he will consent again to be bribed, — which I think will be the case, — I will pay him down whatever he demands before he leaves the room."

"Good! But if he refuses?"

"He will not refuse. After this conspiracy, Methodios will distrust him more than ever."

Julia reflected for a few moments, and was about to answer when the door of the room opened and Janshah appeared. Obsequious as he had been to Wilfred, he was more so to his new master, whom, curiously enough, he respected for his subtlety in obtaining the ring, and bowed profoundly before him as he spoke.

"I had great difficulty in getting the carriage, my lord, but it is now here."

"What is the temper of the people in the town?"

"They know nothing of the trouble at Varzo. We can pass through at dawn without being stayed."

"Will the relief guard be here shortly?"

"Within an hour, my lord. The dawn will soon break in the east."

"Janshah, the princess and the duke will come with me."

"Yes, my lord."

"Now that your servant is here," said Julia, ignoring, for her own reasons, that Janshah had been Wilfred's servant, "show me the gold."

Measurby made a sign to Janshah, who left the room and shortly reappeared, followed by two servants carrying a heavy box.

"Where did these two fellows come from?" asked Measurby, somewhat startled.

"I sent them on to the town four days ago, my lord, in case the designs failed at Varzo."

"You are a wonderful fellow, Janshah. You

think of everything. By the way, how did you bring that box here from Villa Tvartko?"

"On the back of my horse," replied Janshah bowing; and then threw open the box. Julia arose from her seat and looked at the gold shining therein, then turned away with a triumphant laugh.

"Upravado is too avaricious to refuse that. Was it with this money that M. Dacre was going to bribe him?"

"The same, madame," replied Measurby coolly.

"Then how does it come into your possession, and how is it that the servant of M. Dacre now obeys you instead of his master?"

"I can answer neither of those questions, madame."

The eyes of the princess flashed fire, but she dissembled her anger with a bland smile. Had Measurby been a wise man, he would have augured ill from that smile, but he was too busy with his own thoughts to notice such a trifling matter.

"Well, no matter," she said sweetly; "so long as you can bribe this man, I care not what secrets you refrain from telling. This amount, I think, will be sufficient, but, in view of his recent disappointment, Upravado may demand more money."

"You can double the amount, can you not, Janshah?" asked the major, turning to the Indian.

"At Varzo, my lord, I can treble it if you wish."

"You see, madame," said Measurby, with a triumphant smile, "I am not like Dacre. I can do what I say. There will be no failure this time."

"I trust not," replied Julia, with emphasis. "I

may not be so fortunate as to escape a third time. Twice I have left Busk as a fugitive; the third time may be fatal."

"Or fortunate. There is luck in odd numbers."

"Let us hope so. Well, now all is arranged, let us go on and obtain some disguise. It will be difficult."

"Janshah will manage all that."

"And communicate with the cardinal."

"Janshah will do it."

"And get safely to Varzo."

"Janshah will arrange all."

"It seems that this man can do everything," said Julia dryly, turning towards the door. "Let us hope he will justify your confidence."

"One moment, madame," said Measurby, making a signal to Janshah and his servants to leave the room. "What is to be my reward if I place you on the throne?"

"You can name it yourself, monsieur."

"I am afraid it will startle you."

"Nothing can startle me now," replied Madame de Lusignan, throwing a piercing glance at the man before her.

"I will try if I cannot do so," said the major calmly. "My price for giving you the throne of Busk is — your hand."

"What!" exclaimed the princess loudly, turning suddenly pale with emotion.

"I wish to marry you," said Measurby nervously.

Julia drew herself up to her full height and looked at him with flashing eyes.

"Truly, you have not spoken vainly," she said furiously; "you have startled me. Marry you! I — a Lusignan — a sovereign! Impossible!"

"Very well, madame! Then I will leave you here."

"Stay a moment, monsieur," observed the princess, dissembling her rage. "You have taken me by surprise. I cannot answer you now. The question requires consideration."

"So long as you answer it before I pay over the money to Upravado, I do not mind," said the major blandly. "We must wait a week before we can hope to get safely to Varzo."

"A week," repeated Julia quietly. "Well, in a week you will have your answer. Now go and leave me for a moment."

The major bowed and retired, leaving the princess alone. Once left to herself, she gave way to her rage. Her pride was deeply wounded by Measurby's insolence, by his audacious demand. Still, she was playing a deep game, and must win in the end. She would promise this adventurer anything, and when she was seated on the throne, punish him for his audacity. That Richborough should aspire to her hand was bad enough in her opinion, — but Richborough was at least an aristocrat. This offer took away her breath, and some minutes elapsed before she could compose herself sufficiently to leave the room.

"A week," she said to herself, smiling darkly as she opened the door. "In a week, monsieur, you will have your answer, and I will have your head."

CHAPTER XXVI.

SANCTUARY.

A week had elapsed since the failure of the conspiracy and the flight of the princess, during which time Hilda had remained secluded in the palace of the cardinal. Owing to the judicious action of the prelate in remaining away from the fête at Villa Tvartko, no one, not even the most rabid republican, suspected him of having been concerned in the plot. Simulating indignation, he bewailed the audacity of the attempt to overthrow the republic, and in the end succeeded in imposing on all, even on Methodios. His house, therefore, afforded a secure asylum for those who had escaped from the massacre at Villa Tvartko, and, besides Hilda, several prominent royalists were hidden in the episcopal palace.

Methodios had taken strong measures for the safety of the republic after the failure of the conspiracy. He imprisoned several prominent nobles suspected of being royalists, placed a guard of soldiers on Villa Tvartko, and publicly congratulated Upravado on his devotion to the country, which had thwarted the daring attempt of the princess to subvert the government.

As soon as order was restored in Varzo, Methodios

sent out troops to the provinces, and so expeditiously did he act that within the week all signs of the wide-spreading conspiracy were crushed out of existence. The president naturally congratulated himself on this admirable result, and ascribed it to his promptitude of action, whereas the apparent submission of the provinces was due to the machinations of the archbishop.

That wily prelate had received a letter from Princess Julia, who was still in Bulgaria, advising him of Measurby's offer, and asking him to secure to her another interview with Upravado. On receiving this important communication, Gregory at once sent messengers to all the leaders of the revolt in the provinces, and told them to pay allegiance to Methodios, so that in the near future a second and more successful attempt could be made to restore the monarchy. The rebels, recognizing the necessity of apparent submission, at once yielded to the commands of the president. He imprisoned a few of the most prominent, but, afraid of jeopardizing his popularity, left the bulk of the provincial conspirators alone. By this astute manœuvre of the archbishop, the conspiracy was left in nearly the same condition as before the catastrophe at Villa Tvartko, saving that the government at Varzo was now on its guard. To quiet all the suspicions of Methodios and his minions was now the task of the prelate.

Notwithstanding the immense rewards offered for the capture of Julia de Lusignan, she was still at large, and safe under the protection of Bulgaria.

With that promptitude of action which was her most striking characteristic, as soon as she had arranged with Measurby that he should pay the money to bribe Upravado, she went at once to Sofia and claimed the protection of the Bulgarian government. The ruler of that principality was by no means favourably inclined towards Methodios, whom he suspected of being a creature of the St. Petersburg cabinet, and would have much preferred to see the Lusignan dynasty once more on the throne of Busk. Julia assured the prince that if she were restored, Bulgaria would have no firmer friend than herself; consequently, when Methodios sent to demand that she should be given up to the vengeance of the republic, the government of Bulgaria refused to be a party to such a transaction. Having thus foiled Methodios on this point, Julia felt that her liberty was at least secure, and remained safely at Sofia while she made preparations for her second attempt to recover the throne.

Cardinal Gregory knew that the most necessary step to take towards securing this desirable end was, at all risks, to attach Upravado to the royal cause. This was a very difficult matter to accomplish, as, after the failure to secure the money, Upravado was by no means inclined to risk his head a second time. Gregory, however, persistently favoured the suspicions of Methodios against Upravado by insinuations that he was implicated in the late conspiracy, whereat the president treated Upravado in such an insulting manner that he began to feel doubtful of his liberty and life. He knew well enough that Methodios would never dare to quarrel openly with one who was the darling of the soldiers, but there was such a thing in Busk as secret assassination. Upravado dreaded this, and, much perplexed as to his future course, consulted Gregory.

That prelate, delighted at the way in which matters were shaping themselves in accordance with his desires, advised him to join the royal cause, and offered him double the amount of money provided he would support Julia. At first Upravado demurred, being unwilling to be tricked a second time, but at length, while committing himself to no course, promised to call at the palace within a few days in order to discuss the matter more fully.

As soon as Gregory had made this arrangement and fixed a time for the interview, he sent off at once to Julia, upon which the princess, in company with Richborough, Measurby, and Janshah, came in disguise to Varzo, and managed to gain the shelter of the palace without their presence being suspected in Busk.

Things were thus progressing favourably as regards the royal cause; but the affairs of the Dacres were in a very bad way. Methodios, enraged at having been so deluded by the Englishman, had imprisoned him in the Tower of the Sultan, and would have put him to death but that he was afraid of rousing the indignation of Great Britain. Dacre was well connected, and had many influential friends in power; so Methodios dreaded lest, if he were put to death, complications might arise between his government and that of her Britannic

Majesty. He had quite enough to do to manage local troubles without embroiling himself in disturbances abroad; so under these circumstances Wilfred's life was quite safe.

Nevertheless he was strictly guarded and allowed to see no one; but he managed to get a letter taken to his wife through the medium of his jailer, who, though in the employment of the republic, was devoted to the royal cause. In this letter Wilfred explaned the whole mystery of the ring, and Hilda bitterly reproached herself that she had meddled with the talisman. Had she not done so, Measurby would never have become possessed of the ring, and the conspiracy would have been carried to a successful conclusion; but as it was, she was a fugitive, her husband was in prison, and the power bestowed by the ring was invested in the person of Major Measurby.

Several times did she wish to see her husband, but this the archbishop would never permit, as he did not want it spread abroad that he was harbouring a fugitive for whom the emissaries of the republic were in search. Were such a thing known to Methodios, it might awaken his suspicions against the archbishop, and the house would be searched, when not only Hilda, but Princess Julia would be discovered. Therefore, to avert this catastrophe, Gregory advised Hilda to remain in quiet, until the second attempt of Julia was successful, when, of course, Wilfred would be released, and they could leave Busk together.

In his own heart Gregory was not so certain that

Wilfred would be set free when Julia became queen. That royal lady was very bitter against the Englishman, whom she accused of having betrayed her. Certainly she did not believe the story of Major Measurby, but at the same time she did not think that Wilfred had been Measurby's dupe. When the cardinal spoke to her on the matter, she plainly said that when she was free to act, she herself would speak to Wilfred, and it entirely depended upon his explanation whether she would set him at liberty or not. Gregory pointed out to the princess that even though, as she thought, Wilfred had betrayed her, yet he had undoubtedly been of great service to the royal cause, and deserved some return for his efforts. To this Julia made no reply, as she had come to the conclusion that either Measurby or Wilfred possessed some power which gave them command of unlimited money, and she wished that power to become invested in herself. As it was, however, she was completely ignorant of the true facts of the case, and no one could tell her the truth but the two men principally concerned in the matter. With this idea in her head, it was her intention, on regaining the throne, to detain them both until she had discovered the secret.

On arriving at the archbishop's palace, Measurby was in high glee, for the princess had promised to marry him if this second conspiracy was successful. The promise was absurd, and would not be kept, as it was unlikely that a lady of royal blood would marry an adventurer. Still, Measurby believed her, as he thought if he told her the truth about the ring, she would not refuse to marry a man with twenty millions of money. It never seemed to strike him that when Julia discovered the source of his power, she could take the ring from him for her own use, and banish him from Busk. Yet this was exactly the way in which she would have acted had she known all. This, however, the major did not know.

Richborough had read her character better. His eyes had been opened during the last week, and he saw that she was quite a different woman from what he had expected to find her. Instead of a soft and feminine nature, he found her a masculine female of the most unscrupulous nature, one who stopped at nothing to gain her ends, not even murder, as witness the way in which she had shot Upravado's aide-de-camp. Knowing, then, she was not a fit wife for him, despite her royal powers, Richborough, with rare good sense, gave up all idea of pressing her to marry him, and determined, after helping to place her on the throne, to return to England. He gave no hint of his determination, however, and Julia thought he was as much her slave as ever.

Both Julia and Measurby knew that Hilda was in the palace, but neither of them attempted to see her, — the first from indignation against Wilfred, the second because he was ashamed to face the woman whose husband he had so cruelly wronged. On her part, Hilda was equally desirous of keeping out of their sight, as all she desired was the release of Wilfred and permission to leave Busk, where they had suffered so bitterly.

As soon as Richborough arrived at Varzo, he at

once sought an interview with his cousin, and they talked for a long time over Wilfred's unfortunate position. Hilda showed him Dacre's letter, and the duke was much amazed at the contents.

"It is truly wonderful," he said, on recovering from his astonishment; "just like a story out of the Arabian Nights."

"I hope it will have as happy a termination," replied Hilda bitterly; "but at present the possession of the ring has brought nothing but trouble."

"The loss of the ring, you mean, Hilda. Had Wilfred the ring still in his possession, all would be well. What a scoundrel that Measurby is!"

"Do not say a word about it to him."

"Do you think I care about speaking to such a scoundrel?" said the duke angrily. "I never open my mouth to him. I will say nothing about what you have told me to any one. But how can we release Wilfred?"

"Surely he will be released when Julia is on the throne."

"I'm not so sure about that. She is very bitter against him for his supposed treachery."

"But if all is explained to her?"

"I do not think it would be wise to explain all," observed her cousin, after a pause. "It is not desirable that an unscrupulous woman like Julia should learn the secret of the ring. If she did she would at once take steps to get it into her own possession."

"In that case she would come into collision with Janshah. You see what Wilfred says in his letter about an invisible body-guard."

"I've no doubt Janshah can do a great deal against a private individual; but you forget that Julia will shortly be a queen, with the powers of Busk at her command. Nothing would be easier for her than to arrest Major Measurby and threaten him with death should he not give up the ring. Then Janshah will obey her only."

"You seem very bitter against Madame de Lusignan," said Hilda, looking at her cousin inquiringly. "I thought you loved her."

"I did, but not now. I deemed her to be a perfect being, but she is far from that. She is a cold-blooded, selfish woman, who will make an admirable despotic ruler, but a bad wife. No, my dear Hilda, I have no care to marry a Catherine de' Medici."

"I think you are wise. I never liked her. She was arrogant in her adversity, and in her prosperity will forget all that Wilfred has done for her. I agree with you, she will not release him when queen: but I have a plan to release him myself."

"The Countess of Nithsdale business, I suppose?"

"Something like that. See!" said Hilda, producing a small bottle. "This contains an Indian drug which, if administered, sends any one to sleep in a few minutes. I obtained it from Janshah when he was yet faithful to us, in order to get some rest. You know I suffered much from neuralgia last year. Well, I found this of great use. Two or three drops will send you to sleep at once. Now, if the queen does not release Wilfred, I intend to ask her permission to visit him in the Tower of the Sultan; drug the jailer and steal his keys then we can fly together."

"I 'm afraid there is not much chance of success," said the duke, shaking his head; "such escapes only occur in novels."

"Then it will be in keeping with all these events. The ring of Aladdin, a revelation, a conspiracy, — what novel could contain wilder adventures? I will attempt this at all events if the queen does not release Wilfred."

"That she will never do unless she receives a thorough explanation."

"And such an explanation would tell her the secret of the ring," said Hilda quickly. "No! we must keep that quiet and see if we can get back the ring from the major."

"Impossible!"

"Everything seems impossible now. Still, things may turn out better than we expect. If I can release Wilfred and we can escape to England, I do not mind giving up the ring. You know I have five thousand a year settled on me, which not even Janshah can touch, so Wilfred and myself can live on that."

"I will come with you to England," said the duke in a melancholy tone, "for there is no happiness for me here."

"There would be less happiness for you if you married Madame de Lusignan."

"I believe that to be true. However, she will make an excellent queen."

"She is not queen yet," said Hilda angrily.

"But she will be soon. Upravado comes here to-morrow. Measurby has the money ready, and the attempt will be made the next day."

"And Methodios?"

"Suspects nothing. What a fool the man is! In spite of the late warning he takes no steps to root out this conspiracy. True, he thinks it is at an end, whereas it is flourishing in the very heart of his capital."

"If Julia becomes queen she will revenge herself on him, I suppose."

"She will wade to the throne in blood," exclaimed the duke darkly. "She will kill Methodios, Upravado, and Measurby. That is why I want to go away as soon as she is firmly established. I do not desire to witness her cruelties."

"Then you think she is cruel?"

"Very! I am beginning to hate her. It is bad enough for Wilfred to be the prisoner of the republic; it will be worse for him when Julia is queen. She thinks he has betrayed her, and she is a vindictive woman."

"Whatever she is," said Hilda, putting the phial containing the drug in her pocket, "I will rescue my husband from her clutches."

CHAPTER XXVII.

DOWN WITH THE REPUBLIC.

There was no doubt that Julia de Lusignan possessed a truly royal spirit, so dauntlessly did she bear herself in those disastrous days. On the death of her father, Pierre II., the rebellion of Methodios was so unexpected that she had been forced to fly. Had she then gained a few days' respite, during which she could have rallied her partisans, she would, without doubt, have remained queen of Busk. After such a crushing blow as the loss of her kingdom, many expected that she would make no attempt to regain her throne, but they did not know the imperious spirit of the woman.

In England she had intrigued incessantly for the downfall of Methodios, but finding him too firmly established to succumb to diplomatic trickery she had accepted Dacre's offer to replace her on the throne, and had risked her personal safety in the desperate attempt. Owing to the treachery of Measurby, the conspiracy had proved abortive, and by the merest miracle she escaped from the grasp of her enemies. Undaunted still, she used Measurby as the instrument of a new attempt, and was now in the capital itself, making one final effort to regain her sceptre. Cruel she was in many ways, unscrupulous in all things, but no one could fail to admire her dauntless spirit, her genius for intrigue, and her powers of endurance. After suffering all these crushing defeats, here she was as hopeful as ever, presiding over a council of her few remaining followers.

Many of her supporters had perished in the fight at Villa Tvartko, and the marquess Paradiso, her right hand, was now in prison and powerless to help her. Richborough was too honest for diplomacy, Measurby not clever enough, so she had to manage all things with the assistance of the cardinal. Indeed, had it not been for that ingenious schemer, this second attempt would also have failed, in spite of her untiring efforts to bend circumstances to her will. Gregory, however, was a tower of strength, and controlled the intrigues of the provinces. The princess, having been absent for nearly two years from Busk, was but a shadow to many of the royalists, and they looked to Gregory for their instructions.

The cardinal loved to control everything in this manner. His palace was the centre of the web, whither all threads diverged. From all parts of Busk, messengers, in the guise of mendicants, were incessantly arriving. They came to the palace for alms, and, having thus escaped the vigilance of Methodios, there delivered their messages to the cardinal. He transmitted them to Julia, and together they conferred over matters important to the cause. The cardinal was very anxious for the restoration of royalty. He admired the brilliant intellect of Julia, yet at the same time foresaw clearly that, once in power, she would not be an easy person with whom to deal. The late king had been a mere puppet in the hands of the church, but Julia was as astute as the cardinal himself and obstinate beyond words. In fact it seemed to Gregory as though the struggle between monarchy and republicanism would be succeeded by a contest between church and state.

However, he had committed himself too far to draw back, and besides, despite Julia's despotic inclinations, could do more with a queen than with a president; so he pushed on matters as rapidly as possible. Now the crisis was approaching, and this council was being held in the octagon chamber to receive Upravado, who was expected to make his appearance shortly.

There were about a dozen men present, including many of the leading nobility of Busk, principally from the provinces, as the citizens of Varzo inclined more to the republic. In truth, from a commonsense point of view, it would have been wiser to have raised the royal standard in the provinces, but in this instance the capital offered particular advantages for securing Upravado; so Julia had decided to strike her last blow for the throne in the very jaws of danger.

"Your Eminence is certain that Upravado will come?" asked Julia, with an anxious glance at the clock.

"I have no doubts about it, your Majesty," replied the cardinal, suavely; "probably he is waiting now, but I do not wish to introduce him here until the council has fully decided what is to be done."

"The matter is decided already," exclaimed the princess impetuously; "this man is to be bribed. Monsieur," she added, turning to Measurby, "you have the gold?"

Measurby pointed to a large box at the end of the room, beside which stood Janshah.

"It is there, madame. Four hundred thousand francs in gold."

"Excellent, monsieur. This time we will not fail. Once we secure Upravado, and my return to the throne can be proclaimed to-morrow."

"At the cathedral," said the archbishop with a smile of satisfaction. "I have taken care that all those devoted to your Majesty will be there."

"Alas! there are many dead at Villa Tvartko who would have been there," said Julia, with a touch of regret for those who had fallen in her defence; "but this is not the time to sorrow for their fate. When I have regained my heritage and punished my enemies, then will I raise a monument to those who have died for their queen."

There was a burst of applause from those present at the expression of this noble sentiment, skilfully introduced by the crafty princess. All present, save the cardinal and Richborough, believed that she meant what she said; but they knew it was merely clap-trap to please her partisans. The majority present felt that she was indeed a tender-hearted sovereign, who could thus sympathize with her subjects; but in after years they had reason to change their opinion. Julia was pleased at the sensation produced by her speech, and would have gone on speaking, but at that moment the electric bell rang sharply.

"Upravado!" said the cardinal in a joyous tone. "I will go and prepare him to meet this honourable company."

He left the room, with his usual dignity, while those behind remained in a state of great anxiety. Everything turned on Upravado, and if he declined to be bought, there would be a repetition of the scenes at the Villa Tvartko. There was no escape this time, as Julia well knew, and, sitting back in her chair with an artificial smile on her lips, she passed through agonies during the absence of the prelate. It was the most critical moment of her life, for the decision of Upravado either raised her to a throne or condemned her to a prison cell.

"Courage, madame," whispered Richborough. bending forward; "a daring heart wins kingdoms."

"I will be satisfied with one kingdom," replied Julia with apparent lightness. "If I win, I win. If I lose, I lose. For either future I am prepared."

"You have indeed a brave heart."

"I should have been a man," said the princess with a fiery glance; "but though a woman, I will rule like a king."

While the words were yet on her lips, the door opened to admit Cardinal Gregory and Upravado. All arose save the princess, who remained seated, in absolute silence. This conduct seemed to abash the general, who could not but feel that he had acted a cowardly part at the Villa Tvartko: and indeed, but that he was afraid of Methodios, would not again have supported the cause of his wronged sovereign. For a moment he stood irresolute, and then, with a sudden decision, moved forward to the chair of the princess, on arriving at which, he flung himself on his knees before her.

"I entreat you, madame, to pardon my conduct."

"It is hardly deserving of pardon," said Julia, sternly. "I do not care for affection that is bought for gold."

"Madame," said the general, bluntly, "I have experienced the gratitude of princes before, in the person of your late father; therefore it was but right that I should make myself secure."

"Let it be so, then, Upravado," replied the princess, slowly; "this time the money you desire shall be paid to you before you leave this room. If so, will you swear to support my cause?"

"I swear it."

"You swore before," said the deep voice of the archbishop, "but broke your oath."

"Pardon, monseigneur," said Upravado, rising to his feet: "I swore to help the princess if certain moneys were paid. They were not paid, so I was released from my oath. You did not keep your part of the bargain. I did not keep mine."

"And you followed me to the frontier," said the princess, rising in her turn.

"Yes. I would have arrested you if I could have done so," replied Upravado boldly.

A thrill of indignation ran through the assemblage, and several of the nobles placed their hands on their sword-hilts. Julia however, smiled at the boldness of the reply, and held out her hand for Upravado to kiss.

"I like boldness in an enemy," she said suavely.

"I am not your enemy now, madame," said Upravado, bowing, "but your friend."

"And I hope you will be my subject, and the prop of my throne," replied the princess with a bland smile. "Well, the money you desire will be yours. Major Measurby!"

The major bowed and led Upravado towards Janshah, who opened the box beside which he was standing.

"Double the amount you asked for is there," he said solemnly.

"Double the amount!" replied Upravado joyously, "four hundred thousand francs!"

"Yes."

"Good! Madame, I am yours."

He crossed over to the princess, and kissed her hand once more. In doing so, he could not see her face. It was just as well, for it was the face of a demon.

"Will you have that box taken down and delivered to three soldiers who are waiting below?" said Upravado to Measurby; "and then we can settle all farther matters."

"Yes. Janshah will do that."

The Indian vanished, and returned with two of his servants. The three, with great difficulty, owing to the weight of the metal, managed to carry the box down the stairs, and when the door was closed, Upravado spoke once more.

"Now that your Majesty has performed your part of the contract, I will perform mine. Myself and my soldiers are yours."

"And what about Methodios?"

"I hate Methodios!" exclaimed Upravado, fiercely; "he would trick me into danger, and banish me from the country. I am no longer a servant of the republic. Here is my real mistress."

It was an astonishing scene. Here was a man who held the destinies of Busk in his hands, coolly betraying his party for a bribe. True, he was delivering the country to his rightful sovereign; nevertheless he was selling it, all the same. There was neither honour nor dignity in the transaction, and callous as was Julia in many ways, she keenly felt the humiliation of being obliged to buy the influence of this traitor. When she could, she would punish him, but the time was not yet ripe for such daring. Upravado had the army at his back, and could either make or mar her. At present she had gained his support, but she fully made up her mind to punish him when she was able.

Upravado knew perfectly well what was passing in her mind, and it was for this reason that he had demanded the money. Could he have trusted to her gratitude, he would have done so; but having experienced the temper of the Lusignans before, he did not care about making such a risky experiment. With his influence he could have made himself president of the republic, in place of Methodios, but preferred a wealthy exile to an insecure position obtained by fraud. He trusted neither Methodios nor

Julia, and, as soon as he had fulfilled his promise and set her on the throne, intended to place himself at once beyond the reach of her vengeance. That she hated him for the humiliations he had made her suffer, he knew perfectly well, and now that the price of his treachery was duly paid would make himself safe from her hate. Meanwhile, like Julia, he acted a part; and to hear him making all arrangements, one would have thought that he was the devoted friend of the Lusignan dynasty.

The design for the proclamation of the queen, however, was due to the inventive genius of the archbishop, who now placed it before the assembly.

"To-morrow," said Gregory slowly, "as you all know, Methodios has ordered high mass to be celebrated and a Te Deum to be sung in the cathedral, as a mark of gratitude for the preservation of the republic. The president with his friends will be there, but there also will be the friends of our party. In fact, I have arranged that the body of the cathedral will be quite filled with our friends. From all the provinces they will come ostensibly to be present at the festival of the church, but in reality to support her Majesty. The soldiers of Upravado will surround the cathedral during the celebration of the mass, and when the queen is proclaimed, Upravado will at once arrest Methodios. Our friends will throw themselves on his party and disarm them, then the queen will be proclaimed to the soldiers, who will accept her with acclamations."

"You can trust your soldiers?" said Julia, turning to Upravado.

"Implicitly, Madame," he answered, bowing.

"The presence of the soldiers," resumed the archbishop, "will intimidate the citizens, who will not dare to resist; so we will have a bloodless revolution. The provinces will send in their submission to the queen when she is established, and the kingdom of Busk will thus be once more under the sway of its rightful sovereign."

"Then," said Julia with exultation, "we will punish the traitors."

"Methodios first," said Upravado, quite forgetting that he also was a traitor.

"Methodios first," repeated the princess significantly, "afterwards the others."

"You approve of the scheme, Upravado?" asked the cardinal.

"Nothing could be better. Methodios has ordered the troops to be in the great square; so the whole army will be present to assist at his downfall."

"We can trust you?" said the princess, looking at him keenly.

"Madame," replied Upravado in a dignified tone, "I am a man of honour. I failed you before because I was not treated well. Now I have received the money, you may be sure I will do my best to place your Majesty on your rightful throne."

After making this speech, Upravado withdrew, and the council broke up. Julia was left alone with the archbishop, Richborough and Measurby.

"You do not think he will betray us, your Eminence?" asked the princess anxiously.

"No! Rest assured he will keep his word. Methodios does not trust him now. Another conspiracy like this, and he would not trust him at all."

"But he could overthrow Methodios, and make himself president," suggested Measurby.

"Yes! but he will not do so. Upravado is too fond of his own ease to risk such a position. No! He will place the princess on the throne as he has promised, and then, in my opinion, he will fly the country with his basely won gold."

"Just as well," muttered Julia fiercely; "if he stays, sooner or later I will punish him with death."

CHAPTER XXVIII.

LONG LIVE THE QUEEN.

The Duomo of San Hilarion dates from the fourteenth century, and is one of the most superb buildings of its kind in eastern Europe. Finely situated in the square of Tephricé, it rises, an immense edifice of white marble, from the summit of a slight mound. Broad flights of marble steps lead upward to a wide terrace, from whence springs the highly ornate front, a miracle of Renaissance art, which looks like frozen lace-work. With its innumerable pinnacles, its multitudinous statues, and somewhat squat façade, it is not unlike the famous Duomo of Milan. Here, however, all resemblance ends between the buildings, for in place of a lofty central tower the Varzo cathedral has an enormous dome, which swells in the air like a gigantic bubble. Being gilded all over, it flashes back the rays of the sun with intolerable brilliance, so that far and wide, during the day, it shines like a globe of fire above the city of Varzo.

The summit of the dome is surmounted by a crescent, from whence springs a golden cross delicately slender against the blue sky, and this strange mingling of Christian and Mahometan symbols is the first object which catches the eye of the approaching traveller. The people of Varzo are very proud of their Duomo, as well they might be, from its delicate architectural beauties and rare antiquity. The hot air and dazzling sun have mellowed the white marble to the soft hue of amber, but by night, in the silver moonlight, it looks like some palace of enchantment erected by fairy hands.

Nor is the interior less beautiful. Entering by the principal door, the eye is at once attracted by a huge gilt cross placed on high, on which strikes the light from some unseen window. In the semigloom which prevails owing to the multiplicity of painted glass, this sudden apparition of the Christian symbol is wonderfully effective, albeit rather theatrical in its seeming.

For the rest, there is a forest of marble pillars springing from the brilliantly tessellated pavement to the groined roof, a magnificent high altar glittering with jewels, and many banners hanging their ragged folds over gigantic tombs of dead and gone monarchs. All the Lusignans are buried here. From Amaury, the founder of the dynasty, down to Pierre II., the father of Julia, they rest in magnificent sarcophagi sculptured with broad-winged angels and trumpet-blowing cherubs.

The brilliant light of the East pierces the windows filled with stained glass of innumerable tints, and the great church, even at high noon, is full of floating shadows. Away at the end rises the glittering mass of the high altar, brilliant with star-like candles, and flashing innumerable jewels through the dim twilight of the building. The fumes of incense hang perpetually round the building; here and there points of red light burn before some rich shrine; there is a constant mutter of prayer, and over all a feeling of peace and quiet and intense rest.

On this great day, however, the Duomo had awakened from its usual lethargy. The building was crowded to the doors with gaily dressed people, among whom could be seen many soldiers in uniform. Outside, some regiments were drawn up in the square to do honour to the arrival of Methodios. Attended by a brilliant staff, he passed up the church and seated himself on the old throne of the Lusignans near the high altar.

It was a thanksgiving service for the safety of the republic, but Methodios did not look happy. Surrounded on all sides by dangers, his eyes constantly glanced round the church as if to spy out his own enemies and those of the republic. Upravado was there, prepared to betray his country, and all was skilfully arranged for the proclamation of the queen.

Julia, in the jewel-vault of the church, was anxiously waiting for the signal to appear before the multitude. She had assumed her royal robes, and on her head wore the ancient crown of the Lusignans, which the cardinal had so dexterously preserved from the grasping avarice of Methodios. Richborough and Measurby were with her, both outwardly calm, but in reality greatly excited by the crisis which was now approaching.

On the arrival of the president the service at once began. The organ sighed forth its rich music, and from the side entered the long train of priests, bishops, and acolytes, all dressed in the gorgeous raiment of the Romish church. Lastly came the cardinal, in his robes as a papal prince, walking under a canopy upheld by white-robed priests.

No one would have guessed that this dignified prelate was concerned in a conspiracy, and was fostering an action which might deluge the church in blood. He cast one glance at Methodios on his way to the archbishop's throne, and it was so proud, so defiant and confident, that the president started.

"What does that mean?" he muttered to Upravado, who stood near him. "More conspiracy?"

"No, of course not," replied the general hastily. "All that sort of thing was crushed at Villa Tvartko."

"I did not like that look of Gregory's," said Methodios reflectively; "he is a dangerous man, and we must get him away from Busk."

"Nothing less than the keys of St. Peter will tempt him to leave his present position."

"Ah!" replied Methodios, raising his eyebrows, "is that so? Well, we shall see. I am safe now, and can afford to punish my enemies."

Upravado said nothing, but smiled slightly to himself as he thought how soon Methodios would be undeceived. The service duly proceeded with all the pomp of the Romish church. The choir thundered out the sublime chants, accompanied by the melodious thunder of the organ. White clouds of incense rolled towards the roof, and hither and thither flitted the figures of the priests. Cardinal

Gregory alone did not move. He sat like a graven image on his throne, waiting for the time when he could throw off the mask. Looking down the crowded church he saw everywhere the faces of those who he knew would support the royal cause.

Without, the soldiers had planted cannon so as to command the square and intimidate the citizens. Within, the church was crowded with the friends of Julia. Only a knot of men around Methodios, and a sprinkling of others among the crowd, were faithful to the republic. At length the mass ended, the organ was rolling out a final march, when it suddenly ceased and the archbishop arose to his feet.

There was a single trumpet blast, which rang loudly through the church, and in a moment Upravado had sprung from the side of Methodios towards the throne of the archbishop. Terrified by this action, the president remained seated in his chair, white as a corpse, and saw a woman ascend the steps of the higher altar, — a woman in regal robes, with a royal crown on her head. She turned and looked towards the crowd. It was Julia de Lusignan.

Before Methodios could collect his scattered wits, the cardinal spoke.

"People of Busk, I present to you the rightful sovereign of your country. Long live Queen Julia!"

"Long live Queen Julia!" responded the crowd, though here and there were some dissenting voices.

Methodios sprang to his feet and drew his sword.

"Treason! Treason, against the republic! Culin! Upravado!"

"Long live Queen Julia!" cried the general loudly.

"Traitor!" shrieked the president, and dashed towards the higher altar. His officers tried to follow, but were held back by the friends of Upravado. A tumult arose in the church as Methodios, mad with anger, sprang up the altar steps, sword in hand, towards the queen. She awaited his coming with the utmost calmness, trusting he would be stopped before he reached her. His action, however, had taken all so much by surprise that no one moved. He reached her side, he raised his sword, and in one moment would have cut her down, when Richborough, who stood near, threw himself between them. The sword struck him on the shoulder, but the blow glanced harmlessly off, while Methodios, enraged at his object being thus defeated, drew a dagger and closed with the duke.

For a moment the two men swayed to and fro, then fell down the altar steps. Richborough gave a cry, for the dagger of Methodios had pierced his breast, and he was unable to rise. Methodios was on his feet in a moment and ran to the altar rails, but before he could reach them Upravado had cleaved his skull. The president of the late republic fell dead.

The organ pealed out a march of triumph, the people were shouting for Julia, the cry had been taken up outside, and she moved away down the church with Upravado and the archbishop, without a thought of the man who had saved her life.

She did, indeed, hesitate as she passed him, for

even her cruel nature felt that his act had been heroic, but the cardinal drew her on.

"Not now! Not now! Show yourself to the soldiers, or all may be lost!"

The procession moved down the church, and Richborough, raising himself on his elbow, looked after her with bitter anguish.

"Julia!" he cried, in a weak voice, "Oh, Julia, I am dying!"

She took no notice. The organ rolled its triumphal chant, the trumpets blared, the people cheered, all sweeter music in the ears of Julia de Lusignan than the cry of a dying man, even though his death had saved her life. She was a queen now, and had forgotten everything else.

The duke knew that he was dying, — not that the wound was deep, but, in the struggle, Methodios had whispered the one word "poison." The dagger was poisoned, and nothing on earth could save him now from his fate. Yet, to die alone, with no one beside him, to hear these triumphal cries greeting the woman who had so heartlessly left him, — it was bitter indeed, and Gerald Havard, Duke of Richborough, sighed to think that he was left to die like a dog in a strange land, with no one near to comfort his last moments.

Lying there in a swoon, with the blood pouring from his breast, he felt a soft arm round his neck, a handkerchief was applied to the wound, and over him bent a well-known face.

"Hilda! Hilda! I am dying!"

"I saw it all, Gerald. That hateful woman!

You saved her life, and yet she could leave you because she feared for her crown!"

"I am nothing to her now. She has made use of me and now I am cast on one side. I am dying, Hilda."

"No, Gerald, you are not dying. See, the wound is not deep. I am stanching the blood easily."

"It is too late. The dagger of Methodios was poisoned."

"Poisoned! Oh, Gerald, let me go for a doctor. But I know not whence to look for one. Ah, here is Nicolas! Here, Nicolas, quick! Quick, he is dying!"

"The archbishop sent me back," said the secretary, hurrying up, his face sparkling with joy. "The soldiers have accepted Julia as queen."

"What do I care for that? Do you not see my cousin is dying? Call a doctor!"

"There is no doctor to be obtained."

"Will you see him die before your eyes?"

"Nothing can be done, Hilda," murmured the duke weakly, "the dagger of Methodios — poison."

"Ah!" said Nicolas, on hearing these words, "I know that famous dagger of Methodios. Nothing can save M. le duc. He must die."

"He is dying now," said Richborough, whose face had assumed the pallor of death. "Hilda! Hilda! You must escape! Tell Julia, if she has any thought of me, who saved her life, to release Wilfred."

"Oh, my poor Gerald! My poor Gerald!"

"Your father will be Duke of Richborough, now."

"Never talk of it," said Hilda, whose tears were falling fast on the face of the dying man. "Oh, Gerald, that you should die like this! That hateful woman! She lives and reigns, and you die!"

"She is only true to her nature, Hilda. Oh! I feel — I die — Hilda! Give my love to Wilfred — I always loved Wilfred. Tell Julia! Hilda — ah! — kiss —"

She pressed a kiss on his lips, but no breath proceeded from thence. His head fell back. He was dead. The church was quite emptied of its crowd, who had all followed the newly restored queen. Even Nicolas, seeing he could do nothing, had departed, and Hilda was alone with her dead cousin.

She did not shriek or weep. The blow had fallen too heavily for that, but she lifted the handkerchief stained with his blood, and kissing the dead man's face once more, walked slowly down the church. Her face was as set and rigid as that of a corpse, and with the blood-stained handkerchief clasped to her breast, she sought the queen.

Outside, all was brilliant sunshine and shouting crowds. On the steps of the cathedral stood Julia, smiling and happy, a crowned queen, with Upravado and the archbishop on either side. Forcing her way through the crowd, Hilda flung the blood-stained handkerchief before the queen, and, with one look of reproach, vanished.

Julia turned pale at the sight, but in a moment smiled again. The crowd were saluting her as queen, and in that sweet music she forgot that her elevation to the throne had cost the life of a man who loved her fondly.

"At last," she murmured, glancing over the sea of upturned faces, — "at last, I am queen of Busk. The crown is on my head; my enemies are under my feet, and all is as I desire."

Truly, she was more of a queen than a woman.

CHAPTER XXIX.

THE GRATITUDE OF PRINCES.

Thus the restoration of the monarchy was accomplished. Accepted as queen by the army and the provinces, Julia had no difficulty in forcing the people of Varzo to acknowledge her as their lawful sovereign. They were in the minority, and dared not go against the plainly expressed wishes of the whole kingdom. At first, they were inclined to resent the substitution of a queen for a president; but after a time, began to find that the change was for the better. The good people of Varzo were very pleasure-loving and frivolous, so Julia, knowing this to be so, announced that, after settling all political affairs, she would give a series of fêtes to inaugurate her reign. This would give employment to some, and amusement to others; so finding their new sovereign to be of this mind, the Parisians of the East began to pluck up spirit and look forward to a long and brilliant reign.

As soon as Julia was conducted to the royal palace, she at once gave orders for the release of Paradiso, who was still confined in the Tower of the Sultan. The marquess duly appeared and kissed the hand of his mistress, with tears of joy at her restoration, though, at the same time, he lamented very much that he had not been there to take part in the triumph of the royalists. He was delighted to hear of the death of Methodios, but deeply regretted the loss of the duke. When Julia had somewhat recovered from the intoxication of her triumph, she greatly repented having acted so cruelly towards the man who had saved her life. Still, under the circumstances, it would have been dangerous to have remained beside him, as neglect to show herself to the army might have cost her dear. Solacing herself with this idea, she made all the reparation in her power, by giving the dead man a splendid funeral, and ordering a magnificent monument to be erected over his remains in the Duomo of San Hilarion.

A week had now elapsed since she had secured her crown, and with the skilful assistance of the cardinal and Paradiso, she was gradually reducing the affairs of the kingdom to something like order. Shortly, she intended to send plenipotentiaries to the great powers, announcing her restoration; but at present she was too busy with the internal affairs of Busk to do so. Wonderful to state, Russia made no sign of interfering, but the revolution had been so rapid, silent, and complete, that the Czar could hardly find a pretext for meddling with the matter. The queen was greatly delighted at this silent acquiescence of Russia, as it gave her time to form her plans; for she by no means approved of Muscovite designs, and hoped, with the aid of her two statesmen, to baffle the government of the Czar.

Upravado still commanded the army, as the queen

saw it would be dangerous at the present time to harm him in any way. The soldiers who had placed her on the throne were quite capable of taking her off again did anything happen to their beloved leader; so Julia, masking her resentment and hate under bland smiles, treated Upravado with the utmost consideration. She hoped, in the near future, to win the hearts of the soldiers so that they should regard her and not the general as their real leader, and then she could avenge herself on Upravado for the insults to which she had been subjected by him.

Notwithstanding her suavity of manner, Upravado knew quite well that she was only watching for an opportunity to arrest him, and made all preparations for flight. He sent on to London the money he had so basely won, and kept a close watch on all the actions of the queen and her ministers, resolving to fly at the first intimation of danger. As yet, however, he was too powerful to be meddled with, but sooner or later he would fall, and then, unless he was fortunate enough to escape, he would be thrown into prison on some trivial pretext, which Julia could easily invent.

One other person was high in favour with the queen, and his position, although he did not know it, was quite as insecure as that of Upravado. This was Major Measurby, whom Julia had made the captain of the royal guard as a reward for his services. Nothing more had been said about the marriage, for, finding himself surrounded by her partisans, Measurby had been afraid to press a matter which seemed so distasteful to her. He had handed over the money, she had secured the throne, and yet no promise of reward in any way had been made to the unfortunate major. Now that she was queen, Measurby confessed with a sigh that he had lost his chance of marrying her, for she certainly would not wed him, now she had gained her ends.

Unless — and the major laid great store by this — unless he told her the story of the ring, and she was content to marry a man with twenty millions of money. Such a sum could do a great deal in Busk, and Measurby thought that Julia, despite her pride, would be tempted by the immensity of the sum. As yet he had said nothing about the matter, and though Julia suspected that he possessed some secret power of procuring money not unconnected with Janshah, she said nothing to the major. Had she only known the secret of the ring, she would at once have taken steps to have secured it for herself, but luckily for the major she was ignorant of this.

To show her gratitude, she made him the captain of the guard, which the major thought was but the prelude to further favours; and what with the ring on his finger, Janshah at his command, and a possible royal alliance in the future, he esteemed himself the most fortunate of men. He did not know how insecure was his position, and that Julia hoped to rid herself of his presence in a very short space of time. This she did not intend to do until she learned the secret of his power, so she quietly awaited her time until she could make such discovery and turn it to her own advantage. The major, quite ignorant of all this, strutted about the palace in his new uniform like a peacock, much to the amusement of Paradiso, who knew in what light the queen regarded him, and frequently quoted to himself the proverb about pride going before a fall.

All this time Julia had designedly neglected the man to whom more than any one else she owed the success of her attempt on the crown. Had not Wilfred Dacre made Villa Tvartko the headquarters of the conspiracy, she would not have been able to come secretly to Busk, and unless she had been on the spot, nothing could have been accomplished. She admitted to herself that Wilfred had done her a service; but, not yet convinced of his innocence on that fatal night, she refused to release him from prison. Certainly she gave orders that he was to be treated with the utmost consideration, but this afforded but small gratification to Wilfred, seeing that he was deprived of his liberty. Paradiso, who had a genuine liking for the unfortunate young man, tried to induce the queen to let him go free, but Julia determined not to do so until she had learned the secret of the money from either Measurby or Wilfred. She had them both in her power, and watched her opportunity to find out what she desired to know, but, meanwhile, kept one in a palace and the other in a prison, which was hardly a fair arrangement.

Several times Hilda had attempted to see Julia at the royal palace, but each time the queen had refused to grant her an audience. Julia had a very vindictive nature, and greatly resented the behaviour of Hilda in throwing the handkerchief stained with

Richborough's blood at her feet on the day of her triumph. She therefore refused to see Hilda; so the poor girl, unable to gain the release of her husband, remained under the roof of the cardinal in a very unhappy frame of mind. Gregory was very kind to Hilda, and greatly regretted the hostility of the queen, but as he already was feeling the difficulty of dealing with a woman of her imperious temper, he dared not interfere.

Things remained in this position for over a fortnight, when Julia, for no apparent reason, sent for Hilda Dacre to come to the royal palace. The fact was, she had come to the conclusion that, as Wilfred's wife, Hilda might possibly know this secret which she was desirous of learning, and she intended to offer Hilda her husband's liberty as the price of all being revealed.

Ignorant of what was passing in the mind of Julia, and hoping that she would be successful in her prayer for Wilfred's release, Hilda hastened joyfully to the palace, and was at once admitted into the presence of the queen.

Prosperity evidently agreed with Julia de Lusignan. The haggard, anxious look of her evil days had now vanished, and in its place appeared a serene, proud, and confident expression. She greeted Hilda in a kindly manner, for, notwithstanding her resentment against her former hostess, she could not but feel sorry for the troubles of this innocent woman. Such a feeling was rather ridiculous, seeing that it rested entirely with herself to make Hilda happy once more by restoring her husband to her arms; but Julia never acted without due forethought. She received Hilda graciously, because she wanted to get something out of her, and, though she felt a trifle sorry for her troubles, self-interest predominated in her mind.

Hilda was unable to greet the queen kindly. She thought Julia a hateful, cruel woman, who had acted in a base manner, and, notwithstanding the folly of such behaviour, could not help showing it. The queen saw this at once, and immediately proceeded to assure Hilda that she had no intention of acting otherwise than in the kindest and most hospitable manner.

"I am glad to see you here, madame," she said, in her sweetest tone; "and I have to thank you for the help which you afforded me at the Villa Tvartko."

"Your Majesty of course speaks ironically," replied Hilda coldly.

"By no means," returned Julia, a trifle disconcerted at this speech; "I owe much to your husband and yourself."

"Indeed, your Majesty, if you think so, you have a strange way of repaying past favours. I am homeless, save for the shelter of the cardinal's roof; my husband is in prison; I have not been permitted to see him; and the Duke of Richborough is dead."

"You have cause to speak bitterly," said Julia softly, "but, indeed, I am not so ungrateful as you think. I am aware that I owed my life to Monsieur le duc, but had I stayed beside him in his dying hour, all might have been lost. I was forced to appear before the army in order to secure their allegiance. When I returned, which I did as soon as possible, Monsieur le duc was dead. Blame me as you will, but confess that I was powerless to act otherwise than I did."

"Are you powerless to release my husband from prison?"

"No. I am going to do so to-day. It is only now that I have found time to think of anything. Ah, madame, you do not know how dangerous has been my position for the last week! Do you think that because Methodios is dead, and I am acknowledged as queen of Busk, that my safety is secured? By no means. On all sides I have to face and conquer difficulties. This has left me no time to attend to such matters as I ought, otherwise Monsieur Dacre would have been released at once."

"Your Majesty found time to release the marquess Paradiso."

"I required the marquess," replied Julia coldly; "and as to Monsieur Dacre, though I am willing to release him, you must admit that I have just cause to keep him in prison."

"I do not admit that," said Hilda firmly. "He did all in his power to help you to succeed. That he failed to give the money to Upravado on that night at the Villa Tvartko was not his fault."

"Then whose fault was it?"

"Major Measurby's."

"Pardon me, I can hardly believe that. Major Measurby proved no traitor. Had it not been for him, I should not now be in my palace."

"I think my husband had more share in your success than any one else," said Hilda with great spirit. "However, it is no use talking over the matter. Let your Majesty release my husband, and then fulfil Richborough's dying request."

Julia turned pale. Stifle her feelings as she could, she still felt remorse for the way in which she had acted towards the man who had saved her life, and lost his own in so doing.

"What do you mean, madame?"

"When my cousin was dying, he said, 'If Julia has any feeling that I have done her a service, let her release Wilfred Dacre at once.'"

"I will do so," said Julia passionately. "I always intended to do so. I asked you to come here for that purpose. See! the order of release is already prepared."

With a sudden gesture she took up a paper from the table and held it out to Hilda.

"Thank Heaven!" said Hilda joyfully, and put out her hand to seize the paper. To her astonishment Julia drew it back.

"One moment, madame. There are conditions."

"Conditions?" repeated Hilda faintly, hardly understanding the queen's meaning. "Your Majesty is pleased to jest."

"No, I am in earnest. I release your husband on condition that you tell me the real reason of the failure at Villa Tvartko."

"I cannot."

"Do you know it, then?" asked the queen eagerly.

"Yes; but —"

"Then tell it to me at once," said Julia imperiously. "From all I have heard, there was some secret power possessed by your husband which has now passed to Major Measurby. That Indian has something to do with it, and I wish to know the meaning of all these things."

"What does your Majesty desire to know?" asked Hilda, equivocating in order to gain time for reflection.

"Why was not the money paid at Villa Tvartko, and how did that selfsame money come into the possession of Major Measurby? Also, I desire to know the reason why this Janshah no longer obeys your husband, but does whatever he is told to do by Measurby. There is a mystery about all this which must be explained to me."

"I cannot explain."

"You mean, you will not!"

"I do."

"Reflect. It means the freedom of your husband," said Julia significantly. "If I do not learn it from you, I will from him or from this major. Tell me all now, and I will release Monsieur Dacre. Refuse, and I shall not only keep him still in prison, but will send you away from Busk."

"Away from Busk?" said Hilda in despair.

"Yes. So now you can make your choice."

The queen turned abruptly away and looked out of the window, while Hilda rapidly thought over the matter thus placed before her. She saw plainly that unless she told all to the queen, there would be no possibility of removing her suspicions regarding the failure at Villa Tvartko. Yet if she revealed the secret of the ring, Julia would at once take steps to possess herself of the talisman.

Hilda was rather inclined to do this, if only to punish Major Measurby for his treachery. She knew that there was no chance now of obtaining the ring from its present possessor, as he would be constantly on his guard. Unwilling, however, that the major should enjoy the fruits of his dastardly conduct, she decided to tell the queen all, and let her deal with Measurby as Measurby had dealt with Wilfred.

"Well, madame," said the queen, returning to her seat, "have you made up your mind?"

"Yes. I will tell all, but I am afraid your Majesty will think the story too wild for belief."

"I will judge for myself. Tell me all, everything."

Whereupon Hilda related the whole story of the ring, from the time it came into the possession of Wilfred; and to substantiate the statement, handed to Julia the letter written by her husband in prison. The queen listened to the marvellous tale with rapt attention, only interrupting Hilda every now and then with her ejaculations of surprise.

"Wonderful!" she said when the tale was ended. "And do you mean to say, madame, that this ring, now in the possession of Major Measurby, commands twenty millions of English money?"

"Yes. It is a marvellous story I have told your Majesty, but perfectly true."

The queen sat silent, thinking deeply. Already her active brain was at work scheming how to obtain the talisman from the major. With such a sum at her command, she could perform miracles, — extend her kingdom, baffle the craft of Russia, and perhaps secure Constantinople. With this she could drive the Turk across the Bosphorus, reconstruct the Greek empire, and seat herself, a second Theodora, on the throne of the Comneni. As ruler of Busk she could do much, but as owner of the ring she could do more; and there and then she decided that before night the ring of Brahma would sparkle on her finger.

With deep craft, however, she let no hint of her thoughts escape her, but with a gracious smile handed the order of release to Hilda.

"I quite exonerate your husband now," she said, smiling, "and had I known of this before, I would at once have released him. As for Major Measurby —"

"What about the major?" asked Hilda, slipping the order of release into her pocket.

"He is a traitor and a scoundrel. Leave me to deal with him," replied Julia fiercely. "I will punish him."

"If your Majesty intends to do so by depriving him of the ring, let me warn you to be careful. If you use force he may get rid of it before it can be seized."

"True," replied Julia thoughtfully. "I will not use force. I will say nothing to Major Measurby to-day, lest he should suspect from your visit that I know his secret. No; to-morrow I will try to circumvent him."

"You intend to obtain the ring then?" asked Hilda dejectedly.

These words recalled the queen to herself, and she recognized the folly of making Hilda the confidante of her plans.

"No, I hardly think so," she replied carelessly. "Major Measurby will do anything I tell him; so the ring is as good as mine now. But we will not talk of these matters at present. You have now the order of release; so take with you Paradiso and go to the Tower of the Sultan for your husband."

"I will go at once," cried Hilda, joyfully rising to her feet.

"One moment," said Julia, motioning her to stay. "After all that has passed, I am unwilling to see Monsieur Dacre again, and think it as well that you should both leave the kingdom."

Hilda was struck by the ingratitude of this observation, but made no remark thereon, save indirectly.

"I think so, too," she replied coldly. "Rest assured that my husband is as little desirous of seeing you as you are of seeing him. We will leave at once."

The queen took no notice of this pointed speech, but continued to talk calmly to Hilda, as though she were conferring a benefit instead of behaving like an ingrate.

"That yacht which lay off Villa Tvartko is there still," she said coldly; "it was given to me by Major Measurby."

"It was not the major's to give," replied Hilda indignantly; "it is the property of my husband."

"It is the property of the ring," retorted Julia, "and, as such, has passed with the ring into the possession of the major. He gave it to me, and as a reward for your husband's services, I herewith bestow it on him. You can both go on board this afternoon, and sail to-night."

"Why to-night?"

"Because it is my wish that it should be so," retorted the queen in a haughty manner. "Before you leave I shall send down a message to Monsieur Dacre on board the yacht. As soon as he receives the message, you can start at once for England."

"We shall only be too glad to do so," said Hilda in as haughty a tone as that of Julia herself. "Depend upon it, your Majesty, neither my husband nor myself feel inclined to stay in a country where we have received nothing but ingratitude."

"Have a care," said the queen in an indignant manner. "Monsieur Dacre is still in prison."

"I have the order of his release."

"It can be revoked."

"I hardly think after what I have said that your Majesty can be so ungrateful to one from whom she has received nothing but benefits. Besides, my cousin the duke—"

"Go! Go!" cried the queen, stamping her foot. "I owe you gratitude, I admit, so I give your husband his liberty and the yacht. Go, I command you!"

"Farewell, your Majesty," replied Hilda, going

to the door. "You have gained your ambition at the cost of a noble life."

Julia, touched by some sudden remorse, buried her face in her hands, and Hilda, with one last look at the woman who was responsible for her cousin's death, left the room. She proceeded along the corridor for some little distance, when the place seemed to spin around her. The anxiety of the last few weeks, the interview with the queen, the thought that she was about to see her husband once more, — all these things proved too much for her nerves, and she sank down in a faint, on the floor of the palace.

CHAPTER XXX.

FEMININE DIPLOMACY.

WHEN Hilda revived, she was lying on a couch in a small room, and some one bending over her was holding a glass of wine to her lips. She looked up languidly and recognized in this good Samaritan — Major Measurby.

"Here, Mrs. Dacre, drink this!" said the major in rather a shamefaced manner. "It will do you good."

Hilda raised herself feebly on her elbow, and looked at him with the utmost scorn. He was arrayed in the brilliant uniform of the queen's guard, and on glancing at his right hand she saw that he wore thereon the ring of Brahma. So contemptuously did she look at him that the major, feeling abashed by her presence, placed the glass on the table and turned to go.

"Stop!" cried Hilda, struggling into a sitting posture. "I wish to speak with you, Major Measurby."

Recovering his presence of mind, he turned back and pointed to the wine-glass.

"You had better drink that first," he muttered nervously. "You are ill."

"How dare you touch me!" she replied with flashing eyes.

"You fainted in the corridor. In common humanity I could hardly leave you there, Mrs. Dacre."

"In common humanity you can hardly leave my husband in prison, where he is now through your machinations."

"It is not my fault,—" began Measurby in a blustering tone, when she cut him short.

"Yes, it is your fault. Had you not stolen that ring from Wilfred, the attempt at Villa Tvartko would not have failed; had it not failed he would not now be in prison."

"As to stealing the ring," answered Measurby mildly, "I only regained my own property. It is a family jewel—"

"Spare me these falsehoods, Major," said Hilda, taking the glass of wine from the table. "I know all about the ring."

"Has Wilfred told you—"

"He has told me everything."

"How can that be, when he is still in the Tower of the Sultan?" said the major suspiciously. "You cannot have had an interview with him."

"He bribed his jailer to take a letter to me, and in that letter all was explained."

Hilda quickly drank the glass of wine, which revived her greatly, and then sat quietly waiting the major's reply. That individual was thinking of some excuse to make, but could find none sufficiently plausible.

"Dacre stole the ring from me," he said obstinately.

"It is false," retorted Hilda haughtily. "The

ring was given to him by Mr. Lascelle and you had not the slightest claim to its possession."

"Well, I have it now," said Measurby insolently, "and I intend to keep it."

"So far as I am concerned, you are quite welcome to do so, Major. The ring has brought nothing but trouble to us."

"Upon my soul, Mrs. Dacre, I am sorry for what has taken place," said Measurby in an apologetic tone, "but it was not altogether my fault."

"Indeed? Then whose fault was it?"

"The queen's."

"Enough, Major Measurby. Do not lay the burden of your sins on the shoulders of other people. Julia de Lusignan has quite enough crimes laid to her charge already, without adding yours to the number."

"You misunderstand the queen," said Measurby quickly; "she is not so bad as you think. If I go and see her now, I can persuade her to consent to Dacre's release."

"I have obtained that," replied Hilda, producing the order; "she has released Wilfred on condition that we leave the country at once."

"How are you going?"

"By the yacht which is still lying in front of Villa Tvartko."

"But I gave that to the queen."

"Yes! and the queen has given it to my husband and myself."

The major looked somewhat blank at this information, and for a few moments knew not what to say.

In that short space of time an idea had occurred to Hilda which she forthwith determined to carry out. It was none other than to recover the ring, and she hastily formed a plan of action.

On the table was a tray with several glasses and a bottle of wine, which the Major had ordered to be brought in order to revive her from the faint. She still possessed the narcotic given to her by Janshah, with which she had hoped to drug the jailer and thus aid Wilfred to escape. If she could only drug a glass of wine and persuade the major to drink it, in a few moments he would be fast asleep, and she could then take the ring from his finger. It was a desperate chance, but she determined to attempt it, and watched for an opportunity to drug the wine.

"Mrs. Dacre," said the major, after a few minutes' thought, "I am truly sorry for your misfortunes, and I think the best thing you can do is to go back to England in this yacht."

"We have no money!"

"In England you have five thousand a year settled on yourself, which no one can touch. Surely yourself and your husband can live on that."

The cool insolence of the man enraged Hilda, and she could hardly keep her temper. Being desirous, however, of getting back the ring, she suppressed her anger, and answered the major civilly enough.

"When we arrive in England, all will be well. But I speak of money for our journey."

"I thought of that," replied Measurby eagerly, "when I brought you in here. I knew that this interview was inevitable, and desiring to offer you enough money to get back to England, I sent Janshah to my rooms for some. He will be back here shortly."

"Did you think I would go back without my husband?"

"No. I intended to ask the queen to release him, but as you have gained her pardon, there is no necessity for me to interfere in any way. I will give you the money, and you can go at once."

"Will Janshah be long away?" asked Hilda with pretended anxiety. "I wish to see my husband as speedily as possible."

"Probably he is on his way back now," said Measurby readily. "From this door I can see the whole length of the corridor, so I will look if he is coming."

The major sauntered towards the door, whereupon Hilda placed her own glass on the tray on the side nearest to herself. There were four glasses on the tray. One of these she placed beside her own, and left the remaining two on the other side of the tray with the bottle of wine between. Then taking the phial from her pocket, she quickly dropped some of the drug into the clean glass, and replaced the phial in her pocket. As her own glass had still a few dregs of wine at its bottom and the remaining two glasses were on the other side of the tray, she could not make any mistake as to which glass contained the drug intended for the major. All this was done so quickly that when Measurby returned she was sitting calmly on the sofa as though she had never moved since he left the room.

"There is no appearance of him yet," said Measurby resuming his seat. "What is the matter, Mrs. Dacre? You look pale again."

No wonder she looked pale, considering what was at stake; but the major, quite unsuspicious of her trick, poured her out another glass of wine. She watched him closely, and saw that he had filled her own glass. To keep him from handing it to her, she took it off the tray herself.

"Thank you, major, I do feel ill," she said faintly; "this excitement is too much for me. Why do you not have a glass of wine yourself?" she added artfully, as he held the bottle mechanically in his right hand, "and drink to our safe journey."

Had Measurby not been blind to his own good, he would have suspected that last phrase as coming from a woman whose husband he had wronged. But he never gave a thought to the matter; and, readily adopting her suggestion, he poured out some wine into the drugged glass.

"I drink to your safe journey, by all means, Mrs. Dacre," he said, putting the glass to his lips; "and I hope neither you nor your husband will think so hardly of me as you do now."

He drank down the drugged wine and set the glass back on the table empty. Hilda drew a long breath, for she now saw that her enterprise would be successful. In a few minutes Measurby would be sound asleep, and then she could secure the ring. The only danger lay in the unexpected return of Janshah. While the ring was on his master's hand, he would do all in his power to keep it there; but once she placed it on her own finger, he would serve her in- instead of the major. Her heart was beating loudly as she watched the effect of the drug on Measurby, and she talked calmly, though devoured by anxiety.

"You can hardly expect us to think well of you," she said, in reply to the major's last remark. "See what trouble you have placed us in."

"Well, I will get you out of it again," said Measurby thickly; "I will give you money; the queen has given you the yacht, and in England you have five thousand a year. I do not think you are so badly off."

"And what do you intend to do with the ring?"

"Marry Queen Julia."

Hilda laughed scornfully, and arose to her feet.

"You talk nonsense. The queen would never marry you."

"She will when I tell her about the ring," muttered the major drowsily. "Oh, how sleepy I feel."

"You need not trouble to," replied Hilda quickly, "she knows all, — I told her."

"You told her?" cried Measurby, trying to start from his seat, but falling back again.

"Yes! so she will try and get the ring from you, unless I take it in the mean time."

A sudden suspicion crossed the major's mind, and he tried to shake off the lethargy which was gradually benumbing his brain.

"You take — what! Ah! What does it mean?"

"I have drugged the wine."

The words, but not their sense, reached the dulled brain of the major. He looked at her in a stupid manner, and his head fell forward on his chest. In another moment he was breathing heavily, fast asleep. The drug had done its work, and she had triumphed over both the major and the queen. Without pausing a moment she took the ring of Brahma off the major's finger and slipped it on to one of her own, where it hung loosely, too large for the slender joint. A soft step caused her to turn round. She was just in time, for at the door she beheld Janshah.

He came forward in his usual stealthy manner and looked at Measurby, then turned his eyes inquiringly towards Hilda. For answer she held up the hand upon which sparkled the ring.

"I am mistress of the ring!"

Janshah bent forward, examined the ring closely, and then made a profound obeisance to Hilda.

"The ring is yours, my lady, and I obey it."

"Have you the gold for which you were sent by the major?"

"Yes! Fifty pounds."

Hilda laughed at this sample of Measurby's avarice. Wilfred had given him twenty thousand pounds, and he had returned the gift by the bestowal of fifty. She looked contemptuously on the major's senseless form, and then turned away with a smile.

"Go down to the yacht," she said to Janshah, "and make everything ready to start. Mr. Dacre and myself will be down very shortly."

Janshah bowed.

"You go to release Mr. Dacre, madame?"

"Yes!"

"Then I will have a carriage waiting for you at

the door of the Sultan's Tower. You can drive to Villa Tvartko, and at the terrace you will find a boat to take you to the yacht."

"An English crew, is it not?"

"Yes, madame! You need fear no treachery."

"Go then at once, Janshah, and in the mean time I will seek the marquess Paradiso, to release Wilfred."

Janshah once more bowed and took his departure, while Hilda, fearing to lose the ring, so loosely did it hang on her finger, slipped it into her pocket, and went to find the marquess. She was delighted at thus recovering the ring for Wilfred, but saw that they must leave Busk as speedily as possible, as, when the queen came to know of the major's loss, she would at once guess the truth. In that case, both Wilfred and herself would be arrested; so she lost no time in finding the marquess, who was much pleased to see her.

"Marquess! I have come to ask you to go with me to the Tower of the Sultan, to release my husband."

Paradiso shook his head in a melancholy manner.

"Alas, madame! I dare not do that without the express order of her Majesty."

"Here is the queen's order," replied Hilda, giving him the paper. "I have seen her, and explained all."

"My dear madame, I am indeed glad," said Paradiso, running his eye over the paper. "M. Dacre should have been released long ago, and I urged it frequently on her Majesty, but she would not hear of it. You have gained a favour which I could not obtain."

"A favour,—to release from prison the man who placed her on the throne?" said Hilda disdainfully. "I confess that I do not agree with you, Marquess. However, there is no use talking any more. There is the order of the queen to release my husband. Come to the Tower of the Sultan with me at once."

"Willingly, madame," said Paradiso, as they left the palace; "it is not far from here. What do you now intend to do?"

"Go to England in the yacht."

"What, that one off the Villa Tvartko given by Major Measurby to her Majesty?"

"Yes, her Majesty has given it to us."

"I am glad she has recompensed your husband in some degree for his unjust imprisonment," said Paradiso hastily. "You have been treated shamefully. But I could do nothing."

"I know you are our friend, Marquess," said Hilda in a voice of emotion, "and so is the cardinal, but the queen — she is not even grateful."

"Julia de Lusignan is a strange mixture," observed Paradiso, casting a hasty glance around to see that he was not observed; "there is a great deal of good in her, though you might not think so. You will see that she will make an admirable queen."

"I trust so, Marquess, for the sake of this unhappy country."

"It is as well you are leaving it," said the marquess in a gloomy tone, "for already I foresee trouble with Russia. The queen is very headstrong, and matters are not safe yet. She will not be content with Busk."

"Why, what does she wish?" asked Hilda in astonishment.

"Constantinople," replied Paradiso significantly; "and perhaps she will get there. But here we are at the door of the prison. I will speak to the jailer. Wait here, madame."

He went inside the tower, a lofty building of Saracenic architecture, from whence it took its name, the Tower of the Sultans. Hilda waited impatiently for his return, thinking he would come to take her to the cell of her husband. He was gone so long that she was beginning to grow anxious, when suddenly he appeared in the portal, but not alone, — with him was Wilfred.

With a cry of joy Hilda threw herself on her husband's breast, and for a few moments they could not speak, so deeply were they moved. Paradiso, touched by the sight, turned away and left them alone to their joyful meeting. Wilfred looked pale and ill from his long imprisonment, and Hilda cried bitterly as she saw the difference in his appearance.

"Hush, my dear Hilda," said Wilfred, kissing her, "all is over now. We must try and get away to England."

"All that is arranged — by the queen."

"The queen!" echoed Wilfred bitterly, "has she at last condescended to remember my existence?"

"She signed the order for your release. It was my poor cousin's last request that she should do so."

"I heard all about that, Hilda," said her husband in an agitated tone; "my jailer kept me informed of all that was going on. Poor Gerald! to lose his life for the sake of that ungrateful woman."

"She has some gratitude, Wilfred. She has presented you with the yacht."

"What yacht?"

"The Zoe."

"Why, she belongs to me."

"No; she belonged by the laws of the ring to Janshah. When Measurby took the ring, he possessed the yacht and gave it to the queen. She in her turn has given it to us."

"Well, we will use it to return to England. And Measurby, I suppose, still has the ring?"

"No!"

"Then who has it?" asked Wilfred, in a tone of lively astonishment.

Hilda held out her hand, and there, on the outstretched palm, lay the famous ring.

"You are its master again," said Hilda joyously. "Place it on your finger, Wilfred, and never let it be taken off."

"Hilda, you are a witch," cried Wilfred, slipping the ring on his finger with great delight. "How did you get it from Measurby?"

"I drugged his wine!"

"But if —"

"It's a long story, Wilfred," she said, drawing him away, "I will tell you another time. Meanwhile, to obtain your release I had to tell the queen all about the ring. She thinks Major Measurby still has it, and when she finds it is gone she will guess I have stolen it. We must get away from Busk as soon as possible."

"Here is a carriage for you, M. Dacre," said Paradiso, approaching.

"Yes! Thank you," replied Hilda, going towards it; "we drive to Villa Tvartko, and from thence go on board the Zoe."

"Good-by, madame, and you also, M. Dacre," said Paradiso, taking off his hat, "I feel ashamed of Busk when I see you depart like this."

"Never mind, Marquess," responded Wilfred thankfully. "So long as I am free, I care not."

"M. Dacre, I know not the circumstances of that night at Villa Tvartko. Who was the traitor?"

"Not my husband," said Hilda haughtily.

"I never thought so for a moment," replied Paradiso quickly, "you had risked too much, M. Dacre, to turn traitor at the last moment."

"The traitor was Major Measurby," said Wilfred, stepping into the carriage.

"Ah!" said the marquess, in a peculiar tone; "then rest assured, monsieur, that he will be punished by the queen."

"He has been punished already," cried Hilda triumphantly, "and by me."

CHAPTER XXXI.

THE WILL OF BRAHMA.

In four hours Major Measurby awoke from his unnatural slumber, with an aching head and a feeling of giddiness. For some moments he could not collect his thoughts sufficiently to remember where he was. No one had come into the room during his sleep, and all was as he had seen it, saving that outside the brilliance of day had faded into a delicate twilight. He looked at the empty couch, at the glasses on the table, and then sprang up with a loud cry.

He had discovered the loss of the ring.

"The wine," he said to himself savagely, — "it must have been drugged, — the ring has gone, and she has stolen it. Oh, what a fool I have been to trust for a moment to the wife of Dacre. By this time he doubtless wears the ring on his finger, and I have lost all. The queen will do nothing for me now, and I can do nothing for myself. Gone, — gone, after all my pains! Oh, curse the woman who tricked me! Curse her!"

It was no use raging in this manner, for bad language would never recover the ring; so Measurby set his wits to work to think of some plan by which he could get it back again. He knew well enough that if Hilda had given it to Wilfred, it was folly to think he had any chance of success, yet he frantically determined to either get the ring again or kill its present owner.

"Let me think," he muttered, trying to collect his scattered thoughts. "I must think. She said the queen had pardoned Dacre, and she had told the queen all. In that case, Julia will ask me about the ring when I see her again. Ah! what a lot I could have done with it! But now I have lost all. I am as much a pauper as I was in England, save for the remnant of my twenty thousand pounds. That paltry sum instead of millions! The traitress, to trick me so! The wine was drugged!"

He took up the glass out of which he had drunk, smelled and tasted the dregs.

"Drugged!" he said, furiously dashing the glass to atoms on the floor. "What a cursed fool I have been! That confounded Mrs. Dacre said she was going to Paradiso to see about her husband's release, and then to the yacht. I will see the marquess, and he will tell me all. If necessary I will go down to the yacht and force Dacre to give me back the ring, — ay, if I have to kill him!"

He proceeded at once to his own room, and wrapped a heavy military cloak round him so that it might hide his uniform; then, feeling that his sword was safe, in case of need, he went in search of Paradiso. The marquess and the major were not good friends, and convinced as was the former of Measurby's treachery, he found it difficult to meet him with cordiality. Trusting, however, that the queen would find work for the major in some distant province of the kingdom, the marquess veiled his dislike under a mask of scrupulous politeness, and managed to be on fairly good terms with one whom he regarded as a disloyal traitor.

Measurby found the marquess at his quarters, just about to go to the queen, who had summoned him to her presence; and he at once asked Paradiso about the Dacres.

"Is Dacre released?" he asked abruptly.

"Yes. Her Majesty has been graciously pleased to give him his freedom," replied Paradiso coldly, — "the least thing that could be done, in my opinion, seeing how much we are indebted to Monsieur Dacre."

"He is a thief!" said the major furiously, "and his wife, also; they have stolen my ring."

"You forget, Major," replied Paradiso haughtily, "that both Monsieur and Madame Dacre are friends of mine. I cannot permit you to speak of them so in my presence."

"I speak of people as I find them," retorted the major, who certainly did not lack courage. "What I say behind their backs I will say to their faces."

"I am afraid it is too late," said the marquess grimly; "they have left Busk."

"Left Busk!" cried the major, in despair, falling back a pace.

"Well, if they are not gone now, they will leave shortly. They are at present aboard the yacht Zoe, off the Villa Tvartko, and only await a message from her Majesty before leaving."

"Has the message gone?" asked Measurby anxiously.

"I am just going now to see the queen about it," replied Paradiso, putting on his hat. "I must go now, monsieur, and you—"

"You will find me at Villa Tvartko," said Measurby, turning away. "I might go on board the yacht by the messenger's boat, in order to bid farewell to my friends."

"I don't think they will be pleased to see you," said the marquess, looking back. "Madame Dacre spoke of you in anything but a friendly manner."

"Curse her!" muttered Measurby, and, turning on his heel, left the palace without further delay. The information afforded by Paradiso concerning the message from the queen had given him an idea, and he already had concocted a plot, which he now intended to carry out.

At once he proceeded to the palace of the archbishop, and obtained a horse from one of the grooms, in order to ride down to Villa Tvartko. He could have used his own horse at the palace, but distrusting the queen now that she knew the story of his treachery on that famous night, preferred to have his whereabouts unknown for the time being. The groom of the cardinal knew Measurby well as a friend of his master's, so without hesitation gave him the horse he required. The major mounted at once, and was soon outside the gates of Varzo, galloping in the direction of Villa Tvartko.

The four miles were soon covered by his horse, which was young and fresh. Measurby alighted at the villa, and after explaining to an officer on guard — for the villa was filled with soldiers — that he was awaiting the arrival of the queen's messenger, to go on board the yacht, strolled down to the terrace in order to await the arrival of the emissary.

It was now growing rapidly dark, and the light was dying out in the west, but already in the east could be seen the rising moon, rendering everything as bright as day. Measurby, pacing to and fro on the terrace, saw the yacht lying out about half a mile from the shore, and cursed bitterly to think how favourable were circumstances to the escape of his former friend.

"Never mind," growled the major savagely; "I will go on board with the queen's messenger, and once there, I will either get the ring or kill Dacre."

To think of all he had lost was very bitter to Measurby. For years he had hunted after Lascelle in order to gain possession of the ring. By using Wilfred as his instrument he had nearly achieved his object, and at the Villa Tvartko, through the unconscious aid of Hilda, he had gained the wished-for prize. Ah, why had he not refused to aid Julia when he met her on the Bulgarian frontier? It would have been better to go to Constantinople, from thence taking passage to England. Then he would have been still in possession of the ring; but as things had turned out he had been tricked, — tricked by a woman.

"Those cursed Dacres," said Measurby, shaking his fist at the yacht, "they have always stood in my way. First the husband, then the wife; and now they are again in possession of the ring, while I have lost the one aim of my life. It is no use, my staying here. I can do nothing with Julia now, so it will be best for me to leave. If I regain the ring, I may return and carry out my schemes, but as it is it would be folly to remain here exposed to the vengeance of that woman. I know that she hates me, and now that Mrs. Dacre has told her it was my fault the conspiracy of Villa Tvartko failed, she will hate me worse than ever."

The major's bitter reflections were put an end to by the arrival of an officer attended by two or three men. Measurby recognized the officer at once, — a young man called Mostar, for whom he had done some slight service. At once he determined to make use of him.

"Mostar," he said, advancing towards the officer, as he paused on the terrace, "you are going on board the yacht?"

"Yes, monsieur," replied Mostar in French, "with a message to Monsieur Dacre from the queen."

"Good! Let me go with you. I wish to say farewell to my friends."

"By all means, monsieur," assented the officer courteously; and in a few minutes they were in a boat, flying over the waves towards the long, black form of the Zoe.

"And Mostar," said Measurby, when he had achieved this much, "you need not mention to Monsieur Dacre that I am on board. I wish to surprise them."

"Certainly. I will say nothing."

"And do not wait for me to come back. I will remain on board, and ask Monsieur Dacre to let me have one of his boats to come ashore in before the yacht leaves."

"I will obey all your desires, monsieur," said Mostar politely. "I will simply deliver the message of the queen and return to the boat without mentioning your name in any way. In fact, so far as I am concerned, no one will know that you are on the yacht."

"Thank you, I am very much obliged," replied the major gratefully; "that is all I desire."

"I am happy that it is in my power to accede to your request," said Mostar courteously, and then relapsed into silence.

In a remarkably short space of time, the boat reached the side of the yacht, and the gangway being convenient, Mostar sprang up the side quickly. Measurby did not follow him at once, as he guessed that Janshah was on board, and he wished to escape the keen eyes of the Indian. After the lapse of five minutes, however, he cautiously went up the side, and was fortunate enough to reach the deck quite unobserved. Then he went carefully down the cabin stairs, and managed to conceal himself in a receptacle for odds and ends, near the steward's pantry.

Hidden in there, he could hear the voice of Mostar talking to Hilda and Wilfred in the cabin. The officer seemed to be giving them some present from the queen, for he heard Wilfred tell Mostar to thank the queen for her gift, and shortly afterwards they all passed the door of his hiding-place to go on deck.

Listening intently, he heard the parting farewell of Mostar, and shortly afterwards the screw of the yacht commenced to beat the waters. She was under way, and the major had now quite lost his chance of returning to Varzo. Not that he regretted this. Varzo was too hot for him now, owing to the hatred of the queen, and all he desired at the present moment was to punish Wilfred for regaining possession of the ring.

Neither Hilda nor her husband came down again to the cabin, so Measurby, thinking that they were sitting on deck taking a last look at Villa Tvartko, decided to go above. He emerged from his hiding-place, and ascended the stairs. Halfway up he met the steward, who seemed somewhat startled at the sight of an officer in uniform.

"I am here with Mr. Dacre," explained the major calmly, "and I have been resting in my cabin. Are Mr. and Mrs. Dacre on deck?"

"Yes, sir, near the wheel," replied the steward, never doubting for a moment but that the major was a guest of his master's. "Shall I tell them you are here, sir?"

"No, thank you, I will go up on deck myself."

He cautiously put his head out of the cabin door, and to his relief saw that Janshah was nowhere to be seen. Wilfred and Hilda were seated in deck chairs just verging on the shadow of the gunwale. Measurby drew his sword and stole forward with the utmost care. It was truly wonderful that they never heard his approach, but being deep in conversation, they doubtless thought it was one of the crew moving about.

Measurby stole nearer, and saw that Wilfred's right hand, the one with the ring, was resting on the gunwale. A moment before he had risen to his feet and placed his hand in this position, with his eyes fastened on the rapidly vanishing shore. The wrist, bare and gleaming, lay on the wood, and in a second Measurby had made up his mind what to do. Raising his sword cautiously, he brought it down with all his force and severed the hand from the wrist.

With a cry of agony Wilfred fell on the deck with the blood spouting from the stump of his arm, and the major, with a shout of triumph, sprang forward to secure the severed hand which lay on the gunwale with the ring glittering on its third finger. Just at that moment the yacht gave a roll, and the hand fell over into the water.

The ring was gone, the famous ring, for which he had dared so much; and losing control of himself in his frantic terror at the loss, Measurby sprang overboard after the hand. The shriek of Wilfred, the cries of his wife, had summoned Janshah and some of the crew. They found Wilfred lying in agony on the deck, with his wife kneeling beside him. As to Measurby, the weight of his uniform and sword carried him down; he never arose to the surface. In his mad desire for the ring, he had thrown away his own life, and under the blue waters of the Black

Sea lies the famous ring of Brahma, encircling the fingers of a skeleton hand.

* * * * * *

Wilfred was ill for some time. Fortunately Janshah knew something of surgery, and managed to doctor the stump until they arrived at Stamboul. There, Hilda was fortunate enough to find a young doctor who was on a yachting cruise with a friend. The friend was going up to the Crimea, and the doctor desired to return home to England; so he willingly accepted Hilda's offer to go on board the Zoe as Wilfred's medical attendant.

He managed to bring the invalid round in a surprisingly short space of time, for the sword had cut cleanly, and Wilfred being a healthy-blooded man, the stump soon healed. The shock to his nerves was worse than the wound itself, and it was not until they had passed Gibraltar that he began to recover his health in any degree.

One afternoon he was lying on deck, and beside him stood Janshah, to whom he was talking about the ring.

"What will you do with the treasure, now, Janshah?" he asked curiously. "The ring is lost; so no one can command the money."

"It will be used for the service of the god," replied Janshah reverently. "He gave the ring to be used for a time, — he has taken it away again. The power that was bestowed on mortals by that ring has, by its loss, reverted to the god. He will use his own treasure."

"And what will you do with the yacht?"

"The yacht, and all its contents, are yours, my lord."

"Mine!" said Wilfred in surprise. "But I am no longer master of the ring."

"You were at the time I bought the yacht for you, my lord," replied Janshah quietly, "and the ring was lost by no fault of yours; therefore, I give all to you, and I am sure the owners of the treasure will approve of my so doing. Besides, there is on board gold to the amount of twenty thousand pounds, which is also yours."

"Then I am not a pauper, after all?" said Wilfred, with a contented sigh.

"Of course not, my dear," replied his wife, who sat beside him. "I have my five thousand a year, you have this twenty thousand pounds and this yacht. I think myself we are very well off."

"What will you do, Janshah?"

"I, my lord, will return to England. With the loss of the ring of Brahma, my task is ended."

"What adventures we have had!" said Wilfred to his wife.

"Well, all is over now," she answered soothingly. "I am glad we escaped from that horrible Busk with our lives."

"Even at the cost of my hand."

"My poor darling," said Hilda, kissing him tenderly, "how you have suffered! But the man who did it is at least punished for his wickedness. There, now, Wilfred, you are quite exhausted; do not talk any more."

"Well, if I have lost the ring, I have at least my

dear wife," he said fondly; "and of all the treasures which the ring has bestowed on me, I value that gift the most."

Hilda kissed him again, and Janshah, looking on, smiled his approval.

. . . .

On their arrival in London all was explained to Lord Kenny, who at first refused to believe such a marvellous story. But, on hearing it again, and seeing the evidence of Wilfred's handless arm, he was forced to accept it as true. He did this with great reluctance, as it was like believing in the Arabian Nights. Although he promised to keep it to himself, he could not do so, and gradually the story became known in London, as Wilfred was certain it would if confided to Lord Kenny.

He was quite the hero of the season, as every one wanted to see the man who had possessed the ring of Aladdin, and placed Princess Julia on the throne of Busk. Wilfred, disliking such notoriety, retreated to his family estate in Herefordshire, and now spends most of his time there with Hilda. Though not as rich as when they had that famous ring, still they are comfortably off, and Wilfred is far happier than ever he was before in the whole course of his life.

Janshah went to India, and Wilfred never saw him again, but it is rumoured that the Hindoos are conspiring against the British government with a view of recovering their old supremacy; so no doubt the treasure is still making mischief as it ever did.

As to Julia,— she, also, is making mischief. Not

content with her kingdom of Busk, on the throne of which she is now firmly established, she is constantly intriguing for an extension of territory. Paradiso is her prime minister, and does his best to restrain her unscrupulous diplomacy; but he foresees troubles in store for Busk. Upravado is dead, and how he died Julia knows best, though some say he is in exile in England. If so, Wilfred has not yet seen him, and thinks that the queen must have got rid of him secretly, as she always intended to do. Cardinal Gregory is still hoping for the tiara, but if Julia can prevent it she certainly will do so, as these former friends now hate one another bitterly. The queen thinks the cardinal too powerful, and he believes her to be too despotic; so between them they make things very unpleasant in Busk.

The prophecy of the statesman who spoke to Wilfred is rapidly coming true, for Julia is constantly thinking of the reconstruction of the Greek empire, with herself on the golden throne of the Comneni. As yet her schemes have come to nothing, but she often sighs as she thinks how she could have achieved her ambitions had she secured the ring of Aladdin.

FINIS.

www.ingramcontent.com/pod-product-compliance
Lightning Source LLC
Chambersburg PA
CBHW020537300426
44111CB00008B/702